Also by Linda Ingalls

Where do YOU draw the line? – An insider's guide to effective Living Wills, Healing, and Critical Care

Written by Linda Ingalls
Cover art by Dale Beck

The views expressed in this work are solely those of the author. The author of this book does not dispense medical advice or prescribe the use of any technique as a form of treatment for physical, emotional, or medical problems without the advice of a physician, either directly or indirectly. The intent of the author is only to offer information of a general nature to help you in your quest for emotional and spiritual well-being. In the event you use any of the information in this book for yourself, which is your constitutional right, the author and publisher assume no responsibility for your actions.

ISBN-13: 978-1490535968
ISBN-10: 1490535969
Library of Congress Control number: 2013912754

Contact information:
Linda Ingalls: **imlindai41@gmail.com**
          www.lindaingalls.com

I MAY BE CRAZY, BUT IT'S ALL GOOD

LINDA INGALLS

To Love

Acknowledgements

To Love, I am very grateful for all.

To all of my patients, their families, and to my clients, thank you for the legacies of your stories and for helping me to evolve.

To mom Bernita, dad Richard, sister Sue, brother Mike, aunt Jean, friends Fedra, Meryl, Shawn W., and Mary S. thank you all for helping me in the process of creating this book. To Dale for the cover art and for being the male shoulder I cry upon.

To all of my blog readers who read this book as I posted each chapter, thank you for reading and supporting this book

Contents

Forward

YOU ARE MORE THAN YOUR BODY!

My Patients have taught me this. This book of their stories and mine is intended to inform, empower, entertain, and bring hope to you, in Unconditional Love.

Yeah, it's all about Love. I get that now. I thought I'd already had it, but, the more I learn, the more there is to know. The more I am, the more there is to be. The more I do, the more there is to create. Hmm, Life is a wave that never ends; sometimes it sucks you under; and, sometimes it is a spectacular ride. It's always an adventure, for sure!

My name is Linda. I am a critical care nurse and I talk to my patients' spirits. I help them and they help me to evolve even when I really don't want to.

This book is about us and it is for **you**.

1
Tony/Sam

It figures that the first time anything weird occurred, it would involve my co-worker, Sonja. I had told her how, sometimes, I could hear a voice in my head when I was meditating. I saw that she heard me, but, she didn't comment. Eventually, we would both be taking care of Tony and that was when it all began.

Tony was a young man who was diagnosed with AIDS. Back in the 80's, having AIDS was pretty much a death sentence. Although he was alone and distraught, Tony refused to let me contact anyone. He had family but did not want to call them because they didn't know he was gay and he "just knew they would die if they found out". I was frustrated and sad that he was so alone in his fear and grief. He was my patient and I wanted to help, but, I felt like my hands were tied. What could I do?

That night at home I started thinking about Tony. I imagined seeing him in my mind; I could see him lying in his bed. I imagined I was talking with him. I don't remember everything we talked about. I know we discussed his feelings and fears, but, I don't remember what was said. I didn't spend much time, but sent him a lot of love and support.

The next day, Sonja was Tony's nurse. After her initial assessment she excitedly came over and asked me, "Did you do anything unusual last night?"

"What do you mean, unusual?"

"Well, did you by any chance have a conversation with Tony?"

"Yeah, I did. Why?"

She got all excited. "He wants to call his parents to tell them everything. He said an angel came to him in the night. He said they had a talk and he knew things would be alright."

"Really?" Hmm that's weird. Okay, whatever. I could feel Sonja staring at me. "Stop looking at me that way."

"What way?"

"You know what way... with those googly wonder eyes. There ain't nothing happening around here."

She shook her head and left.

Tony did call his family and they were totally loving and supportive of him. They became very involved in his care.

Hmmm, I wondered, is something happening around here? I shook my head. Don't know, can't think, gotta work, get going, Linda.

****

I don't remember how much time passed, maybe a week, a month? One day I was assigned to a young boy named Sam. I don't remember his history, but apparently he'd been in the ICU for a few days, transferred to Pediatrics and now returned, comatose, to the ICU. He'd had some kind of head trauma and now was having seizures. His doctor said he had a very poor prognosis and wasn't likely to live. That is all of the story I had.

I walked into his room. For some reason I just stood there at the foot of his bed and, in my mind, I said, *"Hello." In my imagination I saw a blazingly angry boy.*

He was yelling, "I'll teach them! I'm gonna die and then they'll be sorry."

WHAAAT? Holy moly, what is going on here? Am I really seeing this? I have no idea, but I don't see how I could be making this up. Sooo, in my mind I asked him, *"What's up with you? Why are you so angry?"*

"I'm angry that my dad took me away; he shouldn't have done that. And I'm angry cuz my mother treats me like a baby."

Whoa; is this real? I don't know what the heck he's talking about. What do I do now? What do I say? Okay, Linda, calm down and just talk."

I told him, "Yeah you could teach them really good. You could hurt them bad; but, you're gonna hurt yourself even worse if you die. How old are you... 8, 9? If you just wait a few years, you'll be old enough that no one can tell you what to do. You can do whatever you want. You'll have your whole life to live. Wouldn't you like to do that instead?"

He actually listened. After a few moments he said, "Well I hadn't thought of it like that. You could be right, I'll think about it."

"Well, okay then." I let it go and started doing my nursing care of this comatose boy. I wasn't sure what had just happened and I wasn't sure what to do with it.

Later on, when his mom came to visit him, I started feeling this revved up energy inside of me. I don't know if it was fear or anticipation. I felt like I was going to erupt. I had a strong urge to tell her what I had seen, so, I said to her, "You know what? I was pretending in my mind that I was talking to Sam and, man, he was pissed off. When I asked him why, he told me he was angry at his dad for taking him away and angry at you for treating him like a baby." I held my breath and watched her.

She stared at me and then started crying. She sat down with her head in her hands and sobbed.

UH OH, now what? I put my arm around her and waited.

She told me that, shortly after Sam was born, she and his father had separated. Then his father had kidnapped him. After all this time she had gotten Sam back less than a year ago. She was so afraid of losing him again that she kept a very tight rein on him.

"I don't let him play with his friends after school. I know it bothers him; we are always arguing about it. He tells me I treat him like he's a baby. I know he is more mature than the average kid and needs more freedom, but I am so afraid of losing him again."

She turned to Sam, leaned her head against his and said, "I'm sorry."

That night, after I left work, Sam woke up. The next day he was transferred back to Pediatrics. I was off work for a couple of days, but, when I got back I went to see him. I walked into his room. He was sitting on the side of his bed with his back to me. His mom and her boyfriend were facing me. She smiled and said, "Hi."

I went to face Sam, stuck out my hand and said, "Hi Sam, my name is Linda. I was one of your nurses in the ICU."

He said, "I know who you are and I know what you did." Then he threw his arms around me and hugged tightly.

What??!! Oh my God, I am gonna cry! I don't know what to say or to think. What is happening here? All I could do was to hold onto him. When we parted, I looked at his mom and her mouth was opened. I gave Sam another big squeeze, told him to take care and have a great life; then I left. Actually, I left kind of in a hurry. This was too weird.

What had just happened? Did his mom tell him? Did he remember...how could he? What does this mean? I don't know but it was a profound experience for me.

Hmm I think something is happening here!

Crazily, a couple of months later I was talking about this story to some friends of mine. It turned out they actually knew the family and told me Sam was happier, doing well, and, getting along great with his mom. She had released some of her fear and was letting him live life again. I thought that was cool, but, I tucked it away on the "I can't explain it" shelf in my mind.

So these are my first two experiences in a bunch of experiences over the next 30 years. Are you still with me? Do you want to hear more? Remembering these things makes me feel a little humbled inside. It was the beginning. Wow, what a trip I have been on. I hope you will continue tripping with me.

2
Me/Joe, etc.

When someone asks me how I started hearing peoples' spirits. I tell them I just started listening.

Hmmm, we need a little history of Linda here.

In 1969, at the age of 18, I was fortunate to have an insight that changed my life forever.

Yeah, I better back up more and digress as to how that came about.

Prior to age 18 my life experience had included a whole bunch of fear, violence, abuse, anger and hate with occasional moments of happiness. In particular, from age 11 to 18, I survived on hate while living with my mom's second husband, Joe. Along with our other issues, he had an anger problem; case in point: me, standing on my tippy toes trying to ease the pressure of a knife at my throat while he struggled to get control over his rage.

Despite what my reality was, most people perceived me to be a happy person because I smiled a lot. It's not like I was ever trying to cover up or to hide myself, I just felt better when I smiled. It felt good to laugh, to care about others, to have fun. DUH, go figure! So, when I could do it, I did it a lot.

I also sang. The only thing I appreciated about Joe was that he introduced me to the country music of Loretta Lynn and Hank Williams Sr., etc. In Joe's country music, my mom's standards, and my own 50'/60's music, I found the solace to help me survive. The songs seemed to be communicating to me. The words and music, sometimes, wrapping me in a cocoon of love; other times, ripping the grief and anger from my throat. All of it was therapy for me. Of course, I didn't recognize this then. All I knew was that when I was singing I felt real; I felt truth.

Even now, I will find myself suddenly humming or singing a song in a patient's room and I know it's important to sing that particular song. I don't know if it is because of the sounds or the words. I don't know if it does something to the patient's energy or just to mine which then helps me to take care of the patient. I just know that songs I never think about or even really know will come into my head and out of my mouth. I trust that it's what is best at that time and go for it.

Anyway, by the time I was 18, we had left Joe. Finally, I was free; out of hell.

Yeah, I was out of there, but I was still angry and hating. Somehow, I knew that this angry, hating person wasn't the truth of who I was. Somehow, I became aware of how my reaction to Joe allowed him to still control me and my life. Somehow, I knew that in order to be free I was going have to forgive him and to love him.

WHAT? No way! Oh my God, I **hated** this man. I survived him because of my hate. How would it be possible to love him? And where the hell were all these *"Somehows"* coming from anyway?

I suddenly had a picture of Joe in my mind and he was... just a man. He was another human being, trying to survive in his own frakked up way. He wasn't an intentionally evil person, he just didn't know how to be other than what he was and he had to live in his own hell. I felt a rush of comprehension and love for him. I felt compassion for the road he had been living and would continue to be living. I didn't need to add my hate to his burden.

I began seeing images of my own road of life. Where had I been going before Joe came along? I'll tell ya, I was a wild child. When I was 9 years old, my babysitter would tell my mom we were going to the movies. Instead, we would hang out with the sailors at the USO club and the pizza parlors in downtown San Francisco until two a.m. I was their darling little mascot; backcombing my hair into big poufy do's, wearing makeup, and smoking. My mom went ballistic when she found out and she put a stop to my late night weekend activities.

Unfortunately, mom wasn't home enough to keep an eye on me. My single mom worked her butt off to take care of us five kids. She left before we woke up in the morning and didn't get home until our bedtime. Although, she tried to set up a variety of babysitting situations through the years, they didn't always work out, sometimes in part, due to me being such a handful.

Babysitters or not, I was the oldest and from a very early age, I felt responsible for the care of us all. Daily life choices often came down to me and I made a lot of bad choices. Many of the choices I made were based upon fear and reaction to fear. There was no one around but me to protect us. I did a lot of fighting with abusive relatives and other kids as I tried to protect my siblings. I became tyrannical trying to control my siblings' behavior. Part of that was to protect them, but, I know part of it was also trying to protect myself from having to fight because of them. Life was a battlefield, physically and morally, for me. When Joe came, he took iron fisted control. Now, instead of trying to protect us from the world, I just had to protect us from Joe. I didn't do a very good job.

But, in 1969, at the wise old age of 18, suddenly, somehow, I realized that despite the awfulness Joe had brought, life could have been a whole lot worse if he hadn't come along. Looking back, I knew that prior to his coming, I had been on a major self-destructive pathway. My best friend was pregnant at age 13 and I have no doubt that could have been me; or, I could have been locked up in juvenile hall. Suddenly, I was grateful that Joe had moved us out of the city and onto a ranch. Except for school, he kept us isolated, out of trouble, and laboring hard, seven days a week.

By 1970, due to my new perceptions, Joe and I actually became friends until a few years later when my second husband, Lee, said, "I understand you have gained your freedom by forgiving and loving him, but he's still an asshole, Linda. Why do you want to keep sharing his asshole life?"

You know what? I agreed, and eased Joe out of my life.

Nevertheless, I'd had the valuable experience that the power of Love and Forgiveness could set me free. Without that freedom, I would still be stuck in the hating game. This was huge because being free allowed me to be open to the possibilities of better ways to live. Also, with all these "somehows" of new perceptions occurring to me, I had an inkling that somewhere inside of me was a part of me that knew there was a better way. I was still living my life and making some bad choices, but I began "seeking" too.

I had met my second husband, Lee, in 1976. He taught me that it was not selfish to love one's own self first; that it was okay to be happy, and that it was okay to have fun.

Wow, really? Awesome!

He also taught me to question everything. I explored a myriad of religions, philosophies, self-help books, blah, blah, blah. I would try things on for a max of one year. If it didn't fit by then I'd cut it loose and move on.

I think it was 1984 when I attended a nursing seminar called "Healing the Healer". They had a boatload of self-help books on the table. I'd read most of them already, so I asked the teacher, "What do you recommend when one has read most of these?"

She directed me to <u>A Course In Miracles</u>. I started reading it and couldn't put it down. It's a set of three Christian based psychically channeled books. One book is the text; one book is a year's worth of daily quotes that you are supposed to meditate upon; and, one book is a manual for teachers. You can read the text as fast or slow as you want but the daily quote meditations were to be done no faster than one per day.

I began reading and it began to change my life.

About a week into it, I was getting pretty angry. From my point of view I'd had a pretty sucky life. Yes, I had been moving on, coping, changing my life, and being a different kind of person; but, the reading and the meditating were beginning to stir up my memories, my emotions, and to shake up my beliefs. My entire being was on turbo burn demanding anger and resistance. So it was, that one day, while out in the wetlands walking my dog and ruminating about everything, I started yelling at "God".

"Who the *fuck* do you think you are, trying to tell me how to live? Where were you during all of that shit? If this is your idea of a meaningful life, then you totally suck! I can make better decisions than you do. I would never treat a kid of mine the way you have allowed me to be treated. This world is messed up, man, cuz you let so much shit happen. You screwed up; you are one sick mutha!

"I'm sorry"

"WHAT?!"

"I said, I am sorry"

Uh oh, I've lost it now! I knew I was alone, even my dog was ½ mile away, but I could hear this voice in my head. I stopped dead in my tracks. What the hell is this?

"Who are you?" I thought to myself.

"God."

"Yeah, right. Now I know I am frakking crazy? Okay, I'll play along. Why are you talking to me?

"Because you are ready to listen."

"Okay you sick shit, I'm listening. What do you want to say?"

"I am sorry for all of the pain and fear you have been experiencing."

"Is that right? Well, if you are God why did you let it be this way? And what - am I supposed to say it's all okay, fall on my knees and do whatever you tell me to do now? You make crappy choices and I'm the one who has to live them. I can make better choices than you do."

"Okay"

"Okay, what?"

"I'll make you a deal. I will listen to your ideas and consider them. I ask that you listen to my ideas and consider them too. When we agree which one is best we will try it out, experience it in life, and see what happens. Okay?"

"You are saying that "GOD" is gonna listen to my ideas and maybe go along with them? So, are you saying I might have a better idea than you?"

"I am saying this is what you believe and I am willing to explore it with you. And if your idea is better than mine, we will do it"

What am I getting into here? He says he's God. I don't know; what if he's something else. What if I agree and get stuck?

"Linda, you can always change your mind and choose again. It will be okay."

"Hey! Are you reading my mind?"

Laughs. "I am in your mind."

Hmmp. Ha, Ha. *"Okay, deal, but I get a say in everything, right?"*

"Right."

And that was it. Each day I would read the quote for the day and sit and think about it. I would think about it and then I would listen for an answer. Sometimes all I heard was silence, yet, sometimes in that silence, I would become larger than myself; I became formless, limitless; I was light without a beginning or an end. I was filled with love and joy. It was indescribably awesome. Still, I kept listening. After a while, not always, I would hear a voice in my head. It always had a different perception from my own. From that limitless point of view I would receive a new perspective with which to perceive my life and my questions. Each time I received the new perspective, I would also feel freedom, love, and joy. I was learning to trust my Inner Voice.

It was after this that I met my patients, Tony and Sam.

And, after them, I met Anna.

3

Anna

Anna was a beautiful woman in her mid 30's. After high school she had married her childhood sweetheart, Tom and had two children, Lilly, age 7 and Micah, age 10. They were granola people - hippies living in the boonies of northern California.

Anna had gotten sick, possibly from a tick bite; we never knew for sure. She came down with what today we would call Sepsis, an infection that her whole body was reacting to. Consequently, she also developed ARDS (adult respiratory distress syndrome). Even today, ARDS still has a high fatality rate; but, back then it was nearly a certainty that she would die.

When I began taking care of Anna she was on a ventilator, a life support machine that helps a person to breathe. Her blood pressure was so low she needed life support medicines we call "pressors" to keep her blood pressure high enough for circulating blood. She had a lot of tubes to help monitor her body and to manage fluids for her body. She also had two chest tubes. When a person gets ARDS and the lungs get stiff, it is very hard to breathe or to push air into them. Any kind of resistance can make it harder for the machine to push in air. With the kind of technology we had then, the ventilator used a lot of pressure to push air into stiff lungs. Often, this high pressure would pop the lungs sending air between the lining of the lung and the lining inside the chest wall; kind of like putting air between salami and its lining. If the created air space is large enough it could collapse the lung – a life threatening situation. Chest tubes take out the air and let the lungs re-expand. Despite Anna being heavily sedated to reduce any resistance to the machine pushing in the air, she already had the two chest tubes. Sometimes we had to give her medicine to paralyze her body so there would be absolutely no resistance. It was that bad.

After my experiences with Tony and Sam, I decided to see if my new awareness of talking with a person's spirit could really help. Is it really real? Am I making it up? I don't know, I still don't understand it. Anna is the first patient I had the intent to help with my new awareness. I was not sure what could be done. I wanted to know where this could go, how it could be used, was there more? So, I walked into Anna's room and I said *"Hello"* to her in my mind.

She said, "I'm leaving. I am so tired of living in the sticks. I want to go party. I want to go have fun. I'm out of here." And she left!

"WAIT!" I yelled in my head. "What does that mean? Are you saying you're leaving your body? Does this mean you are gonna die? Wait, what do I do?"

No answer, she was gone. Oh my gosh! I couldn't feel her presence. Her body was still there, heart beating, machine breathing for her, urine flowing. But her spirit was gone. Holy shit! Did I cause this? I don't think so, how could I? Ego, Linda, ego. Yeah, yeah, but this is kind of scary. I am quivering inside. Take a deep breath. Does the body live without its spirit; If so, how long? What do I do? Do I prepare her family for her death? I have no idea. Is this real? Am I making this up? *Again, what do I do now?* Get your self together, Linda. Just put one step in front of the other and stay aware of the vibes.

I continued taking care of her body. I started taking care of her family. I got to know them, giving them my love, attention, and support. Tom and the kids came into visit every day. Gosh, they were nice. They all loved Anna sooo much. Tom was just a quiet-natured, farm-loving, pot-growing, hippie-dude. I could see that his whole world revolved around Anna. They really had been in love since kindergarten. Isn't that amazing? At first, awash in the family's perspectives, I, myself, felt affection for Anna. But, over the next few days as I got to know them and kept an ear out for Anna, I felt something wasn't right.

Yeah DUH, Linda, Anna's frakking gone!

The family moved into town so Tom could spend his days with Anna. Her parents came from out of state to be with her. Her friends would come to visit. They were into all kinds of stuff that today we call complimentary therapy. Then we just called it "crazy shit": crystals, reflexology, feathers, medicine bags, aromatherapy, and acupressure.

Man, I loved having all of that stuff around. I was there doing my critical care nursing while at the same time, being aware of the energy and trying to figure out what I was supposed to be doing with it. At that time, all I knew was to send her body loving energy. One morning, her friend put a heart shaped crystal on her body and it was still there when the chest x-ray was done. The crystal showed up right over her heart. Woooo, so cool. I wanted a copy of that x-ray, but radiology wouldn't let me have one.

Later on, her best friend came to visit. We got to talking and she confided in me that Anna had been planning on leaving Tom and the kids. She was going to move to San Francisco. She was so tired of the country life and wanted the excitement of living in the big city. She wanted to party! Tom didn't know. But *I* did and I believed it because that is what Anna had told me. Now, it was becoming more real to me. Before this I could tell myself, "Oh you're just nuts, making this stuff up."

Time was passing and Anna wasn't getting any better. After just one month in the ICU, she had accumulated six chest tubes. I still could not feel her presence anywhere. I started gently talking about the possibility of her not making it. The family knew. They could see it. We spent a couple of days crying and hugging. It was so heart breaking.

The next day I came to work and I heard, *"I'm back."* I looked around. Yep, it was in my head.

"What? You're back? What does that mean?"

"I missed my family. It wasn't fun being without them, so I came back."

"Does this mean you're not gonna die?"

"I don't plan to."

"Great."

Hmmp. I expected that, as spirits, people would have more awareness and be wiser. I guess people can be just as flaky spiritually as they can be in their bodies. Obviously, they can change their minds there too.

Wow, this was huge for me to see. It wasn't as black and white/all or nothing as I thought it would be. I wasn't sure what to make of this except to stay flexible, go with the crazy flow, and to *definitely* not make predictions.

While I was thinking of all this, I suddenly heard a scream in my head. It was Anna.

"I'm a monster, I'm a monster!" she wailed.

"What in the world are you talking about?"

In my mind came a picture of Anna sitting in a chair. Her left arm was stiffly bent up into her chest. Her left leg, slightly raised, was stiffly bent at the knee and hip. Her limbs were contracted. OH MY GOD. NOW WHAT!

"I'm a monster, they won't want me anymore." She cried and cried. It was breaking my heart.

"Look." I said. "I have no idea what this is all about, but I bet your family would want you back no matter what you look like. I know they love you so much. You listen, I'll ask them"

That day when Tom and the kids came in I said, "Would you want Anna to live and come back to you no matter what?"

"Oh yeah" they all replied.

"What if she came back and there were things wrong with her? What if her body was messed up, crooked, and couldn't work? What if she wasn't the same anymore?"

"Linda, we want her with us no matter what"

"See, I told you." I said in my mind. I heard her sigh. Later I asked the same question of her parents and her best friend. They all said, "Yes."

The next day I was off. That day, Anna's lung popped for the 7th time. But this time her heart also beat erratically. She needed CPR, shocking, and resuscitation meds. Her heart started going again, but her brain had been affected. Anna was not responding anymore.

When I came back a day later I found that her body was flaccid. The ventilator had no trouble breathing for her anymore; there was no resistance to the air being pushed in. I don't know how it happened but all of the problems we had been battling for a month were no longer an issue; they all seemed to resolve themselves. Her vital signs stabilized. Her lungs healed and she was able to come off of the ventilator. But, she wasn't waking up.

Spiritually, Anna was freaking out. I did everything I could to love her, soothe her, and support her through this. As usual, her family stood by her with hope and love. I encouraged all of her healer friends to come do their thing on her; anything to help.

And then one day she started to respond - more each day until she was AWAKE. Man, we were sooo happy. She got transferred out of ICU to the med- surg floor where I would go to briefly visit. It wasn't like Sam. She had no awareness of me or any of our mental conversations. In fact, in all of these years, I can only recall three times when there was awareness - once with Sam, once with my sister, Susan, and once with my brother, Dennis; but, they are other stories.

Anna was eventually transferred to a rehab hospital. I actually volunteered to work there for one day just to see what they would do for Anna and her family. About a month after she was admitted there, I went to see her and it was all I could do to not freak out.

No way Jose, can't this be real!

She was sitting in a wheelchair. Her left arm was stiffly bent up into her chest. Her left leg, slightly raised, was stiffly bent at the knee and hip. Her limbs were contracted! Her speech was slurred and she drooled a little. Tom and the kids were all over her, happily waiting on her, encouraging her.

Oh MY GOD! This is the "monster" picture she had shown me. Breathe, Linda.

I said "Hi" to her, but, she didn't remember who I was. She began to complain about everything; her condition, the hospital, Tom, the kids, her parents, her friends. She bitched and bitched and I could tell this was not a new attitude. This was her normal baseline.

Well, I am only human you know. I knelt in front of her and said, "Yeah, your condition sucks, but you chose to be here. You can sit here and feel sorry for yourself or you can work to make the most of it. I want you to know how much your family loves you, how they stood by you all of this time, never giving up on you, and wanting you no matter what. Get it together and show some appreciation for them and your life."

I know, I know – neither professional nor compassionate. But, I didn't like her; she had such a bitchy attitude.

Wow, just cuz I'd had this intimate relationship with someone spiritually didn't mean I would like who they were as a person in their body. I was unhappy that she hadn't brought spiritual awareness of her choices back into the consciousness of her mind. She wasn't like Tony or Sam. I guess after them, I expected there to be some awareness, some kind of change, at least in thought or attitude; but, no, nothing. Well, maybe it's just her. This is still new to me. I don't know what's normal.

I never went back to see her. I'm not a saint. A year later I heard that they'd moved to another state. She'd had surgery on the arm and leg to release the contracture and physical therapy was helping her to walk. Also, I heard that she'd become nicer, more appreciative of her life and family.

As for me, I was aware that even with my new increased awareness, I was not necessarily a better person myself. Looking back at this, I think it is interesting to note that, in my work environment, I didn't ask or even try to listen to my own Inner Voice. I could listen and hear when I was meditating, but in the life and death immediacy of my job, I didn't take the time to listen. This was an issue for many years.

If Anna was one kind of challenge, Mrs. Jones was a different kind.

4
Emily

Ahh I loved Emily Jones and her four daughters.

Emily was in her 80's. She came to the ICU, comatose, and on a ventilator, after having a stroke from a very large bleed in her brain.

Her four daughters were some tough cookies. Teresa was a lawyer, Joan a banking investor, Mary a college professor and Sarah an RN - all professional women, all self-assured, strong willed, articulate and somewhat intimidating to the nursing and medical staff caring for their mom. They kept a vigil, 24/7, at her bedside even though there was supposed to be no visiting at night. They also kept a diary of everyone, everything, every treatment, and every drug...anything that came into contact with their mom; and, they gave each other report when one came to relieve the other.

Man, I loved it. It didn't intimidate me at all. In fact, I would walk in, tell them exactly what I was gonna do and make sure they wrote it down accurately. I made sure they comprehended everything going on with their mom. I think it is great when families have such good communication. Also, I have to admit, I wanted no mis-communication, no mis-understanding, and no mis-anything with these "liberated, Amazonian" women. They could be wicked scary!

One morning, two weeks into this, I was leisurely driving to work through the beautiful wine country. The early morning sun was just starting to create a soft glow on the fields when into my head pops up a picture of Mrs. Emily Jones. She was in pink calf length pants leaning on a huge boulder at a beach.

She said, "I want you to tell my girls..."

"Hey, hey, hey what are you doing? What's going on here?" I was driving while I was seeing and hearing this little movie in my head. Fortunately, I could multi-task. Did we even use that term back then?

She repeated, "I want you to tell my girls..."

"Stop! First of all I don't believe that this is real. Second, I don't do messages. Third, there is no way I am ever gonna call those WOMEN, girls"

Did she listen to ME? Nope. Remember Whoopi Goldberg playing Oda Mae in the movie, Ghost? It wasn't quite the same as Patrick Swayze singing "I'm Henry the VIII"; but she wasn't letting go.

"I want you to tell my girls, that I am not going to be here to help keep them together as a family. They are going to have to settle their differences and learn to get along with each other. They are going to have to come together to make a decision about me. They have to be there for each other now and when I am gone. Tell them I love them."

Oh man, I can't do this. Are you kidding me? This is exposure, man. This is putting me out there to be shot down. I could get into a lot of trouble. I mean what I do is on the down low. People don't really know about it. Hell, I don't really know about it. I can't do it. I'm not gonna do it. You can't make me do it!

The rest of the drive, my stomach wouldn't stop flopping. I'm scared. I don't know that I really believe in this stuff. On one hand, I feel like I have this awareness, kind of like a gift and I am supposed to be using it. On the other hand, I am scared to death of what I will be required to do. I mean they burned witches; they lock up people who hallucinate; I could be condemned as being possessed. I have my pride, my ego, my self-esteem. I am a good nurse. If I do this, these women could make a lot of trouble for me.

And yet... Linda, their mom wants you to give them a message.

Well, girlie girl, whatcha gonna do? Are you gonna believe, gonna trust, gonna take a risk? It's a big risk. I just don't know. Please help me.

I walked into Emily's room. Mary was there. I didn't say anything besides my usual hello, how was the night, etc. I did my assessment of Emily and left. A little later I returned to give Emily a bath. Now Sarah was there too; time to change the guard.

Come on, Linda, you can do it. I started washing Emily's face; I wanted to vomit.

I plunged, "You know what, this morning while driving to work, I had an image of your mom in my mind. She had on pink calf high pants, leaning on a boulder by the beach." I kept my eyes focused on Emily's face. "She said to me, 'Tell my girls...'"

I heard a big gasp from Mary off to my right. My shoulders hunched up. Oh man, now you've done it, Linda. I snuck a look at her. Her mouth was open, eyes wide, staring at her sister. She started crying. Sarah took her hand and turned to me.

"Our mom was a liberated woman before it became a movement. When we were children she taught us that we were going to be women someday and to never let anyone call us otherwise. But, to her, we would always be 'her girls'."

Hmmm, be cool, Linda. I kept doing Emily's bath. Finally I said, "Well, she wanted me to tell you something. Do you want to hear it?" They nodded and I told them. Mary started smiling, Sarah was nodding. They KNEW. They knew exactly what I was talking about.

Mary called her sisters to come in. Sarah helped me finish the bath and I got the hell out of Dodge. I went to the bathroom, sat down and sighed, even a bit tearful. I cried with relief, cried with awe, cried because I could do this but afraid of what it meant and where it would take me.

The girls did get together. Their first joint decision was agreeing that Emily was not progressing and would not want to live this way. They had us take her off of life support, put her onto comfort care and transferred out of the ICU so that in her own time, in her own way, she could have a peaceful death. It took about two days and she did just that. Meanwhile the girls were resolving issues and re-arranging their relationships so that they could have a cohesive family together.

As for me, I had taken another step on my long path to who I am now. It wasn't the last time I was scared, unsure, and resistive. If I knew then what I know now, maybe this path wouldn't have taken so long. I wish I hadn't been so stubborn, so scared. But, God/ Spirit/ Love/ Source whatever name you accept, had me in a crucible: purifying me, teaching me, clearing me so I could be a better channel and expression of Love.

****

I don't remember telling people, at that time, what I was doing. But, while I was writing this memoir, I received emails from two nurses I had worked with during that time and they shared two more stories with me.

The first story is from Christy:

"I wish my recollections were better. I remember being in room 210 and my patient had expired after many days in the ICU. I am pretty sure that life support was withdrawn, but I can't say for sure. I remember it felt like he was released from a very long period of our good intentioned prolongation of life (i.e. suffering). You were helping me with after death care and you were communicating with him, telling me how he was feeling, and how he was going into the next life. I am sorry I can't elaborate, it was so long ago. I know it was comforting to me at the time to know he was going to a good place after caring for him for so long. I could feel his presence somehow."

The next one from Marti:

"I don't remember a lot of specific details, but I do remember you taking care of Jake (of Jake's Bikes) when he was in the unit. He was comatose. You'd been taking care of him (and talking with him) for a while. His family/friends were in with him a lot. You had debated telling them about talking with him. I don't remember if there was a specific reason you decided to tell them one day--but it seems I remember they were very loving/caring/worried about him--and one day you did tell them about communicating with him. You had told them, and they had said something like, "Tell him to show us if he can really hear you." And just when you had told him that, he suddenly sat upright in bed, and then laid back down. Wow, that really got their attention! That's the biggie from that experience that really stands out in my memory. After that you facilitated their communication back and forth with them/him. When you had just started this, I do remember their comments at times as,

"Yeah that sounds just like what Jake would say." Whew, that was a few years ago! There's my recollection, Linda."

You can see by my stories that I am experiencing these things but don't really understand or know what to do. I was just going with my intuition. I would center and ask, "Now what?"

Wow. Just writing this memoir is a journey all in itself. I can't wait to see what is written next!

5
Psychic/Perception/Matching Pics

One day, in the late 80's, while I was shopping in another county, I went to use the ladies room. As I left the stall I noticed a flyer that read:

Are you an RN?
Do you feel like you can communicate
with your patients' spirits?
If so, come to this class

Woooo! I looked around the bathroom. If this had happened today, I would think I was being "punked". But, dude, there was no one else around. I wrote down the info and went to the class.

It was held in an old house and was an introductory class to clairvoyance, sponsored by The Berkeley Psychic Institute (BPI) which was founded by Lewis Bostwick. In just one class the mystique of clairvoyance and telepathy disappeared. I saw that anyone could learn to do it. So much for me being special – Oy what an ego!

The first important thing they taught me was how to *ground*. Physics tells us that everything is made up of energy i.e. atoms, protons, etc, and that includes our bodies. We are one big mass of physical, liquid, gaseous, emotional, mental, and spiritual *energy*. Today, one might call each of us a "bio-field". I didn't know that term then. I equated grounding to having a three pronged plug for my appliances. That third part of the plug is to send static and excess energy into the ground. No, I am not an electrician, so that's all I am gonna say about that.

When I learned grounding at BPI, I found that it helped me to keep my feet on the ground, not get too spacey, and to let go of or better handle the energy I would experience happening around me. The way they taught me to ground was to imagine and/or feel a grounding cord, a connection between my tailbone and the earth. I imagined different things - a tree root, a waterfall, an anchor, or whatever came to my mind at the time. They told me to make it go deep into the earth to make a good connection. Well, I wanted to really be connected, so I would make my grounding cord super strong and send it to the center of the Earth entrenching it into the core. I figured that way even though I may have created it in California, it could go with me anywhere in the world, right? With amusement, my teachers would tell me I was too intense about it and they would make me create and destroy grounding cords over and over until I finally lightened up about the concept.

They also gave me a word for something I had already been doing. That word was *centering*. Centering is when you bring your attention into the present moment, quiet your mind, and be inwardly aware no matter what you are doing. It can be done even in the middle of chaos. I know some nurses who are like the eye of a hurricane during a Code Blue. They are centered; aware of themselves and what is happening around them all at the same time.

Centering is also done when one meditates. For example while doing <u>A Course In Miracles</u>, I would center my attention on my heart, my 4th chakra, and focus on feeling Unconditional Love. This was my way of getting quiet, relaxing, listening, and opening myself up to new awareness.

I am very grateful to have learned the concepts of grounding and centering. They have helped me to survive and to thrive in life.

I signed up for more meditation and healing classes.

The Institute also offered a clairvoyant training program that lasted about 18 months for younger adults and two years for older adults. Although, chronologically, I wasn't quite yet an older adult, they would only let me into the two year program. I guess my energy field looked old to them. Yeah right! How can energy look old? Of course, this class would cost more and last longer. It was a bit of a blow to my ego to be told I would need more time to train. I mean, look, I am already seeing and talking to people's spirit. Obviously, I don't need them to teach me that. They tried to explain why to me, but I wasn't getting it. I signed up anyway.

One of the things we had to commit to was opening ourselves up to a new perspective. It was like la Tablas Rasa: the "blank slate" referring to the concept that we are born with a blank slate - without built-in mental content; and, that knowledge is created from experience and perception. So, in the program, we agreed let go of our perceptions and attachments to ideas, relationships, jobs, behaviors, etc. It didn't mean that we walked away from them, though some people did. It did mean that we committed to allowing ourselves to see our beliefs, convictions, knowledge, relationships, jobs, hopes, dreams and our truths in a new light, a clear light.

"Older adults" like me had a lot more time and life experiences in which to get stuck in preconceived ideas; stuck in belief systems taught to us by our families and society; stuck in our compliance or rebellion to what we were taught; stuck in fear, denial, and anger; stuck in the conclusions we created about our own personal life experiences. *Stuck, stuck and more stuck.* It was very important for us to realize that as we let go of our poopy attitudes, changed our perceptions, and saw more clearly it could lead to a change in our choices. You can see how terrifying that could be when you have established relationships, careers, and beliefs. We have more to lose! And, although I *said* I wanted to see clearly, often, I avoided it because of my fear of what I might see. Also, my beliefs often had an emotional charge attached to them; a mostly negative charge. I mean who wants to go there?

The Institute had created a way of safely using clairvoyance to clear ourselves. They gave us tools to help us be in a neutral place while we "saw"; and tools, in addition to grounding, to release the energy as we experienced it. They gave us amusement to lighten the heavy, intense visions. They gave us their own clear seeing to support us when the emotions would get overwhelming.

We did clairvoyant readings to help clear out our energy and become more proficient in seeing clearly. In the beginning of my training, I wasn't very clear, (surprise!) and so when I did readings or healings, I saw much of my own self in the person I was working with. These similarities between us were called "matching pictures". Being able to look at a matching picture from a neutral place is kind of like watching a movie - it gives me some distance because I am looking at someone else's issues rather than looking directly at my own. Instead of getting bogged down in my own emotional turmoil and denial, I can be more objective. It provides me with a safe place to realize - wow, the same kind of thing happened to me; wow, I do the same thing in that situation; wow, I believe the same thing. I can safely see my own emotional drama/trauma playing out in the other person's life. I can see my own games clearer. At that point of awareness I have an opportunity to keep my belief as it is, to revise it, or to let it go. I ask myself, "Do I still really believe this NOW? Does the person I am NOW, still want this?" As I ask these questions; let go of old beliefs and emotions; make new choices; and, allow new perceptions to enter my mind, my energy comes into my present time. As I resolve my matching pictures, my vibrations rise, my energy field becomes clearer and I can see others more clearly.

I could grasp this concept because I already had the awareness that everything I experience is brought to my brain through my senses- my physical senses of sight, smell, hearing, touch, etc; and my non-physical senses of clairvoyance, telepathy, etc. I know that as my senses pick up data it's sent to my brain where my mind filters and interprets the data into meaning based upon my belief system i.e. that smells good, that's ugly, and that's dangerous. Everything I experience in life is filtered through my beliefs. It is a great tool for self-awareness because everything I perceive is like looking into a mirror - they are reflections of me, my beliefs. Doesn't mean my perceptions are true, rather, they are just a reflection of what I currently believe.

When I would meet others with a perception similar to mine I used to think that it must be the truth because we all perceived the same thing; but, is it? Well, how often have you seen beliefs and perceptions change depending upon where you live or what century you live in? In the beginning of our lives we are taught what to believe. Hopefully, as we mature we get the chance to review our beliefs and make a choice. There are many philosophies, techniques and pathways to help re-frame a belief system. My clairvoyant training was one of them. My training was quite useful to me in the long run. But in the beginning, as they expected for this older adult, it was not easy.

One of the first things I had to let go of was my training from A Course In Miracles. Why? Because I had a relationship with something, call it God/Spirit/HigherSelf/Love/Source, whatever. To me these were all names for the same energy. The Institute called it a Being and that I was being a trans-medium for this Being. I had to let it go for now until I was clear and could better see its influence on me.

Also, I had to get out of my 4th chakra - heart energy space and get into my 6th chakra energy space - the 3rd eye, center of neutral clear seeing. In other words they wanted me to stop letting my heart dictate my perceptions and, instead, allow myself to see objectively and clearly with clairvoyance.

Lewis said, "I'm not teaching you about love, you should already know it. I am teaching you to see clearly." I thought I understood him and so, I agreed to let go.

It was an amazing experience for me. I was doing energy based healings some times and other times doing intuitive readings. We would read as a panel with three to five readers. Another student would be standing behind the panel, grounding the energy. A client would sit in front of us. In a light meditative state, with our eyes closed, we each took our turn looking at the client's energy and then communicating what we saw. The teachers would stand behind our line up and be there for us, grounding and guiding. Sometimes, I could see so much and I would say what I saw. With amusement, the teachers would say, "Linda, don't give it all away."

I didn't understand what that meant, but it would shut me up and I resented it. I'm like, why? Why don't you want me to say what I see? This client paid us for a reading. Well, I am reading; I'm on a roll. Why do want me to stop? If I was the client, I would want to get it all.

I never got a clear understanding of this until recently. The gist is, what I was seeing and saying would be blowing my clients away. Instead of gently increasing their awareness with their highest good in mind, I was rocking them with an 8.0 on the Richter scale. It was too much too soon. Even later when I was doing readings on my own, it was like that. A client would come to me only once. I would say too much; their eyes would glaze over and it was like Charlie Brown listening to his teacher. All he could hear was, "wah, wah wah". It was too much to take in and process.

I was the same way with myself too. It took me a long time to recognize that even though I *thought* I wanted to know everything, not even I could handle all that I saw. I would blow *myself* away and it could take years to process the information. Why? It's the *fear* and *resistance*, man. I didn't want to let go of my "stuff".

It was scary for me to see clearly when I wanted to hang on to my stuff – whatever the stuff was. To be honest, what I really wanted was to see validation that the stuff I was holding onto was good stuff, true stuff, and "this is what's best" stuff. That was what I hoped to see. That was what I was afraid I wouldn't see. Then what would I do? This is why older adults can have a harder time clearing out.

So, while I really loved my program, I had an undermining resistance, mostly, because I was afraid of losing my husband, Lee. A huge motivating factor in my evolution to be a better person was so I could allow myself to have a great marriage with Lee. I figured if I could keep evolving and healing my own issues then it would help our relationship. BUT, what if in the healing it became clear that it would be better to walk away from the relationship? We definitely had our ups and downs, but, walking away was not acceptable to me. So, I resisted too much clarity.

Once before, in an explosive reaction to an argument, I had left him. The relationship was too hard, too much work, too much drama and trauma. I hopped on a greyhound bus heading back east to find a monastery or a commune where I could just focus on my spirituality.

I was ruminating the whole way, replaying every wrong thing in the history of our relationship. *Oh boo hoo!* Talk about drama. But this is not the important part.

It took hours and miles before I become aware that as I had been replaying each memory in my mind, right behind it came a revised picture, a different point of view. Without my conscious awareness, my thoughts were changing; my feelings were transforming to peace and love!

When I *did* become conscious of this process, suddenly I could hear my Inner Voice talking to me, gently urging me to try looking at the memories from a new perspective – from Love's perspective. Now, as the bus kept traveling, I began to review my thoughts with this *conscious intent.* I would look at a memory, feel the feeling initiating the drama and I would say, "Maybe there is a better way to perceive this. If there is a better way, I choose that way to perceive it. I choose Love's way." Sometimes, I just let go and got quiet; sometimes I had to actually experience the emotion and ride it out to clarity; sometimes I argued my point of view in my head. Eventually, though, I would see from a different point of view. It seemed to just happen. All of a sudden I would see things differently. I think that as I grounded and let go of emotional drama, I got centered and came to peace. Then, my Inner Voice could illuminate a new point of view into my mind.

This point of view was founded upon Love and it changed everything. It was like I was *re-writing my history*! Not that it changed the facts of anything that had happened; rather, it changed my reaction to it. Now, by perceiving from a place of Love, I could act rather than react. I could make a conscious choice instead of being a victim and re-acting. I could love instead of fear. I got off at the next stop, called my husband and flew home to his welcoming arms.

I never knew how my husband managed to stay with me, ha ha. We didn't believe the same things. I was always afraid I would outgrow him as I had done with my first husband. Lee wasn't spiritual; I was. But, somehow, he believed in me and in what I was doing more than I did.

I would come home with a story and say, "Oh my God, listen to this!"

When I finished the story, he would say, "Linda why are you always so surprised? You have these experiences all the time, but you don't believe in them, in yourself, or even in the concepts you say you believe."

I think because Lee wasn't spiritual, he was a grounding point for me. If Lee believed in something I did then it must be real. We didn't walk the same paths, but he always blew me away. Every time I struggled up a spiritual mountain and *finally* reached an epiphany, Lee was always there at the top of the mountain waiting for me. I would say, "Hey, how did YOU get here?" He would point and I could see he had come by another path, his own path. I could see there were lots of paths up that mountain. I could hear God speaking in many languages – whatever language He needed to speak in to reach people's hearts so that eventually they would listen. From my perspective, Love is multilingual, using whatever vocabulary is needed to reach us; supporting us on whatever path we need to take in order to reach awareness. It took me a long time to trust this and to stop resisting clarity.

Well... I mostly stopped resisting...when I would remember to anyway.

I spent three years at BPI and graduated from the program with the title of "Reverend" in the Church of Divine Man. But I wasn't into being a reverend. Worse, in all the neutrality of being in my 6th chakra energy space, I felt disconnected from my fourth chakra – my heart, my Love. So, I did <u>A Course In Miracles</u> again and reconnected myself. From this foundation of love I continued to evolve supported by my own Inner Voice and my clear seeing. I continued to have doubt and resistance, but they kept getting whittled away with experience and the crucible of Love's light. Taking care of my patients plays a huge part in that.

For example...

6
Terry

I did a stint as an agency nurse meaning I worked for a company that would contract me out to whatever hospital needed me for that shift. Experienced agency nurses know that until a hospital's ICU staff learns to trust you, they will avoid assigning you to very critical cases if they can. In truth, agency nurses don't always get a good assignment. So it happened. I went for a shift at a hospital unfamiliar to me and they assigned me to Terry.

Terry was only in her 40's and had been in the ICU for almost a month. She wasn't critical when I met her but she could not breathe on her own; she needed a ventilator. She had a tracheostomy – a tube going through a hole in the neck and directly into the windpipe (trachea). This is where the ventilator connected to help her breathe. She was alert but couldn't talk.

The staff was frustrated and tired of trying to take care of her. They couldn't get her off of the vent. I don't remember what the problem was with her lungs, but to make matters worse, she also had a very short, chubby neck. Due to her neck's shape she would kink off the trach tube and not be able to get air in or out even with the machine's help. Apparently this kinking happened every few days and a Code Blue would be called on her. She would be resuscitated and a new trach would be placed in an emergency situation. The staff had tried everything they could think of. They were tired. They wanted her to be taken off of the ventilator and go to Hospice; but, neither she nor her husband was ready for her to die. By the time I met them, there was a lot of distrust and discomfort between the staff and them.

I have to digress and tell you something. I'm a sucker for jokes because I never can remember them. My husband loved that because he could tell me the same jokes over and over. It got to a point where he would ask, "Do you remember this one?"

"No, but I remember I liked it." He would tell it to me again and I'd crack up again.

The crazy thing is that, by some miracle, when I took care of Terry, I could remember jokes; all kinds of jokes. I was making up jokes! I was an idiot-savant of jokes! Rude, crude, politically incorrect, silly, blonde, and nonsense jokes. Whatever came to my mind... "What do you get when you line up 100 blondes ear to ear"? – "A wind tunnel". Stupid, right? Ahh, but we had a blast. I pretty much spent the whole day in her room, taking care of her and just socializing with her and her husband. I had no history with her; I had no expectations of her; we had no difficulties; and, we laughed all day. So, the staff asked me to return the next day and the next. I ended up taking care of Terry for the next two weeks. We laughed every day, telling jokes, watching videos, and socializing; it was a most unusual experience.

One afternoon, during lunch, a Code Blue was called for a patient somewhere else in the hospital. This was a small hospital, so when the team of people who answered codes went to the code, there were only a couple of nurses and one respiratory therapist left in the ICU. Of course, that is when Terry's trach kinked off. Her oxygen level dropped immediately. I yelled for the respiratory therapist who arrived with Terry's doctor in tow. The doctor just happened to be in the ICU. We were in the room with Terry and they said there was nothing they could do.

What?!

I recently had seen a particular kind of wire reinforced endotracheal tube that was stronger than normal ones. I offered it as a solution, but, they were not interested. I was just an agency nurse; I had no influence. I could not force them into taking action.

What the hell! I could see the energy. It was so obvious, a blind person could have seen it. They were worn out with trying to save her. They were letting her go. So I turned to Terry who by this time was unconscious, with a very low oxygen level, heart rate and blood pressure. She was dying right before my eyes.

I took her hand and in my mind I yelled, "Hey, these jerks are gonna let you die right now and I can't stop them! If your wish is to die, okay, I will accept and support you in this. BUT, if you don't want to die, you better do something really damn quick to save yourself."

Within seconds, out of the blue, an anesthesiologist happened to walk into her room and said, "I was on my way to the code, but decided to come here first. What's happening?"

I blurted out the scenario and, again, suggested the tube with the wire.

He said, "Sure." HE ACTUALLY HAD ONE IN HIS BAG! He took out the old trach tube and put the new ET tube in its place and Terry could breathe again. Everything went back to normal and she was stable.

"Oh my God Terry! YOU DID IT."

Yikes! How awesome! I could hardly believe it! How did this happen?

Of course Terry had no consciousness of this awesome event and there was no one I could tell, except Lee who said, once again, "Linda, why are you surprised?"

I didn't get called back to that hospital for a couple of weeks. When I did return, Terry was dying. She had gone septic, was on multiple pressors, and getting blood, etc. Her body had swollen up to three times her size; her face was huge with the swelling. The nurses said she hadn't been able to open her eyes and she wasn't responding anymore, but, the husband would not let her go. They didn't assign me to her because, yeah, she was critical.

But, I went to visit her anyway and whispered in her ear, "Terry, it's me, Linda. How many mice does it take to screw in a light bulb? Two; the hard part is getting them into the light bulb."

Struggling, she cracked open one eyelid and smiled at me. I kissed her cheek. Her nurse saw it and just stared like I was a freak.

The next day they had me back and actually assigned Terry to me. She had gotten even worse through the night. I listened to the night nurse's report and knew it was the end. I went into her room and whispered in her ear, "Terry, there is nothing else we know to do to save your body now, it's dying. If there is anything you can do, you better do it fast; if you are ready to go, though, I will support you." Her heart rate dropped. "Okay, I am going to call Mike and tell him it's time."

I don't know what got into me, I felt a "strength of conviction", or a certainty, or something. When I called Mike and told him it was time to let Terry go I could hear in my voice a kind of power of authority. I don't really have the words to describe it. I think Mike heard it and I know he trusted me; he knew that I really cared about her. Without hesitation, he told me and the doctor to go ahead and stop everything. He lived a half hour away and would be there as soon as he could, but he didn't want Terry to suffer any longer.

I went to Terry, told her what Mike had said, and, that I was going to stop her treatments. I did, but Terry hung on until Mike got there. As he took her hand in his, she died.

I am very grateful to Terry. She taught me so much. From then on, I have never seen my patients as helpless victims lying in bed. She changed my perspective and my strategy for patient care. I began to focus on the *empowerment* of my patients, helping them to become aware of their own ability to affect the course of their life and their death. I am still doing this, though it is like an onion with so many layers. My patients keep teaching me and I keep learning more and more.

Oh and guess what? Once again, I cannot remember jokes. ☺

7
Lola

I want to tell you a different sort of story now; it doesn't have any spiritual communication in it, but, I so love it and I hope you do to.

It is about Lola.

Lola was in her 40's. She had a neuromuscular disorder that had been developing over time, making her weaker and weaker until eventually it would be fatal to her. Prior to being admitted to my hospital she'd already had a tracheostomy in place that she could plug and still be able to talk. She had known she would need the life support of a ventilator for breathing eventually; but, even at this stage of her process, she was not holding back on living her life to the fullest.

Fulfilling a lifelong dream, she and her boyfriend were en route to see the Grand Canyon when, in respiratory distress, she had to come to my hospital. Initially, she was put onto a hospital ventilator and then had progressed to being put onto a ventilator that she could use at home.

By the time I met Lola in the ICU, she had been on the home vent for a couple of weeks and wasn't progressing in large part because of her anxiety, depression, and agitation. She was requiring a lot of sedation to relax her enough so that the machine could assist her in breathing. She couldn't talk anymore. When I went to her bedside I saw her face was pinched into such a frown. Although, she was moderately sedated, she was still tense.

I said to her, "You don't look too happy."

She shook her head "No"

"Are you saying you are not happy?"

Nodded, "Yes."

"Are you in pain?"

Head shook, "No."

"Trouble breathing, too cold, too hot...?" I went down a list.

"No." She shook her head to all of the questions. Then she reached up and touched her trach.

"Are you unhappy with being on the ventilator?"

"Yes." She nodded.

"I was told you knew you would be on a ventilator some day and that this is what you wanted. Isn't that right?

She closed her eyes and shrugged her shoulders.

"Lola, are you happy with that decision now?"

"NO."

"Have you changed your mind?"

"Yes."

"It's okay to change your mind. You have a right to do that."

She moved her hands, searching for paper and pen. She wanted to write something. "Too late," she weakly scribbled, "I am on the machine."

"Do you feel stuck?"

She started crying and nodded, "Yes."

"Lola, you are not stuck, it is not too late. Yes, you are on life support and, yes, you still can choose what you want. You are conscious and alert. You are still in control of your healthcare. You can choose to continue on life support and have the best quality of life you can make; or, you can choose to stop life support, go on comfort care, let nature take its course and have a peaceful death."

Her eyes widened hyper-alert with hope. She grabbed my hand squeezing it tightly and nodded yes.

"I support you in whatever decision you make. I have a question though. Are you looking to escape? Are you sure you don't just need some more time to adapt to a new life style?"

"No, not escape." She wrote. "Grip reality. I am dying."

"But you knew that."

"Yes and been living life fully. Been happy. But crossed a line now. Now not being happy. Am holding on, resisting my death."

She stared at me to see my reaction. I nodded for her to continue. She seemed to become more alert, almost excited. Her writing became stronger, clearer.

"With my illness I learned to embrace life, let go of the usual expectations and I was happy. Now I want to embrace my death. Bring love and happiness to it. Am I a quitter, crazy, failure? I don't feel like one. It feels right but I don't want my daughters to be angry with me for going."

"Ahhh. I got it. You are an awesome woman. You have a lot of wisdom, thanks for sharing it with me. I am going to help you as much as I can. Okay?"

She smiled and nodded.

"Okay, the first thing you need to do is to be calm. You have needed a lot of medication to calm you down so the machine can help you breathe. Begin embracing where you are right now and stop needing these meds. You will need to communicate your wishes to your daughters and the doctor and no one is gonna believe you if you are depressed, anxious and drugged out. Understand?"

Nods.

"When you are completely drug free and calm, please re-evaluate what you are saying you want. You might not think the same way then. If you decide this is the path you want and you can demonstrate that you are awake, alert, calm, and coping, then talk with your daughters. They are going to need you to communicate your wishes from a place of love, not defeat, and somehow you are going to have to be able to do that. Can you do it?"

Smiles.

"Once you have convinced them, you will have to convince the doctor that you are completely aware of your choice and that it is truly what you want. It's gonna take a few days and effort on your part. How do you feel about it?"

She drew a smiley face.

Well, it took more than a few days. Lola's daughters got it right away. They knew their mom. They felt the love. No problem. Some of the nurses were having a problem, thinking it was an assisted suicide. I shared my perspective that there is a difference between withdrawing life support and assisted suicide. In the former, a body that has been *kept alive by artificial means* is finally allowed to have a peaceful death. In the latter, a body that is still *naturally alive but suffering* is helped to peacefully and comfortably die. This made sense to them and they became comfortable with Lola's decision. The doctor, however, was sympathetic but unsure. He insisted she have a psychiatric evaluation by not one doctor, but two. They finally all agreed that Lola was in her right mind, clearly understood her choice, and had a good attitude. They were impressed with her calm, certain presence.

Me, I was inspired by it!

Once she got the "go ahead", Lola began planning her death just like she would plan a birthday party. The friends and family she wanted to be present were notified. Her minister was notified. I brought in a beautiful aerial video of the Grand Canyon, but, first, she wanted a particular personal video to be played for everyone.

We moved her to the largest room in the ICU. People showed up and had their private times to speak with her. Then we watched her video of a benefit her friends had thrown to raise money for her trip to the Grand Canyon. It was a party with food, drinks, and a live band. The video centered on a particular dance. While the band played "Unchained Melody", person by person would drop money into a jar and take a turn dancing Lola around the floor. Male or female would tenderly put their arms around her and she would look at them with eyes and face glowing in love.

Oh my God, I don't think I can handle this!

It was all I could do to not fall apart. Tears were dribbling down my cheeks as I watched this video. My throat ached from choking back the emotion. I am the nurse, I am supposed to be strong, be professional! I was a wimp. I was being overwhelmed with the emotion. Then I heard Lola's voice in my head, *"Don't resist... embrace in love and happiness."* I grounded and centered myself. I allowed myself to feel the pain and grief and to embrace it until, finally, it moved through to peace and then to love. Without resistance it just flowed naturally to love.

We never got to the Grand Canyon video. She had seen all she wanted - the love shared by herself and the people in the video and the love she was sharing right now with the people in her room. She wrote to me that it was time. I started the intravenous medications that would keep her from experiencing the anxiety that would come with shortness of breath. The intent was to keep her mind and body at peace when we stopped her life support. She drifted into a light sleep. I disconnected the vent. At first, she frowned and grabbed her daughter's hand. Then I whispered in her ear, "You are free now to embrace in love." She smiled, became calm and in a few minutes, holding both her daughters' hands she peacefully passed away.

It isn't that I had never had a patient die before this. I just had never had a patient *consciously choose* to stop life support and have a peaceful death. I had never seen someone try to convince their loved ones that it was okay, the right thing to do, and then support the loved ones while *they* processed and grieved. I had never seen such loving strength, certainty and patience. I had never been so emotionally melted in a patient's case. I learned I could "go there" with my patients and families. I could embrace my humanity within my professionalism and I could become stronger, more compassionate, more of a rock for my patients and families to hold onto during their most vulnerable times. Lola had given me a gift, a gift I embrace still today.

8
Abigail

I had always been an aggressive patient advocate. You notice I said aggressive not just assertive. Yeah, I have been known to holler at a few doctors and to demand or refuse orders when I was advocating for my patient. All of my life, beginning as the eldest kid of a large family, I have been fighting with my mouth, fists, manipulation, resistance, strength -whatever it would take - to protect the more vulnerable within my sphere of responsibility. Adding in the awareness of spiritual communication almost cost me a job. Here is the story:

Abigail was a plucky, 83 year old. She had some kind of an inflammatory process in her lungs causing respiratory failure and a need for the ventilator. She was not having an easy go at recovery. At this time, the only treatment we could think to help her was high dose steroids. Doesn't it just figure, Abigail had an allergy or sensitivity to steroids and needed *more* meds to counteract the allergic reactions. It was complicated. Considering her age, the doctors and her family were wondering if it was worth it to keep going.

She could hear them talking. I could see the doubt in her face and so I snuck in a *"Hello"* to her in my mind. Yes, she was doubtful there too.

She said, "I'm 83. I've had a good life; maybe it is time to just stop."

I am a big supporter of patient rights, but something just didn't feel right to me. *"Abigail, I can see you feel you've had a good life. I am just wondering what you would choose if you could have whatever you wanted. Do you feel you have had enough of this life? Are you finished with living in this body? Is there nothing else you would choose to experience?"*

"No, no. It's not that at all. I really like to live. I am happy with my life. I stay active. It just seems like maybe it's time for me to go. 'They' all think I should go. I am 83 after all."

"83, smatey 3. Do you feel like an old woman? Are you done?"

"Well that's just it. I don't feel like an old woman and up until now I've been able to do the things I want. But maybe..."

She was waffling. I intuitively felt that her choice was crucial in whether she would live or die. *"If you could come out of this illness close to your normal self, would you want that or are you ready to take your 'next step'?"*

"I'd want to live." Finally, a clear statement.

Over the next few days, whether at work or at home, I would talk with Abigail in my mind; supporting her when she was feeling down; re-enforcing her strength and will to live.

One night, while talking with her at home, I knew she'd reached a crisis point. I knew the following day she would have to cross some line and how she did it would determine her fate. I was anxious to get to work to support her. Whatever she wanted would be fine with me. My job, as I saw it, was to help her make a choice based upon Love not Fear.

But, when I got to work, I found I was being floated to the med-surg floor. We had a policy in this ICU, as in most ICU'S, that we took turns floating. But, we also had a policy that the nurses on the telemetry unit who had been cross trained in ICU could be floated into ICU from their telemetry unit to replace one of us when we were floated out to a med-surg floor. It was the dumbest thing I had ever heard of, but, I had done this float many times already. However, this day I refused to go.

I told my charge nurse, "Abigail needs me to be with her today. She is going into a crisis and needs the kind of support I can give her."

O my God, I am sure they thought I was frakking nuts. I thought I was frakking nuts! Yes, I had a good reputation for taking care of patients. Yes, they knew I was a strong patient advocate and that I worked really well with death and dying in the ICU. But, what made me think my patient was gonna have a crisis that day and who am I to think she needed me? I don't think I had told anyone about being able to speak with people's spirits. I am pretty sure no one there knew that about me.

"Linda, you know you can't refuse to float." My charge nurse told me.

"Look, Abigail needs me today. She is in a crisis, I am not gonna leave her. If you make me float, I will resign."

WHAT IS UP WITH ME? Linda what the HELL are you saying? I know you feel strongly about this, but, dude, you're gonna lose your job. Are you just totally losing it? Dang, I can hardly believe the words my own ears are hearing me say. NO! It doesn't matter. Abigail needs me today.

Well, you can bet my ultimatum went over big. Next thing you know the nurse manager and the supervisor were involved.

Unbeknownst to me, they were questioning the off going night nurses about Abigail's condition; about me as her caregiver; and, about me as a caregiver in general. They were talking with my charge nurse. I never knew what went down, but they decided to let me stay and take care of Abigail.

That day, Abigail did go into a physical crisis. As I did the intensive physical cares, I kept communicating with her verbally and spiritually. We took it moment by moment; each moment with love to surround and support her; each moment a choice to live or to die.

"What do you want to do, Abigail?

"I want to live, Linda"

"Okay, I am here with you."

"It hurts, Linda. Not sure, I can do it."

"If you could do it, what would you want?

"To live and be well."

"Breathe in the Love and the Light, bring it right into your body."

All day, Abigail kept choosing Love, Light, and Life. No more waffling. All day we struggled for her body. In the end, she did it! She turned a corner. She chose to survive and to live. She continued to get better over the next few weeks, made it out of the hospital and eventually to home again.

My first nursing award was from that ICU. It was the "Friends and Heroes" award.

I have never put my job on the line again.

I have put my reputation on the line ever since.

I don't wait to let people have awareness of my spiritual talks. I don't try to keep it a secret anymore. I don't wait until "they" know me well enough to think, "Well, maybe she's not too crazy." At every job, there would always be one or two nurses that would know. Over the years, more and more coworkers would know and I would be assigned to specific patients and families that they thought needed my kind of help.

My passion brought me exposure. With exposure came expectation, a need to prove, wanting to do more and more, self-importance, failure, self-doubt, fear, getting stuck, anger, rejection, forgiveness, humility, hope, and renewal.

I suspect I will be writing about this process along with my stories. You see it is through my relationships with my husband, my patients, my family and my coworkers that I have evolved. I have so many stories and as I look at my list, I can see how they have reflected my own issues. I hope you are still with me. I hope you are still interested. Maybe some of these stories will be of service to you, too.

9
Frequency/Form/Fork/Intention

Why did I ever think that I could help heal people? I had an experience in the early 1990's that rocked my world, sent me down a rabbit hole, and has motivated much of my searching since.

Before I get into that though, I need to present a couple of concepts that you may or may not already be familiar with: Frequency and Intention.

Science has shown us that everything is made up of energy. A rock that feels so solid to our hands is still only a construct of vibrating energy particles, - atoms and protons, etc. - with space in between them. Weird, huh? I bet if you hit me on the head with that rock I wouldn't say it felt like spacey particles. Actually, I'd probably be the one feeling spacey! Sorry, I just had to say it.

Energy particles vibrate at different speeds. This is called their frequency. Depending upon the frequency energy vibrates at, we experience it as solid, liquid, gas, light, sound, thought, emotion, etc. One example is ice. It is created by energy particles vibrating at a frequency that makes it a solid, but, if you increase the frequency of the particles by heating up the ice, it will turn into water. Increasing the frequency more will vaporize the liquid into air. You probably know all of this already.

Another example is when light passes through a prism its vibration changes into several different frequencies that produce several colors.

How we interface with energy depends upon how our frequency/vibe is communicating with their frequency/vibe. (See chapters 22 and 28)

Our bodies are made up of several frequencies – solid, liquid, gas (some more than others, ha ha), emotional, mental and spiritual. Science has begun to call our bodies a "biofield". In metaphysics these energies are called the "aura".

Have you heard the saying, "form follows thought"? One day, while I was meditating I "saw", in my mind, a kind of a movie picture showing me *unformed* energy particles being transformed from a "possibility" into a *formed* physical "reality". It was done by changing the frequency of the energy particles from an unformed "no-thing" to a formed "some-thing". For the first time, I was seeing that the so called emptiness of space was actually pregnant with life just waiting to be created into something.

In this picture of pregnant space, I perceived the "basic life energies" as neutral, unformed, energy particles flowing around in space, ready to be molded into an idea. To me, it was like watching little letters floating around in the air waiting for someone to pluck them out of the space and form them into words which could then be formed into sentences to express an idea that could then be created or acted upon physically. I called it potential energy. Now I know they are called quantum particles.

Watching the movie in my mind, it appeared as though just a single impulse created a light ray that would reach out, snag some of those free flowing energy particles out of the pregnant space and bring them into the light web of my personal energy space – my biofield/ my aura. It was like watching an energy whirlpool (vortex) that spiraled and slowed down into my mind, my emotions, and then into my physical reality.

When those free flowing energy particles entered into my space, their vibration slowed down to match the frequency of my thought. I could have stopped right there, let it all go and nothing more would have come of it. BUT, the more **attention** I gave to this thought, the more I developed it, the more the energy vibration slowed down until it matched my *mental* frequency and became a full-fledged idea or concept.

As I gave *more* attention to this idea, the energy vibration slowed down until I developed a *feel* for it on my *emotional frequency*.

As I *continued* to pay attention to my thoughts and feelings, the energy vibration would slow down even more until it would manifest on my *physical* frequency as "some-thing". Maybe it would be an action or behavior on my part; maybe a person or an event would come into my life; maybe I would become ill; or, maybe I would become well, whatever.

Form followed thought.

Again, it wasn't that every thought I had came into my reality. No, the ones that manifested were the ones that I gave a lot of attention to because I either really wanted them *or* I really *didn't* want them. In fact, it seemed almost easier to manifest what I didn't want because I gave sooo much attention to not wanting them. It would have been better to focus on what I did want instead. (This, I learned in later years, is called the Law of Attraction.)

Now, I want to talk about the concept of **Intention**.

In the dictionary intention is defined as an aim or purpose that guides an action or objective. For me, Intention is to consciously think a thought or to make a statement that then provides *direction* for the flow of energy to manifest a desired outcome. For example, in healing work my intention is to communicate Unconditional Love and to achieve the Highest Good for my client.

So, from the concepts of Frequency and Intention, I saw that healing work could happen on one frequency- be it spiritual, mental, emotional, or physical, and could then cause change on the other frequencies. Whatever frequency a person can receive healing on is the *entry* point to helping the total self. If a person is receptive to body work – start there. If they want to pray – start there. If they want psychotherapy – start there.

This brings me back to the original question of why I thought I could heal people. Ever since I had that meditation, I have seen reality as being an energy manifestation - a virtual reality picture - of a thought, a belief, or an agreement. Sooo, I wondered if I could just **change the picture**.

Lee and I were taking a road trip to Oregon. It was going to be a 10 – 12 hour drive. I had a humongous cold sore on my lip. I got them a lot back then and they usually took forever to heal. I decided to experiment and see if I could make it go away by changing the picture. I sat in the passenger seat of our car, looking into the mirror on the visor. I saw the sore and thought my intention to heal it. Then, I put my attention on the well part of my lip at the edge of the sore. I would say to myself over and over, "change the picture", then I would blink and *imagine* I could see more healthy lip tissue instead of a sore. It took ten hours of effort but that sucker disappeared down to the size of pin head.

Holy moly! I did it!

I hadn't told Lee what I was doing, but at the end I turned to him and said. "Does my lip look any different to you?"

"Hmmm," He said vaguely, unsure. "Didn't you have a sore there?" He couldn't really remember anymore. I thought that was interesting. Did changing my reality affect other's realities?

Oh my God, now what? It is so awesomely cool, but, what do I do with this, what does it mean? Do I have to go out and heal the world now? Can I do that? Do I want to? What would happen if I did? What about Lee?

Needless to say I was very excited, but, at the same time, I was aware of my resistance. I could not finish the process and heal my lip all together. It was really frustrating. That damn pin-sized sore lasted almost two weeks.

I scared myself with this experience. The ramifications were 8.0 on the Richter scale - huge to me. If I could do this then why didn't I always do it for myself, for others, or for the world? I had a lot of fear of what I might be able to change in my life. Albeit, not everything I had was good for me, but I wasn't ready to let go of them. What about changing other people's lives? For better or for worse, it is *their* life, their choice. And, even If I could make changes, would that weaken them or empower them? Would they rely upon me and never learn about their own power to heal? Would they get angry and turn on me? Did I want to dedicate my whole life to healing? What about just having fun? What was the right thing to do? I was overwhelmed, afraid, and conflicted.

This was it! **This was the fork** in the road. I can see that now. I wasn't ready to go down that path back then; and so, I wasn't able to change the picture like that again.

BUT, I KNEW! I knew it could be done and I knew I had done it. No matter what rabbit hole I went down, no matter how much I tried to minimize or deny this experience, it was always there, in the back of my mind, motivating me to work through my issues; prodding me to keep going; to keep learning; and, to keep evolving, so I could reach my full potential.

I still did some healing work. Once, I had a patient whose central IV catheter had been taken out, but it wouldn't stop bleeding from the puncture site. Despite direct pressure with my fingers or a pressure bandage, it oozed for hours. Finally, while she was dozing I decided to use energy to see if I could heal it. Without touching her, I just pointed my finger at the site and imagined the energy going to the puncture site of the vein and seeing the cells of the vessel knit close without scarring. She woke up and said, 'It feels like your finger is inside of me." I told her what I was doing and she went back to sleep. The bleeding stopped. My charge nurse noticed this and just gave me a look. Whatever.

Another time, when I was trying to create a private practice, a woman came to me because she had some kind of hard lump on her jaw. She said she had been to see a couple of doctors and they told her it was some kind of "thing" that would go away eventually. But, it had been a year and the "thing" had not gone away. So, we did some guided imagery and Healing Touch. A couple of weeks later she called and said it was gone. I never heard from her again.

Over the years, these kinds of experiences kept me going; kept me trying; kept reminding me of what *could be done*. But, I still had issues and I was inconsistent in success.

Part of me was puffed up with self-importance; wow, look at me, see what I can do, I am special. I hated that arrogance and what it told me about myself... a lack of self-esteem.

Part of me was still afraid to know what could be done because then I would have a responsibility to do it and it could put my life onto a path I wasn't sure I wanted to take.

Part of me wanted to continue being a victim and not admit to the fact that I was creating so much of the shit I was experiencing in my life and that I could change it.

Part of me wanted to be and do "the Highest Good"; to be "my Full Potential"; and, to "be a Light" in the world because I cared.

Fear and conflict lead to mixed desires, mixed signals, mixed energies, and mixed choices that lead to mixed manifestations.

I still didn't trust in a God. O yeah we had conversations; didn't mean I trusted. Probably the biggest issue was that I *still wanted to have whatever I wanted* and I was afraid to find out that what I wanted might not be the Highest Good or what was best. I was always putting myself into positions of rebellion, bargaining, and trying to convince the universe *that my way was best.*

From *my perspective*, I wanted two conflicting things. On one hand I wanted: "whatever I damn well pleased", AND, on the other hand I wanted: "the Highest Good; whatever Love/ God thinks is best".

O man, THIS IS THE FORK IN THE ROAD! Again.

I have *believed* these desires/intentions were two *different* paths that I keep straddling and so I keep experiencing conflicting results. These conflicting results were my proof and reinforced my belief that the things I wanted *were* in conflict with each other. And *because I believe* it all, it has been so. **It is a self-fulfilling circle.**

As I am writing this book, I can see how I am still at that fork in the road, believing I am straddling two conflicting paths. My belief has kept me stuck at a certain level of awareness. I can see now why I have become so proficient in the kind of healing work that I do. It is reflective of my own evolution. Looking back, I can see I have been helping people in "transition". Now, I can see that I, too, have been in transition.

My sub-specialty in the ICU is dealing with "critical" and "end of life" choices. I help my patients become aware of their spiritual self and see that they are more than their bodies. I help them explore what they believe about being out of their body; what they believe about dying. I help them explore their self-image – what they believe about themselves and to see a more truthful SELF. I help restore them to a place of love and self-acceptance. From that place they may choose whether to try to heal their body if they can, or, to leave it.

All of this is going on in my mind and my imagination, but, enough of it has been verified or experienced consciously by my patient's families or my peers that I have accepted the validity of it. My peers often refer patients and families to me, or, they will come up to me and say, "Linda have you talked to him/her yet?" referring to a patient. Further validation to me.

In addition to helping my patients, I try to help their families' transition by keeping them informed; educating and empowering them to make decisions founded upon Love rather than fear. I even wrote a little book entitled, Where do YOU draw the line?- an insider's guide to effective Living Wills, Healing, and Critical Care, to help people before they get into a situation like those I see every day.

People ask me why I don't work in Hospice. Well, DUUUUDE! I want my patients to heal and be happy. It's just that I have learned it is not about what I want. I have to allow my patients to have what they want and to support whatever is their "Highest Good"; sometimes their Highest Good is to make that transition from spirit in a physical body to spirit out of a physical body. When I see that, I want to empower them to do it in Love not fear. In return, my patients keep showing me how making choices based upon Love really does work best. I have seen some awesome transitions with my patients. I call them the" miracles in dying".

10
Mrs. Dodds

One story is about Mrs. Violet Dodds, an elderly woman who developed respiratory and heart problems and was not doing well. She was married to Todd. Her adult children were Tony, Mike, and Madeline. They were a close and loving family. For some reason I always remember Violet as Mrs. Dodds. She was a very sweet woman, very graceful even in her illness.

After I say, "Hello" to a patient's spirit, one of the things I may do is to have them stand in front of a full length mirror in my mind. I have them look at the "truth" of who they are rather than what they have been believing they are. I am always amazed at what they see there. It's different for every person. I don't always understand what I see but it is an awesome healing experience for the patient.

Mrs. Dodds had been in the ICU for almost a month. She had slowly worsened until she was unconscious. One Saturday morning, I was talking with her in my head about her body, herself, what she believed about leaving her body, etc. Then, I asked her to look into the mirror.

Violet's reflection was of herself at around age 16. She had long hair almost to her waist. She was dressed in a kind of white shift or maybe a muslin type nightgown and she was barefoot. She looked so very innocent and sweet to me.

"Violet, you are lovely." She shyly smiled. Suddenly, I could see that she was in a little field filled with daisies. She sat down in the grass and started to make a daisy chain. "Violet, what do you believe happens when you leave your body?"

"Oh, I will go to Heaven, Linda."

"How do you feel about going there?"

"I will be going soon, I know that. I am not worried or scared, if that is what you want to know. I know I will be with my Father there. Truly, I am looking forward to leaving. My body is becoming just a shell now."

"That's beautiful. I am curious though, if you are ready to go, why haven't you gone?"

She sighed, "I don't want my family to feel like I have abandoned them. And..." she hesitated, and then whispered, "Linda, I don't want to be alone when I die."

Later that day, her eldest son, Tony, was visiting. Tony, from my perspective was the most conservative person in the family. He wasn't into "spiritual" stuff at all, so I didn't mention my conversation with his mom, except for one thing. We were standing at the foot of her bed and I asked, "Tony, would you feel abandoned if your mom died?"

His face got all soft and he said. "No. I know mom would never abandon us. If it is her time to go then that is how it is."

I clarified, "So it would be okay for her to go when it is her time. Do the others feel this way too?"

He said, "Yes, we all love mom and want what is best for her. We know she loves us."

Hmmm.

The next day, Sunday, Mrs. Dodds took a sudden turn for the worst. Her heart rate dropped to 30, her blood pressure dropped. She was clearly in a dying process. None of the family was there.

She doesn't want to die alone, Linda. I know, I know. Hurry up, call everyone.

I called, Todd. No answer. I called Tony. No answer. I called Mike. No answer. I called Madeline. No answer. No one was home! I left messages on their machines. Desperate, I called Madeline's office. Her boss happened to be there on a Sunday and said he would try to contact her.

Damn, I can't find anyone; I don't know what to do. She doesn't want to be alone! Okay, Linda, you're starting to panic, just chill out; ground and center. Breathe. Okay, okay, she is dying and there is no one here but me.

Although, I had another patient, I didn't want to leave Violet alone. I asked the other nurses to please keep an eye on my other patient. Then I went into Violet's room, stood at the head of her bed and said, "I'm here, Violet, you are not alone." I started combing her hair, massaging her head and sending her love. It was quite peaceful.

All of a sudden in my mind's eye, I saw this male like figure with huge wings float down through the ceiling reaching for Violet. Then I saw Violet, in the image of the young girl in her white shift and bare feet, float out of her body reaching and wrapping her arms around the angel's neck. He draped her body in his arms and they floated up through the ceiling. Dreamy eyed, Violet, never took her gaze from his face.

Wooo, okey dokey now! Never saw that before. I took a deep breath and kept combing her hair. Her heart was still beating, but she was gone.

Less than five minutes later, her husband arrived. I asked if he had received my messages, but he merely replied, "No, I didn't get a message, I just came." Then, in just the space of another few minutes, one by one all of her kids were there. No one had gotten a message, they were just showing up. As they came into the room and saw the monitor, they all knew what was happening and surrounded her bed.

I asked, "If you could say something to Violet right now, what would you say?" Each one had a little message for her. When they finished, her body died.

Each person then had a little private time with her. When Madeline finished her time, I took a chance and told her what I saw. Her face lit up with joy.

A few weeks later some flowers and a card came for me from Madeline. She related how, at the funeral, people kept commenting that she seemed so peaceful about her mom's death and she would tell them, "That's because I know my mom flew off with an angel."

A few years later, I was in a jury duty holding pen and I heard someone yell my name. It was Madeline. She told me she has never forgotten and how much it has helped her in her life

11
Thunder Woman

Another story is about Emily, a woman in her 70's who had a respiratory problem. She was intubated, eventually requiring the placement of a tracheostomy tube, and, was just not progressing. She had two adult daughters, Martha and Tina who had families of their own but who were also very involved with their mom's life. Martha, especially, was at her mom's beck and call. I would say they had a love/exasperation relationship. She and I had talked a lot about setting limits in the relationship.

Emily was conscious, well informed, and continued wanting to be a Full Code, meaning she would want resuscitation if her body failed. Her daughters supported her decision. After almost a month, though, Emily was deteriorating and communicated to her daughters it was "time to go".

Martha and Tina informed all of the family. The plan was for Emily to go onto comfort care and be detached from the ventilator. The expectation was that she would peacefully die in her own time. Emily's room turned into a kind of a shrine. A table was set up with family pictures on it. There were candles even though we couldn't light them. The room was scented with a beautiful perfume and a cellist came in to play music for a while. Although, the extended family members all came in to say good bye, Emily did not want anyone in the room when she died except Tina, Martha and me. So, after saying their goodbyes, the rest of the family stayed in the waiting room.

Everything was set and when Emily gave the go ahead, we began the comfort medicine and disconnected her from the ventilator. She was unconscious and appeared to be comfortable. Tina and Martha, quiet and reverent in their grief, kept vigil by her side as the day slowly wore on.

At one point when I came to check on Emily, I heard her in my head.

"Tell my daughters that even though my body is dying, I am still here."

"No. You're a powerful woman, you tell them yourself. I am not gonna play this game with you. If you have something to say, you do it." I left the room.

Linda, what the heck are you doing? That wasn't very nice. Yeah, but I've watched all of the game playing between Emily and Martha this past month. I've heard all of the passive/aggressive stories and the guilt tripping. I'm not getting into it. Are you sure, because it sounds pretty judgmental? Yeah, it does. Guilt, guilt, guilt. Hmmm, I don't know, maybe it was too harsh. *HEY, dang, this is the game and I fell for it!* Okay, ground and center. What is best? Yeah, it still feels like the right way to handle this. I am going for it.

In about 30 minutes Emily's alarm went off at the nurse's desk because her heart rate had dropped to 20 beats per minute. I went to check in the room; the girls were stressed and crying. As I walked in, the heart rate went back up. I stayed and talked with them for a bit when, suddenly, I felt the urge to tell them about how Emily wanted me to give them a message and me telling her she would have to communicate to them herself.

As I finished telling them this, Emily's heart rate dropped again and continued to drop. *In the instant* that the monitor flat lined there was a thunderous boom that shook the window. The girls jumped out of their seats exclaiming, "We hear you Mom, we hear you."

I left the room, my heart in my throat. One of the nurses said, "O my God, that was her, she died."

The family members came running in from the waiting room. They had heard the boom, and they, too, felt the sound was from Emily.

A coincidence? There had been no lightening, no storm, no rain, and no loud accident. We never could explain away that sound and, eventually, I stopped trying to. The girls were peaceful, happy and grateful. They would proudly tease, saying, "We come from a woman who can create thunder!"

12
Ted

As I've said, I often don't understand the things I see or do, yet, I am glad to be a part of them. This next story, though, was pretty darn clear to me.

Mr. Ted Johnson was sick and dying in the ICU. He had lived with his daughter, Amy for several years after his wife had died. Amy was a good daughter, very attentive and took good care of him. But, she was a little dramatic and things were always "about her".

The day Ted was actively dying is the day I took care of him. Amy was there with a lot a family including a grandson in his early 20's. Suddenly, Ted's heart rate and blood pressure dropped precipitously. Amy started to loudly cry and people started consoling her. The grandson stormed out of the room, slamming the door. The rest of the family was quietly grieving.

Ted's heart rate and blood pressure came back up to normal.

What?!

Amy calmed down, the grandson came back and they all sat down. Suddenly, Ted's vital sign's dropped again. Once again, Amy started loudly crying, the grandson stormed out, and slammed the door.

Guess what? You got it. Ted's vital signs returned to normal and every one calmed down again.

This time I asked, "Hey, is Ted a jokester? Did he like to play practical jokes on you?"

Yeah he did.

"Well he is doing it now. What do you think he would want you all to be doing right now? Would he want you to be unhappy or would he want you to be remembering and sharing those jokes he played on you?"

They knew that that is exactly what he would want and so they started sharing the memories and I am telling you this guy was a real comedian.

I asked if he had a favorite hat or shoes that he always wore. Yes, he always wore a red baseball cap. It happened to be in the closet. So we put that on his head and the family continued to reminisce about the jokes.

At one point while they were all laughing, Ted's vital signs quickly dropped to nothing and stayed there. But, this time, the family was able to feel the love and joy they had shared with Ted and in that energy they were able to let him go.

Way to go, Ted.

13
Healing/Protection/POV/Movie/Act-React

People often ask me, "Doesn't it take away your energy to do healing work?"

No, because, when I am giving a healing, I am receiving a healing. First, it is because of all the awesome loving energy flowing through me to my clients; I get to have it too! Second, as I mentioned earlier, I am aware that what I notice in someone else's energy field could be a reflection of something I have in my own energy field. Remember how I said that seeing an issue inside of myself may be too hard and that it's much easier to see the issue in another person? When I am doing healings, if I see a matching picture, I can use it an opportunity to heal myself; to make new choices based upon who I am NOW. In this way I am receiving healing as I am giving healing and I am refreshed with it.

Another question people often ask is, "What about protecting yourself when you do healing?"

Well, first, I have all of that wonderful loving energy flowing through me and I am receiving healing as I give it. Second, I don't feel that protection is needed. Remember, earlier, I said that everything I sense gets *filtered* through my personal beliefs and programming. All of my interpretations of what I sense really reflect my own belief system. It's like looking into a mirror. So, I pay attention to what I notice or feel about others and view everything as an opportunity to make a new choice for myself. Because of this I see everyone and everything, including whatever appears to be threatening or pushing my buttons, *as a gift* and an opportunity to choose a new and better perspective. I *allow* a new perspective, founded upon Love and Happiness, to enter into my consciousness. Because I choose to be this way, there is nothing I need to protect myself from. It is *all* a blessing.

Third, as my awareness expands, I don't see separation; I see that LOVE is at the core of everything and it makes us ONE; so, from this point of view there is only Love and harmonious Intent. Once again, there is nothing to protect myself from.

How I am experiencing myself and my life depends upon which point of view I am focusing my awareness and attention from.

Mmmm, I am going to elaborate upon this.

When I am being "mini me" i.e. "Linda", a single, solitary, person in a physical body, all of my attention and awareness will be focused from this narrow point of view. From this point of view I may have a belief of being separate from everything else. If I believe I am separate, it is possible to feel alone, fearful, threatened, angry, or aggressive. From a narrow point of view like this, I can only see a *piece* of the bigger picture.

Let's see if I can make this simpler.

It's kind of like being part of a movie. For example, Clint Eastwood may come up with an idea for a movie, so, he decides to put on his hat as writer and writes a script. Then, he decides to fund and manage the project, so, puts on the hat of producer. Then, he decides to put on the hat of director and directs the movie. Then, he decides to play one of the characters in the movie, so, he puts on the hat of actor and plays the character. Now, he has on the hat of the character too.

That's a lot of HATS! With each hat he has a different *point of view* of the picture. He, also, has different points of view *from which to experience himself.* For example, when he has on his hat as his character, his attention is fully focused upon *being* the character *in that moment.* He might experience loneliness or threat from the other characters because, in that moment, he is experiencing himself from his character's point of view. Conversely, when he has on his director's hat he has a broader point of view. He doesn't see actors threatening each other. He sees them *playing a role to create an effect.* He sees a *bigger picture.*

How does he do it? How can he be a producer watching the budget of a movie; a director telling actors what to do; and still play a character living in the slums, stuck in the memories of a war, grieving his wife's death, and getting involved with the life of the neighbors' kids? How does he NOT get stuck in his character and still remember who he is when it is time to yell, "Cut"?

Of course, a part of him has to always retain the awareness of who he really is so that he can *shift* his point of view as needed. He shifts his point of view from the micro to the macro and back again. Not only can he see the big picture he also gets to play the narrow minded character in it. Sometimes I call this the "mini-me, the big-me and the all-me".

Another "point of view" example is the joke of the 5 blind men trying to describe an elephant. Each of them was touching only a particular part of the elephant; yet, each of them thought they then knew what an elephant looked like. But, none of them got the bigger picture - the whole picture. One, they couldn't *see*, so they each had to feel their way around. Two, they would not *listen* to each other's description. Three, they each developed their *own separate points of view*. Four, they believed that the "other's" differing points of view were a *challenge and a threat* to their own. So, they stayed separate, feeling threatened, needing to protect themselves and their beliefs. Five, they *did not recognize an opportunity* to come together as one, in order to have a broader, and united point of view; an opportunity to see a bigger picture – a whole picture.

Get it?

Where does your awareness and attention stem from? Is it always from the point of view of the person you think you are – the role you are playing? Do you ever get out of your character and look at yourself from a broader point of view, perhaps your director's point of view? Or, in different words, do you ever take time to become aware of yourself and your life from the perspective of Love/ God/ Spirit/ Oneness/ Higher Self/ Source/ Inner Wisdom/ Inner Being/ Universal Consciousness, etc whatever you want to call it? Do you ever look at the big picture of your life, your reality?

There are many paths to obtaining this perspective. When people ask me, I say just make an intention that you want to perceive from a better perspective. I always choose Love's perception; you might choose another word. You have your own path, your own unique way. Ask, and then allow it to come to you. It will.

The point of all of this Self-awareness and bigger picture stuff is that I recognize I am *more* than my body and that I *shape* my reality; I am a not victim to it. I create it by my *thoughts* and my *choices* which are then *fueled by my emotions* and given *form by my words and actions*. When I can remember all of this I can make conscious deliberate choices based upon Love and Happiness. When I don't remember, am not conscious of it, then my choices are made by *default* and that is when I feel helpless and victimized.

To elaborate, if I am being Linda, in my body, and can remember that I am more than "mini me", then, I can allow my awareness to expand and *put on all of my hats*-character/director/producer/creator – *at the same time*. With all of my hats on, I can *listen* to my more aware Self; *see* from an expanded point of view; and have a more complete picture. Then, from my greater awareness, I can make better choices based upon Love rather than fear. My Toltec mentor, Lennie Tan called this, "being awake in the dream". To me that means living consciously with awareness of the bigger picture.

When I am doing this, I *act* rather than *re-act*. I tend to see all situations as an opportunity to make a conscious choice to have Love and Happiness instead of fear and anger. The next story is a good example of this.

14
Jonas/Challenging my Spirit

For a long time in my life I had to deal with a lot of bullies in one form or another. For a long time I did it with my fists or my words. But I have changed.

I had started a new job in an ICU. During the first shift I met a nurse named Jonas. Jonas was a BIG guy with long hair and had a kind of a tough guy persona. He would point his finger at people and say, "Target, target, target" while mimicking shooting them.

Yeah man, right off there was friction with us. He was aggressive and would make derisive comments about people that were teasing but hurtful. He only did it to me once. I gave him so much derisive shit back he never did it to me again. But, he constantly did it to others. Our coworkers would laugh it all off, but, I don't let people bully me nor anyone else around me. Whenever Jonas made a smart ass bullying comment to someone, I would comment right back. I never let him slide and it was apparent to everyone we worked with that there was going to be trouble.

The problem was we *did* have to work together, sometimes with the same patients. Oh my gosh, it was hard. We had such different intents and approaches to patient care. This culminated one afternoon when we were admitting a patient together who had to go to surgery right away; halfway through the process we were glaring at each other over the patient's bed.

What the HELL am I doing? I am ready to go off on this guy! Dude, this is not who I am anymore. This is not how I want to be. It's got to change now!

That night, at home, I got into a light, relaxed, meditative state and began seeing from my "director's point of view". I imagined I was sitting up high in the last row of a theatre. Looking down at the stage, I could see Jonas and myself snarling at each other. Usually, watching from this point of view would give me enough objectivity, but, this time it didn't. I could still feel myself seething. So I pretended the actor Steven Seagal was on stage playing Jonas and the actress Sigourney Weaver was playing Linda. Then I watched them go through their sparring. NOW, I had enough objectivity to see the games; to see what matching pictures I had with Jonas; and what buttons were being pushed. *They had been hiding from me*! They were things I did not want to look at, hard things; things that made me scared, angry and caused me to want to fight.

Right then, I knew I had an opportunity to heal myself if I chose to. I had to get out of my character's perspective and see a bigger picture. First, I chose to forgive Jonas of my perception of him as an asshole. I chose to recognize that I perceived him through the filters of my own beliefs. I wasn't really seeing him. Second, I chose to perceive from Love's point of view instead. But, it wasn't that easy for me. I had a hell of a lot of emotional baggage. So, I allowed myself to feel my emotions, to see what I was afraid of. I let myself be scared, and angry, playing out fighting scenes on the stage below me. I kept doing it over and over until my emotions were played out and I started laughing at the ridiculousness of it all. This is what I call "walking through the valley of the shadows of death." I kept plodding through the murky darkness of my emotions and beliefs knowing with full certainty that there was a light on the other side of the valley. When I finally got to that point, I thanked Jonas for pushing my buttons; for making me look at what I had been hiding from. I thanked him for being my angel and giving me this opportunity to heal and to love myself more.

When I got back to work, I felt nothing but Love for Jonas. Somehow everything changed. He became soft and sweet when he was around me. I began to wonder if he was really different or only that I saw him differently. I never found out because I only saw and heard good things from then on. My reality, my picture had changed. I'll tell ya, it's a whole lot better than fighting.

Sooo, to reiterate, I see me playing the character, Linda, in a movie picture. When I get out of that point of view and into a broader one, my awareness, perception, attention, and focus changes. I see a bigger picture. As my awareness expands I see no separation between us; LOVE makes us One. It's very cool.

Having this awareness has taken a significant amount of fear out of my life. Yeah, I am not perfect, but I am a lot better. Sometimes, friends say I don't have enough fear because I will do things that others might consider risky. I try to tell them it is a matter of perspective. To me there was no risk, there was no danger, because in that moment I was One; I was aware of myself and my connection to all; I was comfortable in my skin, and this made the energy of the situation a loving one.

Don't get me wrong. This doesn't mean that I am ignorant of the dangers I can get myself into when I am lacking awareness; when my point of view is narrow; and when I am caught up in game of my character and story. I am very aware of the stupid choices I can and do make. I do try to not "challenge my spirit" by putting myself into dangerous situations and thinking, "Well if I am truly an evolved spiritual being, this should not hurt me." No way! If I am in a situation where I am having *that* kind of thought, then I am already in way over my head. No, I try to not be stupid. It's just that now I recognize I am not alone. The part of me I call "Linda in a body" is the mini-me, the small portion of who I am. Now I know there is the big-me and the all-me. There is Love.

As a child, my point of view was such a sad thing. Growing up I used to feel so alone and responsible; I sometimes felt abandoned. If I met a challenge I had difficulty with I might get angry or feel like a victim. Sometimes I gave up; most times I pushed through it, because, hey, there was no one else to take care of it. Over the years, little by little, as I have become aware of my Inner Self and Oneness, I have learned a new way. I learned that when a situation becomes too hard, too scary, or too much for me to handle, I can just say something like: "I give! / Uncle! / Love, I need you to help me". And you know what? The pressure relaxes and I can cope. Sometimes, the situation changes and I am not even aware of it until after it has happened. I know I'm not alone; I know something has my back; and I can live from Love rather than fear. I have learned to trust this. But... I do forget to use it. ☺

15
Mr. Sands/Fetus

I love to watch how my patients' points of view change when they become aware that they are more than their bodies; that they have a non-physical self. This is huge. It is awesome to watch then as the non-physical spiritual being begins its transition into a larger awareness of itself. I see how the physical self was never really alone because their non-physical Self was always there with them. Whether I am working with clients transitioning out of their bodies, or, trying to heal their bodies, or, I am working with family members, I intend to bring their awareness and attention to this part of themselves. I help them to see or hear it. From my perspective this is the Core Self. I call it Love.

I love this next story:

Mr. Sands can be a harsh, cranky man. I went to school with his son, Jake, and I witnessed some of the hard times he'd had with his dad. Unfortunately, Jake has already passed away. But, his sisters, my friends, Patty and Josephine are still coping with their dad.

Mr. Sands was in the hospital for an extended time due to complications from surgery. They thought he wouldn't make it a few times, but, he did and now he's in a nursing home, being grumpy and not cooperating with his recovery.

I received an exasperated email one day from Patty; she was venting and trying to cope. While reading the email, without warning, I found myself saying, *"Hello"* to Mr. Sands.

I see him standing by the side of his body.

Despairingly, he runs his hand through his hair and mumbles, "I know I'm a grump. It's who I am. I'm tired. If I go into the "life review" shit now, what am I gonna do? I've been a shit for so long. To change now would be so out of character for me. What! Am I suddenly gonna get religion and be a different person? What for?"

He continued to ramble, "I can't even bring these thoughts to conscious awareness in my body. If I try to think about them when I'm awake, I just fall asleep. But, here in this place, these thoughts are needling me; I can't get rid of them!" He sounded desperate and walked away from his body.

Turning toward me, he exclaimed, "Look, can you imagine the grief it will cause me, if I start looking at all of the shit and pain I've caused? I mean, how could I survive all of that? And what good will it do? It's already done. I can't take it back!"

Agitated, he paced back and forth. Suddenly, he stopped. I could see a new thought had occurred to him.

*"I don't know how to make myself be different; but," he speculated, "maybe, if I start **acting** like this other part of me that is bugging me, I will just **be** different."*

He sighed, "But, I don't think I can handle the guilt. This is why people die; so that they can start over."

He cast an accusing glance my way, "But, here you are, talking to me, making me aware, and I can't even be mad at you for doing it. I know I've been a shit and I am sorry. I just don't know how conscious I can be of this and let myself be different. It's just so much pain to become aware of; so much regret."

He nods his head at his body, "I know that I am more than he is. I don't wanna be that guy anymore. I don't really like him. But, I don't know what to do."

I started to give him a hug.

"No! He reflexively backed away. "I don't want hugs and love!" He paused and thought, "But, then again, that's something he would say. He doesn't believe he deserves them, so he rejects them." He sighed, "But, I can see it's not the truth."

I notice he still didn't let me hug him. Instead I take him to the mirror, curious as to what he will see.

He sees a happy little boy in an outfit that kind of looks like an old style railroad engineer. He has on one of those old blue and white striped caps. I ask him who the boy is.

He smiles and says, "That's me. Look how cute I am. I love that kid."

The child reaches out of the mirror to hug him. Mr. Sands pulls him out of the mirror and holds him; then starts sobbing. "How did I go from being this kid to being that guy over there? I am so sorry." He mourns to the child, to himself, and to all whom he has caused pain. "I can't make it up, I can't change it. Jake's dead."

In that moment, I see Jake coming toward his dad. Mr. Sands falls to the ground and Jake goes down to hold him. Mr. Sands is in so much pain. I can sense it and I feel my own grief at seeing Jake. I am crying so hard I can hardly write this. I have to stop!

Whew, wait, hold on! What the frak's going on? I need a minute. Dang, that was a sock to the heart. I'm crying like a water fountain!

Jake had been one of my first crushes and I was very sad that he had died before I got to see him again. Obviously, I haven't dealt with my own issues. In our grief, Mr. Sands and I have matching pictures. In order for me to help him, I have to help me first.

Uhh, I don't know if I am ready. Tough shit, ready or not, get it together! Okay, Linda, use your tools; feel your grief; acknowledge and embrace your issues; forgive them and choose Love.

Hmmm, I need a moment.

To be honest, it's quite a few moments before I finally get to a place where I am grateful for this opportunity to clear myself so that I can unconditionally love myself and Jake. Now, I can get back into clear- seeing:

"I am sorry, I am sorry, I am so sorry." Mr. Sands cries to his son.

Jake replies, "And I love you so."

They stay like that until Mr. Sands has cried himself out. Then he asks, "Now what do I do?"

Jake answers, "What do you want to do?"

Mr. Sands says, "I don't know, son. I don't know how much of this I can bring to my consciousness. I don't want to be that guy anymore. I don't know how I can live with what I have done. Even now, I don't understand why I had to be that way. Is this the time I am supposed to get enlightenment, fall on my knees and say, praise Jesus? I don't think I can do that even now."

I stepped in and said, "Well, how about if you just realize that, in truth, you are not that guy and make a choice about whether or not you want to be who you really are? Just make the choice and see what happens. I can tell you for sure that whatever happens will not be more than you can handle, even though it can feel that way."

He clarified, "So, I can just make a choice that I want to be my true Self? I don't have to become conscious, I don't have to make any changes?" He frowns, "Then what good is it?"

"Making a choice is a decision, a statement of intent. It changes the flow of your energy. It's like a lighthouse giving you a direction, guiding you back to your Self. Whether or not you are conscious about it or make any changes in your "Now", in your body, it will happen." I reassured him.

"I can live with that. I want to live with that! Okay, I choose to be the truth of who I am." He walks over to his body, looks deeply into his body's eyes and says, "I choose to be the truth of who I am. I don't know how that will look, but I will trust that I am heading in the right direction."

He turns to Jake, who is smiling, and says, "How's that?'

Jake says, "It'll do for now." He and his dad shake hands, hug, and then Jake leaves.

Mr. Sands sits down, stares at his body, and waits.

I suggest, "Try beaming it some love."

"What will that do?"

"I have no idea, but it feels good."

He laughs and starts doing it.

I sent this story to Patty in an email and added: "I don't know what will happen. As I have said, most of my patients have no awareness of our work together. But, *you* do, so maybe, you can hold the awareness that inside of your dad there is a part of him that wants to be Love. Make it your secret awareness. Don't believe the grumpy lie. You don't have to buy into the grumpy man bullshit and let him beat you down. When he is being a shit, look past the poop to the truth of the loving man he is inside. Communicate with the loving man and ignore the other stuff. It may not have an effect on him, but, *you* will feel better because you will see through his mask, through the game. You can stop playing ball. When he throws you a poopy curve ball, let it drop; you don't have to throw it back. You might even start laughing at the ridiculousness of it all. This is a way of loving yourself, taking care of yourself. You are stepping out of the game and being in Love's truth instead.

I have no idea if your dad is going to get better. He will evolve in his own way, in his own time. Just as we all do. All you can really do is to show up and care."

I received this email a week later:

"Hi Linda,

We hadn't known what to do to help my dad. We brought him food; he wouldn't eat. He was refusing physical therapy and his medications. I was afraid of telling Josephine about you connecting with dad last week because so often I make her upset by talking about Jake or my mom. But I finally mentioned you had connected with dad and maybe helped him with some things he was anxious about.

The day after you had connected, he showed huge improvement. He wasn't distressed like before. He was loving. He was hungry. He was getting up for physical therapy. We weren't sure if it was real progress because we have been on such a roller coaster ride between one day and another. After the fourth day in a row of him improving, Josephine said, 'Okay what happened with Linda because I think that was our turning point.' So, I sent her a copy of your email. Also, my son, Tom, read it to his siblings at Sunday night dinner.

Josephine wrote back: 'Thanks for everything Patty-especially connecting with Linda. Hard as it was to read, I find comfort in any pleasantry around our brother. I miss him so much it is almost unbearable at times.'

Linda, I am grateful for your help.

Love, Patty"

A recent email from Patty tells me that Mr. Sands is still improving and making home visits now, but he is often unbearably grumpy again. So, I said, *"Hello"*, again.

"It's too hard, it's just too hard." He ranted.

"Okay."

"I am telling you, I can't do it. It's too hard." He insisted.

"I understand; it is too hard. It's okay"

He squinted his eyes at me, "Well, maybe it's not too hard." He confessed, "I just forget to choose to be the truth of my Self."

"I get it. I understand, believe me. I won't bug you about it."

"No!" He blurted, "You should come remind me more often." He paused. "Hmmm, boy, are you sneaky!"

I smiled, "I'll be baack."

****

I said my work was mostly dealing with people in transition at the end of their life, helping them come out of their characters and back into awareness of their Self. But I had this very cool, very different experience:

Recently, I said, "Hello" to a friend's fetus. It was about 24 weeks old.

I couldn't see anything; it was all foggy. I kept searching in the fog for clarity when I suddenly heard, "Hey, stop it. Can't you see I am trying to get into my character here? You're distracting me by making me be conscious of my Self. Don't wake me up; I have to get into my story."

"Whoa." Okay, never heard that one before. I realized I was communicating with someone at the beginning of their life's story; just getting into their picture. Very interesting. I backed off.

16
Jean

Jean was a youngish woman in her mid 30's and married to Sam. She came to us from New Zealand via Mexico where she was receiving treatment for cancer. She'd had cancer a few years before and had received a holistic therapy which appeared to cure her, but, eventually, the cancer came back and it had spread. She was in Mexico to treat this. Jean was strongly into holistic medicine and was a very positive thinker.

Jean and Sam had two young children back home in New Zealand. Sam, being very tech savvy, had set up their laptop computer so that Jean and the kids could communicate face to face via the computer. Sam was a very supportive husband, deeply in love with his wife.

They had been in Mexico for several weeks when Jean had suddenly begun to decompensate so Sam had her transferred to a hospital in San Diego for treatment. On the way to that hospital she became unconscious, needed emergent care, and was brought to the nearest hospital which turned out to be mine. She was admitted to the ICU in a coma and obviously not doing well.

I don't remember how my mental talking began with Jean, or what we said. I do remember telling Sam something and he believed me. He told me, he often felt as though he could communicate with Jean in a telepathic way. Later that day, he revealed to me that he felt he could communicate better with Jean when I was present.

Okay...

The next day, Jean was deteriorating. Sam and I were in the room when I started telling him things to say to his kids. He stared at me and I realized what I was saying. I stopped.

What the heck am I doing? Where did *that* come from? I haven't even said, "Hello" to Jean and I am saying these things!

He asked me to go into a private room with him. I asked another nurse to watch Jean for me and went. Sam had a pad and pen and asked me to repeat what I had said.

I looked at him, opened my mouth and started saying this very clear message, "Tell my children I am not abandoning them. I have tried very hard to stay with them and they should know I will always be with them."

He interrupted and asked what this was for.

I said, "This is Plan B."

He became tearful but continued to write.

When we were done he told me that when Jean's cancer had returned he had, over the year, been suggesting to her to have a "Plan B" which was to write letters to the kids in case things did not work out. However, Jean was a very positive thinker and refused Plan B, focusing instead on getting well.

Oh my God, I don't know how this stuff comes out of me, but I am very glad it means something to him and that it helps.

We returned to the ICU and Sam went to Jean's room. I could see from her monitor that she would be going soon. Sam came out and asked me to come into the room. He said, "I can communicate clearer with you here. Please stay here while I talk to her."

So I did. I stood holding her hand while this man verbally poured his heart out to his wife with very intimate, loving words as if they were alone in their own room. In my mind I could see her hearing it all and just saying over and over. *"I love you too, I love you too."*

Aaaaaah! I am going to explode with all of these emotions! So much love, grief, remorse and I don't know what. I want to be here to help but I am going to fall apart. I gotta get out of here.

I couldn't handle it anymore. I whispered to Sam, "She hears you Sam and she loves you too. I have to go now."

I left, grabbed Dale, one of my close co-workers, went into the lounge and sobbed onto his shoulder.

Holding and comforting me he said, "Linda, you shouldn't be taking care of these patients." He knew I still had periods of grieving over my husband's death.

"No, it isn't that. I am happy to be here and to help; it helps me, not hurt me. It's just that, I am human and the things Sam is saying to Jean are very private, intimate things. Yeah it was sad, but, it was also profound and touching to me. I am glad to be a part of it. I just need to cry."

And good friend that Dale is, he let me.

Jean died within the hour. Sam was grieving but also fortified knowing she had heard his words and he had the letters to bring home to his children.

17
Lee

I forgot to tell you about my husband dying.

Lee had a lung problem that started when we began training for an ironman-length triathlon.

I was in my mid 30's and he was in his late 40's. He could already bike 200 miles and run/walk 30 miles. I could do 100 miles on a bike, and was running about 18 miles. We both needed to learn how to swim and signed up for classes. Although Lee was already a certified scuba diver, he didn't like to swim.

During the first lesson he inhaled the pool water and that night ended up in the ER due to difficulty with breathing. He was told he had end- stage emphysema and would die within the year. I knew this couldn't be right, but, it hit Lee like a ton of bricks.

It was the beginning of the end for him; a slow decline that progressed over the next 20 years. Initially, he became the "boy in the bubble", developing allergies to almost everything, and was, essentially, housebound. I would come home from the hospital and he'd have difficulty breathing because of the soap I washed my hands in at work.

A year later, he developed bronchitis and went to a different ER. There, we learned he had been misdiagnosed and mistreated. Yes, he had some emphysema but definitely not end-stage. However, over the past year, he had developed very bad environmental allergies to perfumes, dyes, and most chemicals. Adjustments in his meds and being reprieved from a death sentence helped him a lot. He was able to change his perception and to utilize his own natural ability to heal. Eventually, he was able to tolerate being out of the house and around people, in open air. He tried to go to work again, but, with all of the perfumes, dyes, and chemicals found in a closed office environment, he needed to use his inhalers so much he had a mild heart attack.

So, Lee became the house person and a more spoiled wife I could not be. All I had to do was go to work. He did everything else. No wonder men like having wives who stay home and take care of them! When we bought our first house I pleaded with him to let me clean the toilet. I felt it would be a bonding experience with my new home. ☺

Over the years, Lee would try to be physically active again. He tried to cycle, to run, etc. but his breathing didn't allow him to develop. He tried to resume sailing, but, even that was too much. He did start golfing some and that was cool. He especially loved playing with my Dad when we visited my parents. Those two didn't keep score and they allowed "do-overs". They had a blast.

Dad was Lee's best friend. We always had a great time being with my parents. One time, while playing cards, Lee said, "Linda, if we ever get a divorce, I am staying with your Mom."

"That's right!" Mom said.

"HEY!" I protested. But, I was so grateful.

Lee had been a grammar school drop-out, yet, during this time at home, he taught himself grammar and how to write. He completed two novels that never reached publication. Back then I don't think people could really allow themselves to be confronted with the issues Lee wrote about. The novels were gritty with some horrific, sordid, real life story lines; but, his main characters were males who overcame these tragic experiences and grew into very cool men. I perceived the novels as love stories as it was always Love that enabled these men to change and grow. You know what? I should publish those puppies. I think that, in today's world, people might be able to appreciate them.

Lee's health continued to spiral downward. As I learned various ways to do energy healing, I would work on him. He always said he felt better afterwards so I kept doing it. It spurred me on to learn more techniques; explore more religious beliefs; examine more philosophies; do more meditation; and, create more of a relationship with my Higher Self. I wanted to become MORE. I wanted to DO more. I still worked as an ICU nurse and did healing on some of my patients. I also began an energy healing practice in my home to work on others.

But I was getting discouraged and doubtful. Although my clients said they loved it, they did not return for further treatments nor did they refer other people.

Maybe it's all bullshit. Maybe, I'm not really doing anything. Why am I even bothering to try? I don't see any effect. People do not jump up from my table and say, "Hallelujah' I am healed!" My patients at work are not suddenly awake, alert, with normal vital signs, and able to walk out of the ICU. I don't SEE anything happening! More importantly to me, *Lee was not getting better.* He would tell me I was keeping him alive; that he would have died a long time ago if it wasn't for the therapy. But, it wasn't enough and I really doubted.

I think it was early in 2002, while working on him, I saw a huge blackness in his chest and couldn't make it to go away. I freaked and didn't tell him about it. I never worked on him again. I also stopped my home practice and pretty much stopped trying to fix my patients too.

Yeah, I am good at the mental, emotional, and even the telepathic stuff, helping people with end of life and other issues; but, I want to fix, to cure, to heal, and to do miracles on the physical frequency.

I want to fix my husband!

It wasn't happening. I stopped believing it could. I stopped believing I was making a difference. It didn't matter how much people observed and commented on the work I was doing. I wasn't getting what I wanted.

The fork in the road just got bigger.

I continued doing my spiritual work, but I stopped trying to do physical healings. During this time, I did write and self-published that little book for the public about end of life issues, healing, and critical care. I thought it was such important information and would help empower so many people to make choices based upon Love rather than fear. I thought it could help change the perspective of the nation. I thought it would help our healthcare system if people were more informed and empowered. So much for *my* thoughts. Lee had edited it. He thought it was a great book and very helpful. So did my coworkers and the manager of the ICU I worked for at that time.

The ICU bought the book and gave it to patients and families. I, myself, gave a lot of them away to people who were interested and needed the info. It did have a helpful effect on a number of people, but, again, I began doubting. The book never went anywhere; it never spread in "that way" - the way in which a person says to others, "O my God you need to read this book." You know what I mean. And so, again, I stopped believing in what I was doing. I couldn't help Lee and I couldn't help others. Yeah, I was losing it. I was spiraling downward and didn't even know it.

In 2002, Lee had built a beautiful wooden/fiberglass ocean kayak and was helping me to build mine. He dreamed of us kayaking the Puget Sound up to Alaska. As he began practicing and training, though, I could see he had underestimated the work kayaking requires. He never said anything, but I think this was his last straw.

That year, breathing hard and struggling to do heavy yard work, Lee had another small heart attack. His lungs were not able to support his body very well. He became short of breath just going to the mailbox; tolerance for activity was way below what was acceptable functioning for him; and he didn't have the quality of life he wanted.

In January 2003, his lungs got acutely ill on top of his chronic problems. He ended up in the hospital and, eventually, in my ICU.

He said, "I am circling the drain. You told me I have a choice. You said I can go down the 'fix me path' or the 'peaceful passing path'. I don't want to go on a ventilator or other life support. It isn't going to fix my body. At best I'll come back to how I am now and that's not good enough anymore. I don't want to live on long term steroids. It makes me wired/tired and I still can't live the quality of life I want. It is time for me to go, Linda; you have to let me go."

Circling the drain; let me go.

Time stopped. I heard his words, but, they seemed so far away.

It's time for me to go, Linda; you have to let me go.

How much do you love him, Linda? As a nurse, you know he's right. He edited my book. He knows the issues; knows his rights;

and he's making his choice. Can you practice what you preach? *Can you let the love of your life go?*

Suddenly, I recalled an incident that had happened a month earlier. We were driving somewhere and out of the blue Lee said to me, "You're gonna have a hard time when I die aren't you?"

"Yep."

"We could intend to die together; not a suicide, just the intention that when the time comes, we would go together."

I thought hard about it; it was so very tempting; I could hardly bear the thought of life without him; but, I sighed and started getting teary, "No, I can't be going yet. I feel like there is a bunch of stuff I am still supposed to work out and to do. It's like I have a mission or something."

He nodded and held my hand, "It's okay; I get it."

I had no clue he would be at death's door a month later.

Lee didn't believe in life after death, but, in his last hours, I asked him, "If there *is* a life after death, what would you want it to be like?"

He thought about it and got a soft, sweet smile on his face.

I thought, "Yeah, keep that thought, my love."

Lee had his peaceful death in my ICU, in his own way, in his own time with me and his son present.

As for me, I began the rest of my life...

18
Me

I just re-read that.

What the frakking hell do I mean: "I began the rest of my life?" NO I DIDN'T! Are you kidding? Life stopped. I *wanted* Life to stop!

I had been preparing myself for Lee's death for a while. I wanted to make sure I did and said all of the things I wanted to, so that I would have no regrets when he died.

So the fuck what! I'm still angry. I'm still sad. Just when it seemed like long term issues we had had were resolved; just when it seemed I understood about creating reality; he frakking died! What the hell does that mean? Am I *supposed* to be alone now? What for? What did I say? Oh yeah, I've got things to work out, I've got a mission.

Who cares?

I don't!

What have I done? I told the love of my life that I couldn't go with him; that I had something more important to do than to be with him. I am so fucking crazy. What is wrong with me? Why would I want to stay in this world without Lee? I made a mistake; I should have gone with him.

I can't stand this pain.

One reason Lee felt okay about leaving is he knew that the great friends I had at work would be there for me just as they had been there for him in his last days. But, I don't want to see anyone. I don't want to do anything.

Brush my teeth? NO!

Comb my hair? NO!

Get out of my pajamas? NO!

Clean the house? NO!

I miss Lee and I am frakking wallowing! I cry for hours every day, totally zoned out with grief. I relate so well to Hilary Swank in the movie, P.S. I Love You. That was real to me; it was how I felt.

Over the week, as I was spent from my emotions, I could feel Love in the background, holding me, supporting me, telling me that I had made the right choice and to just take some time. I was so confused; I didn't want to know.

But, I had to go back to work, and guess what? On my first day back I had a patient in the same room Lee had died in. I also had the patient in the next room. And guess what else? Yeah, you got it - the patient in Lee's room died that day! Oh my God, I don't know if I can deal with this, but, I have to. Suck it up, Linda; you have a grieving family to help.

The next day, the other patient died. It was like a slap upside my head – a message - saying, "Hey, Linda, get your head out of your ass and get on with it."

A month later, I received the "Excellence in Nursing" award from my peers and the hospital management. This meant I was to attend the hospital's gala. Needless to say I wasn't in the mood to go; I wasn't going to go; but, my friends strongly encouraged me to attend.

So, I had to shop for a gown and that turned out to be fun.

I had to dress up and that was fun.

I took my friend, Nancy B, as my date and that was fun.

The gala turned out to be fun.

Damn, I had fun.

When I got home I felt sooo terrible I cried all night.

Life wasn't gonna stop no matter how much I wanted it to. Eventually, I got my head out of my butt and back onto my shoulders. I remembered I was here for a reason and I had to get on with my evolution. I figured Lee would be continuing to grow wherever he was and I had to keep up so that, if we met again, I would be ready.

BUT WHAT THE HELL! I was still the same old me! I was still conflicted. I still didn't believe. I still didn't trust. Do I "Let go and let God?" Do I get involved with a religion? Do I use the Law of Attraction and Deliberate Intent to create? Do I continue trying to do healing work? Do I meditate more? Do I do any of these or a mix of these? *What actually works?*

I can see I am on a path of evolution and self-awareness. I can see I am not alone on this path. What I can't see yet is how to be more effective! If I am supposed to go down the path of uniting with my Inner Being, my God Self, in order to be a more effective creator then what the hell else do I need to do or to let go of to be that? Or, am I supposed to trust, to surrender to God's will and to float upon the mystery of "His will"? Do I ask in Jesus' name? Do I chant the Buddhist "nam myoho renge kyo"? Okay, cool, I do it all. But every time I go down that road it leads me back to uniting and being a partner with God, using the Law of Attraction, Deliberate Intent, etc. – and that is the *other* path. I am going around in circles! What works?

Since Lee died, I have had lots of different experiences and I know I am moving forward, but I feel like I am missing something. Lee was right...I was having a hard time without him. In addition to missing him so much, I didn't have my grounding rod. If he agreed with something I did or saw, then it was real to me. Now, it was all on me; I had to figure things out on my own.

The first thing I had to figure out after he died was how to start living again.

So, I created a project - a CD in tribute to Lee. Using karaoke, I sang our story. If this was American Idol, Randy would say, "Dawg, some of those songs were a bit pitchy but I like what you were trying to do."

Ellen would say, "I don't care if it was pitchy, I loved it."

Kara would say, "I agree with Randy and Ellen. Yes, some of it was pitchy, but, you have a good voice and I love how you told your story; it touched me."

Then Simon would shake his head and say, "Look, Linda, I have to be honest with you. It was all a bit Karaoke..." The other judges would start to protest. Simon would stop them and say, "It's true, but, it doesn't matter. It was a beautiful thing to do."

Yeah it was. It was my therapy; my memorial of Lee and our relationship. I gave it to family and friends. They liked it too and I think it was helpful.

At least it got me moving forward.

19
Toltecs

I knew I had to get the ball rolling on my spiritual path again. A book had been floating around at the hospital and I decided to read it. It was entitled, The Four Agreements, by don Miguel Ruiz, the Toltec Nagual in the Eagle-Knight lineage. I resonated so much with this book that I read the Mastery of Love, too.

I felt this Toltec wisdom as taught by Miguel was something valuable for me to explore; so googling, I found a Toltec Mentor in Vancouver, BC named Lennie Tan who was a graduate of don Miguel's dreaming classes. She became my new mentor.

Within the space of a couple of months, I had several important experiences that propelled me along my path. One, I began taking lessons with my beautiful teacher, Lennie.

Two, I was to attend a family reunion in Sonoma County, CA and saw, on- line, that there would be a Toltec meeting led by Allan Hardman, another graduate of Miguel's classes. I don't know what got into me, but, I rearranged my days off and my flight schedule so I that could attend this meeting. During the question/answer part of the meeting I had questions but I didn't want to voice them. They were about my relationship with Lee. Suddenly, Allan started speaking and answering all of my un-asked questions. I was stunned, listening in amazement, crying and, finally, grateful in the peace I felt.

Third, on impulse I left Sonoma Co. and, instead of flying home, I flew to San Diego to meet Miguel's mother, Sarita. I had no logical reason to go; I just had a desire to meet her. Mother Sarita, as she is called, is a well-known curandera, a healer. I made an appointment with her and her apprentice, Rebecca Haywood. Sarita asked me what I would like healed and I told her I had not come for a treatment; I just wanted to meet her. We talked and they gave me a healing anyway. It was wonderful. With their encouragement, I signed up for a three day healing seminar with them. It was going to be in two weeks. I wondered how the heck I was going to get more time off in such short notice? I called my wonderful boss, told him what was going on and he just arranged the time off for me. People at work really were taking care of me.

I had a very strong desire to meet Miguel and hoped he would show up at the class. Well, he did, but we were in a deep meditation at the time. Then I heard he had shown up at the home I was staying in but I had already gone to class. Dang, we keep missing each other. On the last day of class, while we were in a light meditative state, I felt hands upon my shoulders. I opened my eyes, and looked up into the smiling face of Miguel. I blurted, "Finally! It's about time." He laughed, gave my shoulders a squeeze and I went back to meditating. Yeah, short but sweet!

When I returned home to WA, I signed up for a spiritual journey to be held at Teotihaucan which is located north of Mexico City. Teo is a large complex with pyramids, learning centers, and quarters where a community of Toltec people had lived and studied. Miguel said that these Toltecs were artists and that Life was their canvas. I liked that; I wanted to be an artist too.

This particular journey was to be led by don Miguel and several of his apprentices. It was a very large group of 60 to 80 people and it was too late to sign up. I was put onto a waiting list and, at nearly the last minute, I got in. Whew, made it! YAY! I was all ready the morning of the trip, waiting for my shuttle, when I realized I had misread the time of the flight and had missed it!

DUDE, are you kidding me? What does this mean? Am I not supposed to go? I don't get it. I started to get angry and flustered, but, suddenly, I became strangely calm and decided to meditate about what to do. I grounded, centered, and chose to let Love decide what was best. Suddenly, I peacefully got up, called the airline and got a new flight; then called the place we were staying in Mexico and, somehow, with neither of us speaking each other's language, arranged a new pick up time from the airport in Mexico City. As my town car drove me to the airport, it began snowing and I almost missed the second flight.

Somehow, I stayed calm.

It was very late at night and I got lost at the airport in Mexico City. Unable to communicate with anyone, I couldn't find my ride; on and on it went. I was amazed at how much resistance energy I had to this trip. The whole time I kept grounding, centering, choosing and trusting Love to guide me. Finally, my ride and I connected and I was safely off to Teo. I arrived in my room after midnight and found my roommate to be restless and nervous.

She said, "I can't rest, I am feeling all revved up. I think it is the energy here, I can't get into synch with it." I could see she was on the verge of panic.

I offered to do some Healing Touch on her. She agreed and was asleep in just a couple of minutes.

Hmmm what a day it has been today. There has been so much energy to move through and then to end the day like this. I feel like I have been walking with Love today. I like it.

You can visit Teo independently; you can go with a tour guide; but, until you go with a Toltec teacher taught in the lineage of don Miguel Ruiz, you will probably not fully experience all that Teotihaucan can offer you. Teotihaucan is a powerful place that can grab you and take you on an amazing journey of self-awareness and growth. The teachers know how to utilize the energy and the various places in Teo to help students have enlightening and enriching experiences. You can bet that each visit will be different.

Over the next 18 months, I journeyed to Teotihaucan so many times I have lost count – at least six, maybe eight times. I went with large groups and small groups of less than 10. I went with groups of first-timers; groups with repeat students; and once, I went with Barbara Emrys' dreaming class. Each journey was a unique, wonderful, personal experience for me.

The first journey from home to Teo was an event all by itself. Then the next day, my first trip from the hotel to the compound, as I approached the museum entrance to Teo's complex, I was overcome by a visceral emotional response. I began sobbing; my nose was dripping as I clutched my body. I could not think nor analyze what was happening. I was just aware of how grateful I was to be home.

HOME??

I continued walking through the museum and into Teotihaucan where I sat on the ground, crying with joy, so happy to be home.

Welcome to Teotihaucan, Linda; holy cow what an entrance that was! I didn't understand it at all, but it was okay.

It was also on this first visit, that I experienced the compound called, "The Women's Place". It is the "Red Tent" of Teo; the place where the females would go to have their monthly cycles, to have babies, and whatever strictly female things were done. The compound is underground and tourists are instructed by the museum guard to walk, single file, without stopping, on a raised walkway. The teachers would arrange permission to have ceremonial experiences here. In all of my journeys I have to say that whether I was the student, or, the one time I happened to be the leader, these experiences were always awesome. However, it was on my first journey into the Women's Place that my biggest "wow" moment occurred. It happened as we were leaving the compound.

Just before the exit, the walkway passes in front of a large stone structure I call, "the bleachers" because they were large, wide stone steps. *The first time I was walking by the bleachers, I saw Toltec women and girls of all ages, sitting, lying, resting, or, talking.* Whoa! What is this? I looked at my fellow students and I could tell none of them were seeing what I was seeing. *I looked back at the women and, as I passed, some of them looked at me, smiled, waved, and said, "Welcome, where you have been? We have missed you."* WHAT?? I couldn't stop and stare, I had to keep walking. But, my heart was wide open, I felt so much love for them, and I didn't want to leave. I stood outside and longed to return to them.

This was the first of several awesome journeys to Teotihaucan. Each trip was special to me and significant to my growth. Each trip was different because of the teacher, the people in the class, and what Teo would provide for us to experience, but, always, no matter what the group class did, I would visit the Women's Place to see the ladies. It was different each time, but, they always welcomed me; and always, I would have a hard time leaving them. I didn't understand it, but I felt so connected to them.

On another journey, I went with a large group led by Miguel's son, don Jose and his wife, donya Judy. Miguel had already announced that Jose would be his successor as Nagual. During this trip, while we were all   meditating in front of the compound called the Nagual's rooms I had an amazing experience. *I was sitting in front with my eyes closed when, in my mind, I saw an intense bright light swirling like a tornado or vortex inside the doorway to a room. I could see Jose standing there and he was beckoning me to the light. I sped out of my body and jetted into the light.*

*I found myself in the center of the light. I had no physical body; I was the light. I noticed a ray of light coming from out of my center. I followed it with my awareness and saw it ended on something like a movie screen, only, more holographic. I watched and was aware that I was **in** that movie, but, I wasn't **Linda**. I was another person and I was living a life in that movie. Then I became aware that there were many rays of lights coming out from my center and going to many movie screens. I was in all of them. I had different forms, different sexes, different ages, different roles, and different relationships.*

*Then I noticed a particular movie and in it were Lee and Linda, only not in the physical bodies I associated with Lee and Linda. Rather, it was the essence of Lee and Linda that I was seeing. My attention became riveted to the movie. My heart yearned to be there with Lee. I felt my consciousness moving down the ray of light toward the movie... **STOP!***

I was back in the center of my light Being. I noticed another ray of light going to another movie where Linda was sitting on the ground meditating in Teotihaucan. In that moment, I knew I had a choice to make. Where would I put my attention, my consciousness? Where, what movie, did I want to experience myself living in?

Oh my God. Here it is again. The same choice: be with Lee or continue to follow this path I am on. This is so not fair! Yet, this time I knew what I had to choose. I wasn't done being Linda.

Suddenly, I was back in my Linda body, sitting on the ground in Teo. I got up and walked away. I was so mixed up. I missed Lee and, yet, I knew I was still supposed to be here. Part of me felt so guilty for not choosing Lee. Part of me was sure I had made the right decision to follow my path. All of me was hurting.

Despite the issue of Lee, I was also so aware of what a phenomenal experience that was. What was it? Was I merged with God and seeing from that point of view? What was I seeing? Were all those movies, places I could put my consciousness into in order to experience myself in various situations? Why would I do that; for fun; to know myself better; to test drive new ideas and directions of my evolution; all three; is there more? What happens to all of the other movies when I chose one movie to focus upon? Do they disappear? Are they only potential realities; or, do they continue to exist while my consciousness and attention are focused upon one reality? Or, are tiny parts of me in *all of the movies at the same time* and my central God consciousness is aware of everything all at once? Holy moly, my mind is spinning!

On another journey, a few of us decided to visit the neighboring Toltec complex called Tetitla. I loved going there and meditating in the Eagles' Place. *This time I was in a deep meditation when I felt a tap on my forehead. I opened my eyes and in front of me was an old Indian man in light ceremonial robes.*

He said, "Ah, good. You are awake."

I looked around me and instead of ruins I saw Tetitla as it must have been in the past. Around me, there were people meditating. I looked down at my body and it was a full grown adult male. UH OH, TOTO, I am not in Kansas anymore. I looked up at the old man.

He said, "Your heart is divided between two places. You must choose."

In that moment, I knew he was right. I knew I could choose to stay in the reality I was seeing now or I could return to Linda's world. I loved Teotihaucan and the people I could see there. I had been considering moving down there. My heart, indeed, was divided. I thought about it and, once again, I knew I wasn't done with being Linda. I didn't say a word, just looked into his eyes. He nodded and tapped my forehead. I was back in my Linda body, again. I opened my eyes and silent tears ran down my cheeks.

That was my last journey to Teotihaucan. As I write this, I can feel the tug on my heart to visit again.

Hmmm, as I read what I have written, it occurs to me that there may be another layer to this, i.e. being with Lee or being on my path. I feel like I still have things I have to accomplish, yet, my heart does yearn to be with Lee, still. Why do they have to be separate paths? Or, do they?

Hmmm, an even deeper layer, I am divided between my Human Will and my Divine Will...I still want what I want whether it's what is best for our Highest Good or not.

The fork is still in the road.

20
"Gettin Movin"

During those 18 months, in addition to experiencing Teotihaucan, I had other adventures that I will relate over the next few chapters.

Remember, Lee had gotten sick while we were training for an ironman triathlon. So, I decided, at the age of 52 and 40 pounds heavier, to do a sprint level triathlon. I dedicated this triathlon to Lee and me and started training with the YMCA's tri group. Man, I was the slowest in everything. No matter, I signed up for the "My First Triathlon" to be held at Lake Wenatchee, WA. It was a ¼ mile swim, 12 mile bike ride, and a 5k run. My friend, Nancy B. came to provide moral support. I had borrowed my friend Clarise's shorty wetsuit. Sure, Clarise is a few sizes smaller than me, but hey, I could zip up the wetsuit and I figured that's all that counted. Underneath it, I wore my riding clothes and my old running bra.

I started the swim with a bang, but just a few yards into it, I couldn't catch my breath. I flipped onto my back, kept swimming and struggled to breathe. Unbeknownst to me, I was going round and round in circles. A race guide in a kayak came to check me out. I told him my problem. He thought it was anxiety, but, I wasn't anxious. I asked him if a too tight wet suit could be the problem. He didn't know. I unzipped the suit and tried to swim again. I got a few strokes in and had to go onto my back again. He offered to tow me to the finish line, or, he said, that I could go closer to shore and actually walk the water course.

NO WAY! I wanted to do this race. It was important! I zipped up the wet suit and I continued to swim a little/ float a little toward the finish line. As I rounded the pier, Nancy was there. I gasped out the problem and kept going.

As I neared the finish and was able to stand up in the water, I could hear Nancy yell at me, "UNZIP YOUR BRA!"

What? *My bra?* I did it and whoosh, the air rushed into my lungs.

Hmmm, I guess it was just a little too tight.

I continued with the race, biking and then running. I did have to do some walking, but I made it to the finish line. Nancy was there congratulating me, but, I needed some time alone. I sat on the grass and unpinned the sign I had been wearing that said, "For Lee and Me". I held it and started crying, telling Lee I had made it. I felt like I had closed a circle for us.

****

I did a second sprint triathlon in an all-female race, sponsored by Danskin which supported research for cancer. I dedicated this one to my mom; my sister, and to my step-son's mom. They were all cancer survivors. This time I swam an unintentional ¾ mile because the wind had moved the buoy.

Did I care? Hell no! Dude, I swam *3 frakking quarter miles*. RIGHT ON!

****

For my next adventure, my friends, Diane and Perry, talked me into doing the three day bike ride of the Tri-Island Trek. We would ferry from Seattle to Bainbridge Island, ride and spend the night; then ferry to Whidbey Island, ride, ferry to Orcas Island and spend the night there; then ferry to Vancouver Island, ride and end in Victoria, B.C. From there we would ferry back home.

Hey, I had done long rides in the past, and I knew I wasn't prepared for this; but, they reassured me that each day would only be about 50 – 60 miles, so I thought maybe I could do it.

NOT!

Dang, that first day on Bainbridge was hill hell. It got so bad, that I stopped looking forward more than 50 feet in front of me. I did not want to see another damn hill. I walked up pretty much all of them. I was skipping the rest stops and the snacks so that I could make up time. And my bike chain kept coming off. The race mechanics were tweaking it but they finally concluded my shifting technique was the problem.

Whatever.

That night when I arrived at the overnight stop, I was pooped and I was having a bit of pain in my neck and right shoulder. But, I had made it! Hopefully with a good night's rest, tomorrow would be better. I went to dinner and Oh my God, my body must have been starving because it was out of control. I hoovered in that food! Guess I won't be losing weight on this trip.

Next day, we got to Whidbey Island. Thank God, not a hill in sight. I started to ride and within about five miles I had to stop. The pain in my neck and right shoulder was bad. I massaged the sore areas and started riding again. Five miles later, I had to stop again. This time, I massaged and did a little energy work on it. I rode again, stopped again in another five miles; and that is how it went. I was one of the last people - the riding wounded. Finally, I got to the lunch rest place and stopped to eat. Some of the other people were quitting. One girl had to, her knee was so injured. They encouraged me to stop too. But, no, I just wouldn't do it.

I took off again. By now, my neck and shoulders were in constant pain. I continued to ride and stop every 5 miles, but by now, I was massaging, doing energy work, praying and crying. Still, I refused to stop.

On one good note, I had been able to ride up the hills so far. I got to the top of one and could see it would be straight down with a sharp right turn and then back up another hill. *I can do it.* I got down the hill, made the turn, began the uphill, and my chain came off. Even worse, my feet would not come out of the cleats.

Okay, Linda. You can lean toward the left, fall into the street and maybe get hit by a car or a bike. You can lean to the right, fall into the ditch and maybe break something. Hmmm... street; ditch; street; ditch? DITCH! I leaned right and, yay, my foot came out of the cleat, hit the ground and I was safe. Whew. I fixed the chain and kept going.

Finally I got to the top of the hill just past Deception Pass. This time I couldn't see the bottom. It was gonna be a long one. There had been road work done, leaving the pavement uneven and gravel scattered in places. I flashed on the memory of riding down another hill in another time and place where I had squeezed my breaks so much they had glazed over and wouldn't work; I ended up walking down that hill. I couldn't do that this time; there was a time constraint and I needed my breaks. Ok, Love, I need some help with this one, cuz I am scared to death. Briefly, I closed my eyes, took a deep breath, let go of my brakes, and took off. I was going faster than I ever had before. I couldn't take my eyes off of the road cuz it need attention, but, at one point I think my speedometer said 45 mph. Wheeeee!

After that hill, I continued to stop and go, limping my way to the ferry. I was third from the last. Diane and Perry greeted me with congratulations, but, I was not a happy camper. I tried to sit, but my bottom hurt. My right arm just hung at my side. I could barely move my head. I tearfully leaned on a wall. Diane tried to massage my neck and shoulder but I couldn't stand to be touched. It just hurt sooo bad.

I think it was dark when we got to Orcas Island and I think they bussed us to the camp. Seriously, I cannot remember that night except I know that I hoovered in the food again.

The next morning we started in the dark and were supposed to ride on a dirt path up this crazy steep hill! Wouldn't you know it...it had rained that night and the hill was totally muddy.

Really? Yeah, no way was I riding my bike. I had a hard time even walking it up that darn hill.

When I finally made it up, it was light enough that I could see the silhouette of the trees and tell the difference between the road and the ditch; Uh, I think I can anyway. I started to ride. Hey, I am stronger. My neck and shoulder still hurt and I still have to stop, but I can ride further than the day before. I am passing other riders! Yay, I am not gonna be last this time! I am at the top of a hill; I see it is a short fast downhill then a sharp right turn and, yay, up the last hill. I know the ferry is just on the other side. I can do it! I sped down the hill, turned the corner on a dime, began the uphill, and...

My frakking chain fell off again.

All the other riders passed me by.

Can I just say it?

Mother Fucker!

I fixed my chain and was the last one to get to the ferry. Oh well. Off we went to Vancouver Island. The sun was out, it was a beautiful day and I really was feeling sooo much stronger. When we docked I took off. Yes, my neck and shoulder still hurt like crazy and I still had to stop, but I knew I could make it to the finish line.

I took a break by one of the sag wagons where they were passing out juice.

One of the drivers said, "We have been following you for the last couple of days. We knew you were hurting and weren't sure if you could keep riding. But you just kept going and going. It was very cool to watch.

Awesome. I told him what was wrong and he started massaging my neck and shoulders. Mmmm, it felt great. Finally, I was done and took off again.

I was passing other riders, left and right. I felt like I was zooming along. All of a sudden the sag wagon pulled up ahead and stopped me.

"Linda, you are not gonna make the ferry in time. We have to bring you forward."

"Are you sure? I feel like I am doing good."

"We're sure."

I was so bummed as I got into the wagon with some other cyclists. I didn't know what "bring you forward" meant and, at that moment, it didn't matter.

I wasn't going to finish the race!

I needed to forgive myself, my body, my chain, God, and everything. I needed a better perception, but, I didn't have one yet.

After a bit, the wagon pulled over to the side of the road. The driver told me that, if I wanted to, they would let me out here and I could bike in the last few miles.

DO I WANT TO? YEAH, MAN!!

They handed me my bike and I flew away. I don't know if it was five or ten miles, I pumped it as fast as I could, crossing that finish line with no slowing down. I stowed my bike and started walking around the loading area.

Eventually, I saw the sag wagon. The driver came over to me and said, "Where the hell did you go? I turned around to get the other bike out and when I looked you were nowhere in sight.

We kept looking for you, afraid you had taken a wrong turn. There was no way we could have missed you. How fast were you going?"

"Fast enough."

21
Dolphins/Air Combat

On one of my trips to Teotihaucan, I came home via Puerto Vallarta. While there, I fulfilled one of my dreams which was to swim with the dolphins.

I was like a child, splashing over to dolphins, invading their space, and wanting to touch them. They kept swimming away from me until I realized what I was doing. So instead, I sent a mental message telling them how happy I was to be there with them; how grateful I was for their patience; and told them that, if they wanted to visit with me, I would be here. Right after that, the large male dolphin in my group swam over to me, stopped, and allowed me to stroke him. He swam to the other members of my group then back to me and stopped again. He did this five times getting closer and closer until our bodies were touching. My heart was so filled with love and appreciation. If you have ever wanted to be with dolphins...do it!

****

The year after Lee died, I attended the hospital gala again. While there I bid upon and won a session with Air Combat USA to be a "fighter pilot for a day" thus fulfilling another dream.

I had flown a plane twice before in two different introductory classes. The last time, I got to do the whole thing: pre-flight checklist, take-off, fly, and land the plane. But, I really wanted to do aerobatic flying; you know: loops, spins, etc.

Air Combat USA is the original civilian dog fighting school. You get to do air combat dog fighting with another plane! The deal is this: You arrive at the airfield, put on a flight suit and a parachute; then go to ground school and learn air combat maneuvers. Next you get into your two seater combat SIAI Marchetti plane with your pilot who is an actual ex-combat pilot - some of them are from Top Gun. He does the take-off then turns over the controls to you. The two planes fly in formation out to the combat area where they separate and go to each end of the air space. Flying head on toward each other and while doing aerial maneuvers you try to shoot each other with lasers. There are six combat runs. At the end you fly back to base, again in formation. The pilot takes over and lands the craft. Then you have a post flight debriefing and get your DVD.

IT IS SOOO FRAKKING COOL!

I actually got there a couple of hours early to watch the other civilians fly. When I first arrived, a plane had just landed. The guy couldn't get out, he was so sick. He was what they called a "six bagger"; he vomited into six different barf bags. Okay, it was a hot day and he was in his 60's. Give the guy a break. I headed out to the plane to see if he needed help but by the time I got there he was out and walking.

I waited and watched the next guy who was much younger. When he was done I heard him tell his wife he'd had a bag ready because he almost hurled.

Hmmm. Looks like this could be more challenging than I thought. I went back to my car to meditate upon it and choose Love's perspective. By the end of my meditation I was calm again. I knew that I was going to have fun and love every moment of the experience.

I went into the office and, surprisingly, they found a suit that fit me. I got the chute on and went to ground school where I met my opponent- a big guy in his 30's. We had our lesson, and then went out to the planes. For some reason, one of the Marchettis was out of commission and I would be flying an Extra 300L which is an aerobatic plane. Yay, what synchronicity. My pilot would be sitting behind me, rather than beside me. I liked it, I felt like I was alone and that the plane was mine.

The pilot did the take-off, got us into the air and then turned over the controls to me. Dude, I loved it! We flew in formation out to the combat range. The other guy set the course and I kept as close to his side as I could without hitting him. That was cool, tricky, and scary. Then we got to the combat area and started our fight. I was heading toward him when my pilot yelled, "Pull up...keep pulling." I did and next thing I know I am upside down looking at the brown earth. Wheeeee!

I came back around, took a hard turn and I was rolling. Another, wheeeee! Then I was head on with the other plane again and smoke went up...I was shot! No biggee to me, I was having sooo much fun looping, spinning, and rolling.

We kept at it. Truthfully, I was so short in the seat, I could not see the laser sights, so couldn't see to shoot the guy. Did I care? NO WAY. My pilot was wondering what was going on though, so, I did finally cop to him that I couldn't see and so he scored a couple of hits for me.

On the way back, I set the formation and the other plane had to line up with me. This was tricky too because I had to fly in a stable pattern that he could match. All too soon, the pilot took over and did the landing. I got out, not even a little bit sick, having had way too much fun. We did the de-brief and I got a DVD of my flight. Guess what it showed? Yep, I was smiling the whole time.

22
Fire

I had another cool, well actually awesome, experience one weekend on Bainbridge Island - I walked on fire.

I attended a Toltec workshop taught by Heather Ash and Raven. I don't remember the name of the workshop. I do know it was great, but truthfully, what I really remember is the fire walking.

We had been in class all day, a moderate group of maybe 15 people. Now, in the very black of night, we went out into the field and there it was, a bed of glowing red hot coals with licks of flames shooting up. It was only about 12 to 15 feet long but it looked like forever to me.

We gathered on each long side of the fire. Heather went first, leisurely walking down the fiery path. Then Raven went; he stopped in the middle and did some graceful dance moves then continued.

Is this for real? My stomach is churning. I am excited and scared to death at the same time.

Raven and Heather taught us to approach the fire by bringing our frequency/vibe into alignment with the fire's frequency/vibe. Apparently there are other ways, such as going into a trance-like state, but, our intention was to bring our energy and the fire's energy into a state of communication. We would do this, first, just by having that intention. Then, standing beside the fire, we kept our bodies gently moving, swaying side to side and saying hello to the fire. By staying conscious and clear we would know when there was a connection to the fire.

At one point, I thought I was ready and went to the head of the path. I looked down at the fire; all I could see was burning red and yellow coals with heat radiating toward me.

"No frakking way", I thought.

I "about-faced" it and walked back to the side. I most definitely was not ready. I saw one of my classmates go into a trance state and woodenly walk down the path. I knew I could do that, just disassociate and walk; but I wanted to be in communication, I wanted to feel the Love and to be one with the fire.

I kept swaying at the side and saying "Hello" to the fire. Suddenly, I *knew* I was in communication. It was like, duh, what took me so long to hear the Love? I felt like I was with an old friend. I went directly to the head of the path and without hesitation walked into the fire and continued to the other side. I felt so embraced in Love and Joy. I got to the other side and started jumping up and down, like a five year old, "I DID IT, I DID IT! OH MAN I DID IT!"

I was elated, joyful and awe struck. I cannot find the words to describe how I truly felt. I walked the fire again and again – six times total. Then it was over.

On the way back to my room I became aware of a small burn on my right heel and thought, "Oh I'm out of communication with the fire." I sat right down on the ground, got back into communication and the red burn spot disappeared!

Oh my God, I learned that "reality" is not what I thought it was. It really is a matter of perception, agreement, and communication. My mind was blown wide open by the possibilities. Yes, fire burns; but sometimes it doesn't. **What else is possible?** What is reality? What is truth?

What a great adventure we are on.

23
Hawaii/Costa Rica

That is the end of my adventures for the 18 month period after Lee died. Please bear with me because, now, I want to flash forward to 2008 and tell you about another cool adventure, and then we will get back to the rest of the book.

I had just watched the DVD, "Riding Giants" which is a historical documentary of surfing very large waves. There was something in the way Greg Noll spoke about the waves that captured my heart. It reminded me of the loving communication I'd had with the fire. I watched that DVD many times and I just had to go see these giant waves. So, I went to Oahu's North Shore in December 2008.

I had three intentions for my visit to Hawaii; first, to see the giant waves; second, to try to surf; and third, to buy some kind of a cool dress for the ICU Christmas party. At home, people had told me I wouldn't find the kind of dress I wanted in Hawaii, but, after walking on fire I knew anything was possible. This party was important because my friend Dale was making his singing debut. We were going to be singing a karaoke duet of, "Baby its cold outside". Plus, I was working on the song, "Santa Baby".

I was sooo excited as I drove up to the North Shore; but, that soon changed. The surfing competitions were going on at Sunset Beach and traffic along the North Shore was terrible. I couldn't find parking or a place to pee. Even worse, I had missed the big waves. The swell had ended the day before. I was really disappointed and working myself into a very unhappy place.

I needed to get a grip. I did my thing of forgiving myself, blah, blah, blah and chose to have a better perspective. I still wanted to be pissed off, but, had just enough awareness and self-control to not totally ruin my vacation. I needed a change of scenery so decided to leave the beach and go into the North Shore town of Haleiwa.

Leaving a disappointing day at the beach, I put on my practice tapes and started singing my duet with Dale. I drove into Haleiwa and pulled into a little shopping center. As I pulled into the parking space, I saw, directly in front of me, a beautiful evening gown displayed in the window.

Wow!   Where did *you* come from and do you have any sisters?! I had to go into that shop. I walked in and the music overhead was playing, "Baby, Its Cold Outside". What?? Directly in my line of sight was a whole row of beautiful gowns. Heaven, I'm in heaven. I walked over and started perusing the selection. Just as I reach for one particularly cool dress the music overhead started playing, "Santa Baby"!

Okay, Okay, I got it. This is where I am *supposed* to be; right here, right now. Dude, I tried on that dress and loved it.

Triiiipy; it all worked out. It always does when I just trust and go with the flow. When am I gonna get that into my thick head?

I returned to my time share at Makaha and found out that the next swell would be in a couple of days so I spent time sight-seeing Oahu. When the swell came in, I drove back to the North Shore. Traffic still sucked, but I was able to park and watch the competition for a little bit. The surfers were being very careful, the waves were big, and some had already broken their boards.

I left Sunset and went to Pipeline. Now that was awesome! It breaks so close to shore and the waves were huge. There were surfers going for it but you never knew if it would be a surfer or a big swoosh of water that would be squirted out the end of the pipe. Either way was cool to me.

Then I went to hang at Waimea and that took my breath away. This was what I had wanted to see.   I walked to the shoreline, noticing there were very few people on the sand. Most of them were sitting on a little knoll at the end of the beach. The Lifeguard was yelling at some clueless swimmer to get out now. I had never seen waves like these.   Yes, there were really big waves breaking out at the usual distance from the shore, but there also large waves coming almost to the shoreline and then breaking. The surfers on the outer breaks weren't even trying to surf, but, there were a couple trying to ride the shoreline waves. In amazement I watched when, suddenly, there was a really BIG wave, way over my head kind of wave, breaking right in front of me *at the shoreline*. Holy shit! It's gonna pummel me! Turning, I sprinted inland, but a look back showed that sucker still chasing me. Ahead, I saw a pond where waves must have been dumping. Hard right, Linda, take a hard right! I pumped my legs; got out the wave's path; and it crashed into the pond without me. Whew, made it! No wonder those folks were on the knoll. After that, I kept a safer distance and just enjoyed watching those waves. It was reported they had reached 23 to 26 feet that day.

I planned to try surfing at Waikiki on my last day. My neighbors, Frank and Chris, had hooked me up with "beach boys" from Aloha Beach Services, a multi-generational "beach boy" family service begun by Harry S. Robello in 1958. Harry was one of the original Waikiki beach boys and nephew to Duke Kahanamoku. You can find their concession right on the beach at the Moana Surfrider hotel.

The day finally came and I froze. *I can't do it.* I was so afraid; afraid of being in the water; afraid of making a fool of myself; afraid of failing. I had to sit down and take a walk into my personal "valley of the shadow of death". I had had two scary incidents at beaches. One was as a child watching helplessly from the shore as my little sister almost drowned. The other was getting pinned by a wave and held under. Plus, hey, I am a fat old lady of 57. I am gonna look like an idiot trying to surf. But worse of all, what if I just can't even get myself onto the board? Once again, I had to move through my emotions and get to Love.

Finally, I came out the other side, quit my boo hooing, and went down to the beach. I told the girl who registered me for a private instruction, "I want someone who will be gentle with a scared old lady."

She said, "I have the perfect guy. His name is Josh".

Hey, that's my step son's name. I met Josh and told him what I wanted.

He said, "I love scared old ladies. We will have fun." And we did. He took such great care of me.

I got myself onto that big old long board as easy as could be and we paddled out. To be honest, there were only baby waves, people; not even a whitewash. The wave came; Josh told me what to do; I stood up and surfed a few feet before I fell in. IT WAS AWESOME! After that, I stood up every time and I even caught a couple of waves to ride all the way into shore. Life was good. I was sooo happy.

When I got home from Hawaii, I was still so stoked I found the Surf Divas in La Jolla. This company was initially created by two sisters for women who wanted to surf. They offered a week long, women's only, surf boot camp in Costa Rica. I had to go!

So, for my 58th birthday, I went to Costa Rica to learn how to surf. Ladies, if you ever wanted to learn to surf, do this trip. It was incredible. There were five women in my class. We were all there solo. Our ages ranged from the 20's to me at 58. Our hostess was the wonderful Emilea who took such great care of us even though we were spread out over three hotels and had a variety of needs. Our teacher was the incredible Melissa. I mean it when I say incredible because she made it her business to know her students, who they were, and what they needed to achieve their dream. She saw right away that I was new to the ocean and a bit nervous. She had me playing in the water while learning to surf. One day she taught me how to boogie board. Right off, I pearled the boogie board – flipped nose down, feet overhead. It was a blast! I learned how to have fun in the ocean and that was a great gift to me.

Then, I was back to surfing. Soon, I was paddling into any wave that came at me. I got very good at turtle rolling. I was even able to paddle out beyond the break. It was exhilarating and exhausting. At first I thought it was just my age that made me so tired, but, after a few days, all of the ladies were pooped. Thank God for the Yoga classes, the massages, and the wonderful food. Talk about an appetite after a workout. OMG.

Disappointingly I still hadn't been able to stand and ride a wave in; I was getting discouraged.

Wednesday was a half day and we were free to do other things. I went ziplining through the jungle canopy with the help of five young male guides who I fell in love with. Ooowee, those boys were cute and they knew how to take care of an older lady. You couldn't call me a cougar, hell; I was more like an old sabre tooth tiger. But I did love all of that sweet, flirty, attention!

On Thursday, it was back to boot camp. In the morning, I hurt my right arm and had a hard time getting on my board. In the afternoon class I hurt my left arm and had to sit out on the shore. My arms were giving out. I had to come to grips with the fact I wasn't gonna get to surf a wave in. Once again, I had to let go of my expectations and judgments and to love myself for the great experience I was having. Is the glass half full or half empty, right?

That night, we celebrated my birthday. Two of the ladies and I went to a local club where I partied hardy with the locals and a big group of college alums vacationing from New Jersey. It was down and dirty dancing, baby. I had a total blast.

The next day was the last day of surfing. My arms were done, I wasn't sure I could even lift my body up onto the board. I walked my board out as far as I could, then kind of floated onto it and sort of paddled out. Melissa was with me. She held my board and told me to wait for the right wave. I waited. Suddenly she yelled, "Paddle!" I did. I stood. I rode. The wave just kept coming. I HAD CAUGHT A WAVE AND I WAS SURFING ALL THE WAY IN TO SHORE!!!

Majorly awesome, dude! I was toast; but it was worth it!

The whole surfing/ziplining thing was a wonderful experience and left me with a hankering for more. But, the entire week I was in Costa Rica I was experiencing an even more awesome sub-story...the bug story.

I had gone to Costa Rica during the rainy season...when the bugs are abundant. My first night, as I lay down in bed to sleep I noticed some movement out of the corner of my eye. When I looked, I saw the floor was covered with *baby spiders!*

Yeah, I have a thing about spiders. When I was a little girl crawling around in a little cave I came out covered with daddy long legs. Spiders have been a challenge ever since.

SPIDERS!

I'm in the jungle at night with spiders! Breathe, Linda, breathe. Spiders! Panting. Breathe slower. Spiders! Choose Love. Huh? **Choose Love now!**

Immediately, I grounded myself, then ran Universal and Earth energy into and through my body to calm it down. I set my bio-energy frequency to Love. I forgave the spiders of my perception of them and chose to have Love's perception instead.

I fell into my familiar natural rhythm of running Love energy. I became calm; I was feeling the Love. I sent a message of Love and Oneness to the spiders and made an agreement with them that they could crawl on the floor but not on me or my bed. Then I sent out energy lines of Love from my body to all corners of my apartment and filled my apartment with Love. In that energy, I was at peace and fell asleep. The spiders stayed away.

The next morning I found that the other ladies had had major difficulties with bugs in their apartments. They continued to have major problems the rest of the week. For me, in the next six days I saw only two bugs, each on separate days and right out in the middle of the floor. I blessed them and took them outside. My apartment had become a bug free zone. Each day I expressed my gratitude at the power of Love!

24
Mr. Cho

My work with patients hadn't stopped and they continued to help me as I helped them, so let's get back to the stories.

Mr. Cho had been in our ICU over a month. He was unconscious, on the ventilator, had chest tubes, and was in a steady general decline. He had a large family that included his wife and adult children.

I hadn't been his nurse, but, now and then, I was in the room to help boost him up in bed or to check on alarms that would go off. So, during those times, I got to say "Hi" to various family members.

I knew the nurses were having a hard time taking care of Mr. Cho and, truthfully, I was trying to stay out of the whole thing. From their experience they knew his prognosis was poor. They felt we were causing him unnecessary pain and suffering by trying to keep him alive on the "fix me path" rather than providing him comfort care on a "peaceful passing" path. Some of the nurses, who had a past history with Mr. Cho's doctor, felt that the doctor was not giving the family accurate or clear enough information about Mr. Cho's poor prognosis. They felt he gave the family false hope and so, eventually, they requested an Ethics Committee meeting.

Ethics committees are usually comprised of folks from various backgrounds: doctors, nurses, social workers, ministers, volunteers, etc. They listen to the issues about the healthcare of a patient and act as a neutral sounding board. They may give advice, but historically, have not made treatment decisions. Anyone could request an ethics meeting; for example: families who feel their wishes are not being followed; doctors who need some objective perspective, and nurses who are trying to advocate for a patient's best interest.

Thursday, the day before the meeting was to occur, I happened to go into Mr. Cho's room to answer an IV alarm. I said hello to his daughter and could see she was really angry.

"You look upset, is there anything I can do to help you?"

She spit out, "Who do these nurses think they are, interfering with the doctor? He is doing exactly what we want in taking care of my father. Who are these nurses to be making trouble? They have no right to do this."

Uh Oh.

I replied, "Well, I am not really informed of the issues, but I will tell you that no one can make you change how you care for your father. These committees are a place to work out differences of opinion so that a patient receives the best unified care we can give. You will be able to say whatever you want and it will be given high regard. I want to reassure you that the nurses care very much for your father's well-being as well as yours. They are trying to do their best to help and to relieve his suffering."

She was still angry, but, appeared to be thinking about this perspective. I really did not know the issues and was trying to be politically correct. I knew one of the nurses was Barb and there was no doubt in my mind she was trying to serve Mr. Cho's best interests. She is an excellent patient advocate.

I backed out, and didn't get further involved. I did give Barb a heads up about the daughter's feelings though. The meeting was the next day, Friday. I heard it was highly charged. The nurses truly did care about the patient and the family. They heard the family's wishes and their confidence in the doctor. They had done their best to advocate and they let go.

The next day, you guessed it, I could hear Mr. Cho's voice in my head at the same time, I could hear the charge nurse telling me I was being assigned to take care of him. Holy Moly!

I walked into his room, stood at the bedside and held his hand. I said, *"Hello"*.

In my mind, he bowed to me and I bowed back. He told me he was at peace and ready to move on, but knew his family was not ready, in particular his daughter.

That is all I remember of my first conversation with Mr. Cho. That day, most of his family came to visit, all at the same time. They tended to hang out much of the day. I gave them updates on Mr. Cho's condition. They saw how I took care of him and seemed to be comfortable with it. I knew they had already been through so much stress; I didn't want to add to it; so, I tried to keep the conversation light.

But, then I had the urge to say, "I know you have been visiting the hospital for quite a while now and you are very informed about the equipment and disease process, but I am going to give you a copy of this little book I wrote. It has three parts, and in the last part of it talks about the different machines and equipment being used here in ICU. You probably already know all about them, but maybe there will be something in the book that will be of interest to you." I got the book, gave it to the son and pointed out the part about ventilators- what they do and how a visitor can help someone who is on one. He started reading and I went back to caring for Mr. Cho.

The son was actually reading the book. At one point, out of the corner of my eye, I saw that something he'd read had struck him, because he called his sister over and they read it together. Then they were showing the other family members. I have no idea what caught their interest. Other than that, the day went by pretty much uneventfully.

That evening at home I started talking to Mr. Cho in my mind.

He again expressed concern about his family, in particular his daughter. So I said, "Well, let's call them in." Suddenly, in my mind, his family was there.

Wow, I never did this before.

The daughter was draped around the father, sobbing; the wife was a few steps back, hands folded in front and her head bowed; and the sons were standing helplessly around. It was like watching a movie. Mr. Cho sat down and cradled his daughter until her crying quieted down. I asked them to all gather around and then asked Mr. Cho to tell them how he was feeling. He told them he was at peace.

Then I asked all of them if they had anything they wanted to say to him. The daughter clung to him. She was very emotional, ranging from angry, to reprimanding, to sad. He listened to it all then smiled at her, stroked her face and said, "My precious, butterfly, do not worry for me because I am at peace. Please know that I am so proud of you." This made a difference to her because she became peaceful in turn.

She got out of her father's lap and let her brothers approach him. They each had their turn and then the wife came and bowed in front of him. He stood, raised her up, embraced her, and kissed her hands. As they all came in for a kind of group hug. I tuned out.

Wow! That was the first time I'd ever had a family conference in my head. I didn't know I could do that. I had never had more than one person before. Very interesting.

The next morning at work, I told my charge nurse, who just so happened to be Barb, about talking to Mr. Cho. I told her about the family conference in my mind and we wondered what it meant. At the moment we were talking, the son came into the ICU.

It was not time for visiting, but he came up to us and said "We want to take my Dad off of life support and do comfort care. Would you please call the doctor for us?"

My mouth dropped open; I just nodded yes. The son went to see his father. Barb and I looked at each other and said, "WOOOOOOO".

I called the doctor who actually came right in. He spoke briefly with the family, then came out to talk with me and asked me how I wanted to handle it. I told him what I wanted to do and he said okay. He wrote the orders, went back in and told the family I would be taking care of things now. He was amazingly accommodating.

When we finally allowed him to, Mr. Cho peacefully died with his family calmly surrounding his bed. His daughter, though tearful, actually had a small smile on her face. The family, including the daughter, expressed their gratitude and gave us all hugs.

Then they were gone. It was all quite quickly done. After all that time and drama; part of me was a bit blown away. A part of me was grateful that even though I was still not curing people and doing miracles at least I was helping and making a difference.

And now, I knew I could do group sessions in my mind. Cool.

25
Mrs. Reed

Another story, a little different, was with Mrs. Reed. She was in her 80's, married and had an adult grandson whom she was very close to. The Reeds were informed people. They had already discussed their desired "quality of life" issues; and, they knew each other's wishes regarding resuscitation. So, when Mrs. Reed came to the hospital with a massive stroke, Mr. Reed knew she would not want to be kept alive. He requested that she be taken off of life support and allowed a peaceful death. Her grandson, who was on his way to Arizona to partake in a vision quest, agreed with this plan. They were all spiritually inclined people and were comfortable with this decision.

So, that is what happened. Mrs. Reed died peacefully.

I lived 60 miles from work and there was going to be some bad weather that night. My supervisor arranged for me to sleep in an empty wing at our Hospice hospital up the hill. This wing was being renovated and had been empty for a few months. It was separated from the occupied wing by a long empty hallway and large double fire doors.

It was late and I was tired; I got ready, turned off the light across the room and went to bed. I was just getting to sleep when the light across the room turned on and the door to my room flew opened. Sleepily I got up, closed the door, turned off the light and went back to bed. Just as I was drifting to sleep, the light went on again and the door flew opened. I groaned tiredly and said out loud, "Okay, who is it and what do you want?"

It was Mrs. Reed. I could see her in my mind as I laid there in bed. I said, "Hey what's up?"

Ooooo she was pissed off. "What do you mean by letting me die?"

Huh?

"That is what you wanted. You planned that with your husband. Why are you so mad?"

"I NEVER GOT TO SAY GOODBYE!!"

"Oh." I thought about it and said, "Well, let's do it now."

I called Mr. Reed and the grandson into my mind. Mrs. Reed threw herself into their arms and cried a little; but, then became joyful and told her grandson, "See, spirit is real, so go on your vision quest and find yours."

They said their goodbyes, then Mr. Reed and the grandson left my mind. Mrs. Reed turned back to me, smiled and said, "Thank you."

"You're welcome." I yawned. The light went off, my door closed and I finally went to sleep.

The next day, I asked the nurses in the occupied wing, whether anyone had come down to my room. They gave me a curious look and said no. Hmm. I know I was awake. I know it happened. I am amazed at how calm and matter of fact I was about the whole thing. I don't know why I wasn't freaked out about it, but, even now when I relive it, I am still kind of calm about it all. Better than getting freaked out, I suppose.

26
Gary

Mr. Gary Davis had been in the ICU for a week, I think, before I became his nurse. He'd had some kind of cancer process that was now overwhelming his body. His wife, Gail, was an RN but not a critical care nurse. While she had some information, she was still a bit unsure about being in the ICU and what course of treatment would be best for her husband.

Gary was obtunded, close to becoming comatose. Gail had already decided to not have him intubated and put onto the ventilator. The night before I met them she had also decided to make him a "No Code"; but she was still shaky about her decisions. She tried to be strong and knowledgeable in front of her adult kids, but I could see she had doubts.

In addition to cancer, Gary had mucositis which is an inflammation of the lining of the mouth and can be very, very painful. Even unconscious, he would resist having his oral care. The night shift RN told me it was a struggle to keep his mouth clean yet it needed cleaning because the mucous lining was bleeding and sloughing off. I don't know why, but, for some strange reason, I never had a problem. He always relaxed his mouth and let me clean it. It was weird how easy it was. I didn't understand it. I do have a way to do oral care that I adopted from the novel, Jubilee Trail, by Gwen Bristow. I adapted the way Florinda helped Garnet take in fluid when she was pregnant and so sick. Crazy, huh? But, it has always worked for me. Still, I knew Gary's mouth was very painful and I was surprised at how he allowed me to clean it. I couldn't explain it. Anyway, when Gail saw this it gave her some confidence in my care of her husband.

One day while Gail was at lunch and I was standing at Gary's bedside, I suddenly saw a man standing on the opposite side of the bed looking at Gary. Yes, I saw him from my mind's eye, but, he was more tangible than I had ever seen before; I felt I could almost reach out and touch him.

I said, "Hi" and he smiled at me. I realized it was Gary looking at himself. So, I asked him what he was thinking about and suddenly, in my mind, I was in a Technicolor meadow. I kept turning around to look at things. The colors were brilliant; I'd never seen anything like it.

Then a huge white stallion came galloping up and bowed in front of Gary, who asked me, "If I go, can I come back?"

"Yep." I was still a little in awe of this Kodak moment.

He hopped on bareback, no reins, and they took off down the field. After a while they returned, he got off and thanked the horse who galloped away.

He turned to me, "Thanks for helping me to have that moment," smiling, he continued, "You know, I am not afraid to die. I know there is more than what meets the eye. I appreciate all you have done for me." He got a twinkle in his eyes, "I am going to die while you are here."

"It would be an honor to be present at your passing, Gary, but, please do it when it is best for you; don't time it around me." He just smiled.

Suddenly, my consciousness was back in the hospital room with the unconscious Mr. Gary Davis.

When Gail returned that afternoon, I asked whether her husband liked to ride horses and she said no. Hmmm, I don't get it. Maybe it was just some weird thing in my head. She kept staring at me like she was waiting for an explanation, so, I took a chance and told her what I saw.

She mused, "I don't really know how he feels about horses but he is very interested in color photography and is in love with making colors as vivid as he can." She became very excited and when their adult kids came she told them about it. They got excited too. It must have meant something to them all.

About an hour later Gary's heart started beating faster and his blood pressure was dropping. At the same time, all four of his doctors showed up and they debated what to do. The cardiologist of course wanted to start medicine to stop the fast heart rate. But Gail was seeing this as a sign that Gary was ready to die. She was standing on one side of the head of his bed; I was on the other side. The kids were standing or sitting around the foot of the bed. Gail said to them, "Maybe this is Dad's way of telling us we should let him go."

"Yesh," came from Gary's direction.

WHAT THE HECK WAS THAT?

Our heads snapped to look at Gary, then at each other. Naw, it was nothing, just some air escaping his mouth.

Gail turned back to the kids and again said, "So, maybe we should not give this medicine and just let Dad go."

"Yesh," again was heard from Gary's direction.

We snapped our heads toward Gary again.

She grabbed his hand, "Gary are you saying to let you die?"

"Yesh." He replied.

I said, "Are you sure you are saying to let you die, Gary?"

"Yesh." He repeated.

Oh my God! Oh my God! This man has not had one physical interaction in days.

Gail looked at the kids, me, and then Gary. "All right darling that is what we will do."

He did not respond again after that. We went together to tell the doctors that Gary was ready to go. Gail told them to switch from the "fix me path" to the comfort care and "let me die peacefully" path. The cardiologist wasn't happy but finally quit arguing with the Oncologist and left.

We gave Gary just the right amount of medicine to make sure he was not in any pain or anxiety and then his family sat around the bed and waited. Gary's vital signs dropped rapidly, but, then held steady at a non-life sustaining level. I encouraged the family to say everything they wanted to say and left while they were doing it.

Time was passing and still Gary held his vital signs at impossibly low levels; but, he did not die. I went into the room and found a very distraught Gail.

"We are doing what he wants; it is hard enough to make this kind of decision; he can't live with these vitals. Why isn't he going?"

She was crying and tearing at the tissue paper. I held her while I told them all, "When we get out of the way and allow a person to have it their way, they will die in their own time and style. In my experience, in a situation like this, I feel like Gary is waiting for something to be said. Has everyone said everything you want to say?"

Gail, still crying said, "Yes, yes, we have all said our goodbyes."

I replied, "Well, I think he is waiting for something." I left the room. Just a few minutes later the alarms went off and Gary flat lined. I rushed back into the room and asked what happened?

Everyone was smiling at me.

Gail said, "I thought about what you said and I told the kids this: 'Your dad and I did not get along well together for quite a few years and I know you all saw that. We even thought about separating. But, in the last couple of years we found each other again and have been so very happy. I am grateful to have had this time with him. I think he would want you to know that sometimes relationships can be tough and you may go through hard times, but to trust your love and let it guide you through.' When I finished saying this, he died, just like that!"

They were so happy, giving me big bear hugs. As they were getting ready to leave, one of the sons asked me the official time of death. It was 6:50pm. Hmmm, I thought. I get off work at 7:00pm. Thanks, Gary.

Another example of the power of my patients' spirit.

27
Connie/Nancy/Jose/Life Coaching

I took a year- long program and trained to be a Life Coach. What was crazy about this is while my Inner Voice urged me to take this course it also told me I wouldn't finish and get the certification.

"Why the heck should I do this then? It's expensive."

"It is good information and you will be able to use it in many ways."

"Okay, okay".

As usual, my Inner Voice was right. I was very good at coaching and I loved it, but, I did not finish the certification process; I came this close! Guess I had received all that I needed. Instead, I began a home practice utilizing life coaching, guided visualization and healing touch. I found this to be a very gratifying way of doing healing work.

Often, my clients had experienced the death of a loved one and had unresolved issues. Using the coaching and healing techniques I could teach my clients how to communicate with their loved one in a way that would resolve issues and release emotions. It was very lovely to watch the healing happen. It was also very cool to see some of my clients utilize their new skills to enrich other's lives.

One of my clients was an ICU nurse. Her dad had cancer. When she would try to talk with him about his wishes regarding code status i.e. resuscitation vs. peaceful death, he would not discuss it. Finally, she said, "Dad you won't tell me what you want, so, I am going to tell you what I think is best for you; if you don't agree with it, you better tell me now." She told him her plan and he didn't comment. When the time came, she made him a no code and allowed him to have a peaceful death.

When she came to me she was 95% okay with her choice but she really wanted to talk with her dad. So I led her through some visualization processes until she could talk with him and come to 100% peace. It also gave her a new way to help her patients as she, sometimes, uses her ability to communicate with spirit to help them.

Of course everything is not about death. ☺

I gave a session to one of my friends, Nancy B, for her birthday. I will let her tell you her story:

"I fell in love with the boy-next-door when I was 16. Pat was my first true love, not a girlhood crush. We dated six years, lived together for a time, and planned to marry. I was even sewing my own wedding dress when I suddenly got cold feet. At 22, I was not yet ready to settle down.

We broke up.

After a few years of being on my own I felt I was ready. I knew who I was. I knew who I wanted to marry. We *would* be together; it was just a matter of time. I *knew* it would all fall into place!

"Magically", one night he came by to see me. I couldn't have been more sure of our love for each other and the rightness of us as a couple. Two days later, I found out he had asked someone else to marry him the very next day.

My heart was broken! Literally.

I knew he had come to see me that night to be sure he was over me. I didn't blame him for that, but it was of little comfort. I moved out of state within the month so I wouldn't have to watch him marry another woman.

Fast-forward 30 years. I had married the next year and divorced after 7 years. I had 3 children that I raised as a single mother. During their growing up years I didn't date at all. Then for a year or two, I dated sporadically. I routinely "fell in love" with men who were completely inappropriate or unavailable. I finally reconciled that I would be okay if I spent my life without a partner. I worked with Linda in ICU and saw firsthand the way she was able to communicate with souls. It was amazing to observe, I never doubted the veracity of what I saw time and again, but had no words to describe it. We became dear friends. As a gift, Linda offered me a healing. I arrived at her place without any notion about what I was really doing, but as always, I trusted her. After settling in her living room, she asked me what I wanted healed.

Without missing a beat, I replied, "My heart." That surprised me.

After some prompting, I related the story of the boy-next-door. Linda then led me into a guided visualization. During this time, I imagined Pat and myself as spirits floating among the stars. Love engulfed us in its warmth. I was supremely happy. I suddenly realized that our love for one another was not bound by time or space. We could love each other eternally despite the fact that we were living separate lives.

After this, Linda did not ask what I had experienced, she simply led me to her treatment room, where I lay upon a table and closed my eyes. I peeked once, and saw Linda holding her palms over my body. I did not peek again, but simply gave myself up to the experience. When I left, I had no physical, emotional, or intellectual sensation that anything unusual had occurred. A month later, I returned to my home state for a high school reunion, celebrating our communal 50th birthday. I have 4 girlfriends who have remained close over the years, and we were excited to be together again. The night of the reunion, we entered the bar where the activities were being held. Suddenly, one of my girlfriends hollered out, "Look, there's Pat!" Mind you, Pat didn't graduate from my high school, much less the same class as mine. I didn't expect him to be there, but, there he was with his wife. I approached to say hello and they explained they were here to see a friend who was performing in the bar that night. They were as astonished as I that my class reunion was being held there. We visited for a while and then they left to watch the performance.

The next time I looked up, I saw the basketball player I'd had a mad crush on. I approached to say hi. I even told him I'd had a crush on him. (What's gotten in to me?)

Shortly later, Pat found me. We spent a bit of time catching up, and arranged to meet for dinner the next night.

Then, wonder of wonders, the gorgeous fellow who had been editor of the school paper approached and started flirting with me. We ended up together for the night. I watched the sun rise with the incredible knowledge that something amazing had happened to me the previous night. Linda had, indeed, healed my heart. My four girlfriends were agog at what had occurred and pressed me to explain it. Of course, there are still no words for the process of grace. Pat and I reconnected in a profound way that left me at peace with the fact that we were not meant to spend our lives together, but this does not diminish our love for one another. Three months after the reunion, I started dating a wonderful man who is perfect for me. We are now married and blissful. When he wonders aloud why we didn't meet earlier, I smile and I tell him I wasn't ready for him. I needed to have my heart healed first."

It was amazing to watch Nancy B, oops, I mean Nancy L, heal herself and I was glad to be a part of it. The wedding was great. I even got to sing a song as Nancy danced down the aisle. Then I got to sing a musical version of their wedding vows. It was such an emotional, cool privilege. I just received an email from Nancy telling me how fantastic her marriage is.

I really loved doing my healing work in this way. I felt it was effective. The only problem was that doing my practice *part time* and my nursing *full time* was leaving me *no time* for myself. So, when I moved I did not restart my practice.

Hey, I forgot to tell you about moving. Well, let me back up a minute and explain how it came about.

After I stopped journeying to Teotihaucan, I began taking the dreaming classes with Jose. Often, Miguel would be there teaching too. They were wonderful classes and I loved them. I would fly from Seattle to San Diego, drive up to Encinitas and stay the weekend.

One day, after our class had been meditating outside at the beautiful Swami's yoga garden in Encinitas, I was crossing the street, returning to the classroom, when my Inner Voice said:

"You're moving back to San Diego."

"No, I'm not."

"Yes, you are."

"NO, I AM NOT!"

"Yes; you are."

Big sigh. I got to the other side of the street called my agent friend, the incomparable, GG Getz and told her to sell my condo cuz I was moving to San Diego. She tried hard to talk me out of it.

She said the prices were way inflated. It didn't matter; I knew I had to go. She easily sold my condo and I easily got my old job back. But, I stayed in Washington a few more months with my friend, Jane, so I could save money. On the internet I perused potential condos to buy. There was one I fell in love with but knew I couldn't afford. Still, when I flew to San Diego looking for a new home I just had to see it in person, so, it was the first place I went to see. I knew I couldn't afford it; it wasn't even in my price range. Somehow though, I was able to buy it and, somehow, I am still able to live in it. I am very grateful.

My parents helped me move my stuff down in the winter when both Washington and Oregon were having snow storms. My Dad was very worried about this, but I kept the intent, "It's possible we will have clear weather and roads all the way down." I sent a "Hello of love" down the highways to our destination. It was pretty amazing because we did have a good trip the whole way. Ahh Love, I just love you!

When I finally did relocate, I stayed with my friend, Merle, until I could actually move into my new home. It was all a convoluted, but smoothly flowing process and...I was back in San Diego. GG was right, it was indeed hugely over inflated, but, I do love my place.

So, here I was in San Diego and taking the dreaming classes. From my perception, Jose's message was a simple one and one I already knew. It was about Love; realizing the God within; and that your best teacher is your own Inner Self, your God Self.

I know that!

"Yes, you do. So why are you taking these classes?"

"Well, they're cool; it's great to be around other like-minded people."

"Mmm Hmm."

"Okay, it does tend to take my attention off of my Inner Self. Yeah, I get it; I've got to do it on my own again, alone."

"You are never alone, Linda." Warm fuzzies.

"I know. It's cool." I stopped taking classes and focused on my inner teacher once again.

28
Dennis/Mood Matching

I am always amazed at what I see when I first say, "Hello" to people's spirits. Their initial responses; what they see in the mirror; who comes to visit them; and what they believe happens when they leave their bodies are unique, often surprising, and always very interesting. Many times they will show me the "white light" as a kind of doorway. When I ask them if they want to go explore, they often say something like, "If I go, can I come back?" Sometimes they don't believe me when I say yes, so, we tie a rope around our waists and they go off exploring while anchored to me. So far everyone who has gone to explore comes back lit up with happiness, love, excitement, and anticipation. It is a pleasure to share their stories with you and, now, I want to tell you the story of my brother, Dennis.

Dennis was in his mid 30's and dying from AIDS. When he came to stay with us, he was slightly demented, had no more social filters, and was so much fun because he laughed a lot. I have always believed it was his sense of humor that kept him alive so long back in a time when we didn't have the kind of drugs we have now to treat AIDS.

He had been staying with Lee and me for a few months and my mom came to help the last couple of weeks.

I worked full time, so Lee was Dennis' primary caregiver. They had a blast together. Lee was writing one of his novels and he would read parts to Dennis. One day I called home and they were busting their guts laughing. Lee told me he had just read a part of the novel to Dennis who had been listening attentively, and then very seriously commented, "Hmmm, I really like the part about the dog." Well, there was no dog in the story and Lee started laughing, then Dennis started laughing, and they became hysterical. It was crazy; you never knew what was going to come out of his mouth.

As he became more debilitated, he would hole up in his room because he didn't want to use a wheelchair. I told him we could be having so much fun if he would use one. He finally agreed and, one day we went to the mall. I left him outside the bookstore where he could watch people. In just a few minutes I could hear him laughing and laughing. I went out to see what was up and there was an older black woman in a wheelchair sitting next to him. He was holding her hand and she was laughing too. As we left, I asked Dennis what had happened. He said, "She was just sitting in the corner looking so unhappy, I told her, 'Come on over here, honey, and visit with me.'" Yep, that's Dennis.

One day he and I were at the super market. It was the day before a holiday and totally busy. We were in a long line for checkout and the cashier, a guy who at baseline was grumpy, was now on a slow burn. Suddenly, Dennis started laughing loudly and saying, "Oh I love that commercial. Abock, abock, abock." People start to back away from the "crazy guy", and give him dirty looks. I noticed, but he didn't and he wouldn't have cared anyway. So I went for it. I asked him what commercial it was.

"Abock abock abock. You know the one where the chickens fall out of the truck on the freeway and are flying into the car behind the truck and saying abock abock." He was laughing so hard he had tears.

I knew it was a funny commercial about chicken products; I liked it too and started laughing. Pretty soon, I noticed the folks around us began to smile and to laugh. Soon, they were relating their own favorite commercials. The whole line got into it and they were all laughing. By the time we got to the cashier even he smiled and told us his favorite commercial.

I stared at Dennis; he didn't even know the effect he had had on people. He was in his own world and enjoying himself. Their social mores didn't affect him. Despite the disapproval around him, he had kept his own energy frequency and ended up changing theirs. It is what Lee had called **"mood matching"**. I already knew and practiced "mood matching" but this was such a great, unconscious, demonstration of it. I learned a lot from watching Dennis in his uninhibited, demented state.

I know you have experienced mood matching. It begins with the "Vibe" you pick up from everyone and everywhere all of the time. We know we communicate on a verbal level and we know we communicate on a non-verbal level with our "body language". We also communicate on an energetic level with our vibrations; if you meet someone who is angry, dude, you can feel it. Conversely, if you are in a bad mood and meet someone who is happy, or hear a cool song you like, then pretty soon you may find yourself feeling okay again. You are picking up the vibe, feeling the energy around you, and matching it. Mood matching can happen with any emotion, positive or negative.

You have all seen it and experienced it in some way. It happens when a charismatic speaker changes an audience's feelings and gets them all onboard with his own feelings. It happens when you walk into your home where there's been an argument. You can feel the tension, so, you start getting yourself ready to deal with it. It happens when you walk into a room with a group of your co-workers and you can tell who's in a good mood and who's not. Do you hang with the dude who is upset or do you hang with one that is happy? Who are you drawn to? Who do you stay away from? Whose energy do you have a *match* with? Is someone looking for an argument? Are you looking for an argument? Well, there you go, you just found your match. Are you looking for a hug and there is a loving person in the room? Just get on over there for some loving. You can become aware of your own internal environment by seeing what kind of energy you hang with; or, how you deal with whatever energy is around you. It can all be a very illuminating mirror.

Sometimes you will find yourself in a situation where the energy is very different from your own. You might find it so uncomfortable you have to leave, *if you can*. If you can't, you may automatically try to shield yourself from the energy. Sometimes, you might find yourself *changing* and getting into the energy around you. Dude, you just matched!

Sometimes, *if you can maintain your own energy,* it is possible that you can change the energy around you. This is stepping up the vibrations, just like playing a low C on the piano then playing it an octave higher, your vibration is higher, and just like tuning one instrument to another, if you can maintain the tone, others will tune to you. How often have we seen one person come into a group situation and change everyone's mood for better or for worse?

If you are *conscious* of mood matching you can recognize it when it is happening and you can choose whether you want to match or not. Perhaps, it is your intention to change the mood surrounding you. For example, when I am working with families, I am aware of the energy frequency around me; it is often fear, grief, guilt, regret, and anger. I check out where inside of me I may be matching, just like I did when I was doing the intuitive readings I mentioned earlier. If I am matching, I release the energy. Whether I am matching or not, I choose to be the energy frequency of Love and I hold onto it no matter what is happening. Love guides my words and my actions and soon it will change the frequency of the folks I am speaking with; they will match the frequency of Love that I am communicating. It is quite healing when this happens.

I speak with my families in whatever way communicates Love to them – be it professionally, jokingly, reverently, or even rude and crude. One of my charge nurses, Angela, tells me I am fluent in "street and crazy" and that's why she gives me those assignments. Hmmm. ☺

To be honest, I am not perfect, nope, I am far from perfect. However, over the years, I have learned to recognize when I am mood matching and to get out of it, if I have time. I get out of it by examining what "button" in me is getting pushed. When I am done examining myself, I imagine a red rosy balloon and I put the offending, button-pushing energy into it. I imagine adding all of my matching mental, emotional, and physical energy into that balloon. Then I choose to be grateful for the opportunity to clear myself; I forgive all the energy in the balloon of my "mini me" perspective; instead, I choose Love's perspective and put all of *that* energy into the balloon. Next I let the whole thing go into the Love's Light to be transmuted into Love and re-cycled. Finally, I inhale a deep breath of Love into my body.

Sometimes, I don't have time to examine my internal "button" and will have to table that process; however, I can still acknowledge that there is a match, release the energy and choose Love.

Still, *sometimes*, I don't recognize that I am mood matching; or, perhaps, I am just in a bad mood and want to stay mad/sad. This begins a "momentum" of my negative energy combining with the matching negative energy around me and then spiraling into more and more negativity until it eventually swamps me. At some point of discomfort, I realize what the heck I am doing and I have to *intellectually* remember that this is not my normal chosen way of being and feeling. I have to ground, center, *reset my intent* to be my Self again and then go through the process of releasing the energy and choosing Love and Happiness.

To be honest, I think sometimes I just wanna be mad or sad. You know what? I have to embrace that and let it be okay, or I will just be adding judgment, etc onto the whole shebang. Oh well... I am human and still evolving. I am sure you have your own way of dealing with all of this; I am just sharing my way cuz maybe it can be of service to you.

Let's get back to Dennis.

Dennis once told me that his greatest sadness was when people had stopped touching and holding him because of his illness. No way was that going to happen with us. When I got home from work, I would hop into bed with my little brother, hold him, and we'd watch TV together. All these years later, I am so grateful we had that time together.

When he got sicker and his level of consciousness began to decrease, Dennis would sleep a lot and I would sit at his bedside meditating for hours. One day, I said, *"Hello"*.

He was standing there waiting for me. I asked, "Dennis what do think happens when you leave your body?"

He pointed to a doorway of white light, then grabbed my hand and pulled me through it with him. At first we saw some people who were waiting for him. I hung back while he visited. There were some family members including our other brother, Bill; there were some of Dennis' friends and old lovers; and, there was a little doggie that jumped into his arms and licked his face. The next thing I knew Dennis grabbed my hand again and we were flying up into the air like Peter Pan and Wendy, higher and higher, out of the atmosphere and into space where he began exploring.

We whirled around one planet and then flew to another one where he let go of my hand and dove in to explore. He came back out and flew into another one while I just hung out in space. This planet was so colorful and beautiful.

Suddenly, my attention was back in my body and I opened my eyes. Dennis was trying to get out of bed to go to the bathroom. Afterward, as I got him back to bed, I said, "I saw those two planets you flew to."

He grinned and said, "There were three; weren't they cool?"

THREE planets! Yeah, there were three and he knew it!

That day he stayed awake, making phone calls to family and friends to tell them goodbye. It was the last time he was fully conscious. I knew my sister and my aunt, who were in California, were having a very hard time, feeling guilty, and sad. So, in my mind, I talked with both of them. I got Dennis in there and encouraged everyone to say their piece and end in love. Later that day my sister, Sue, called me. She said she had called our Aunt Jean and discovered they were both feeling better about Dennis. She wondered if I had been working on them, so she called to ask me and, I told her I had been.

My sister's sensitivity amazes me. She is the only other person beside Sam who ever gave an indication of awareness of our work together. Well, actually, Dennis did too now that I am thinking of it.

Dennis' wishes, regarding death, were that he would die at my home with Lee, Mom, and I present. He wanted to be peaceful, look good, and have the sun shining on his face.

He had been somnolent for several days. I was going to have to go back to work; Mom had to go back to California; and, Lee, who had been playing primary caregiver, would not be able to give the full time 24/7 care Dennis would now need.

I was meditating by his side and told him, "Hey, what do you want? You said you wanted to die in a certain way and I agreed to it. But you are dragging this out, being a little dramatic and "queeny" about it and that's not okay. I am going to have to put you into a nursing home in the next couple of days. I am willing to do this if it's what you want, but no more games." Dude, I didn't play games with him when he was living, I wasn't gonna do it in his dying either.

The next day, I shaved and bathed him. As I was turning him to change the sheets, his breathing stopped and he lost his pulse. I laid him on his back; yelled for Lee and Mom to come now. His breathing and pulse came back. I said, "Okay, sweety; Mom, Lee and I are here. The sun is shining on your face and you look bee-oo-tiful Dahleeng." One more breath and he died, exactly as he had wanted to.

Dennis taught me another big lesson: It is okay to set limits with the living and it is okay to set limits with the dying. From my perspective, the living have the right to not play games with the dying. Family dynamics can be very interesting to watch and never are they more apparent than when someone is dying. Often a patient who, while alive, played games with one or more family members *could and would* continue to play games in their dying process. I had seen it a couple of times already. Sometimes it was a happy game as with Ted the jokester and sometimes it wasn't. As I would get to know the family better and see how frustrating the relationship had been for them, I would tell them that it was perfectly okay to set limits on what they were willing to experience. This was what I had done with the "Thunder woman". It was why I wouldn't pass on the message to the daughters and told her to do it herself. She knew her game and she got over it. Very cool!

29
Dream/Oscar/Hermonia

I used to go with my patients when they wanted to explore "what was beyond" their bodies. As I already related, my brother saw his friends then went planet surfing. Gary rode a white stallion in a Technicolor meadow. Most of them saw the "white light" thing and walked through it as if it was a doorway. Many of them saw friends and family that had already passed. Some would see a particular person often an angel or a religious figure.

I soon realized they always saw something comforting. I wondered if that was to provide a buffer, a way to ease them into the process of leaving their bodies. I began to see it as a gentle way in which their souls could welcome them back and ease the transition to greater awareness.

I once had a dream where I was sitting by myself on a crowded bus. I couldn't see the faces of anyone on the bus because they were turned away from me or sleeping with a hat pulled down or, whatever. Behind me was a young couple. They were having a tough discussion. It sounded like the woman was ill, possibly dying. I turned in my seat, introduced myself to them, and asked if I could be of help. They both looked up at me and got huge smiles on their faces. I didn't know what to make of it. I glanced up and saw that everyone in the bus was now looking at me with huge smiles. I looked around at all of them and realized these were all people I had helped in some way with the transition of leaving their bodies. In that moment, *I knew they were there for me.* It was me who was now in transition and they were there to escort me in love. I turned toward the front of the bus and sure enough there was the light. I woke up from the dream with tears in my eyes and joy in my heart. I thought how cool it would be to have that experience.

I would watch my patients go into the light, come back, go, and come back again. When they came back they'd often look at the condition their bodies were in, or the condition their families were in, and start to think about what they should do. These experiences and the processes people went through *before* making their decisions is what I found the most interesting and where I might be of some assistance to them; it was kind of like "soul coaching". Hey, I just made up that term, right this minute. I like it!

Probably the most powerful help I gave was when I would say "Hello" to a patient's spirit. Often, the spirit was startled or surprised that I could see and hear it. It would look at me then look at its body and recognize that the body was in no condition to be communicating; and so the spirit would wonder how it could hear me talking. At THAT moment is when most spirits would realize they were more than their bodies. It's a very powerful experience to watch that first awareness of being more than just a physical body. Oh my gosh, some of the reactions were so beautiful to watch. In particular was one time when I watched a spirit go to his body and embrace it with love and gratitude for all that it had gone through for him. It was so very moving.

Sometimes a spirit would look at their body then back to me and ask, "Can we fix it?" Surprisingly, not too many of them would ask this. I don't know if it was because I, myself, didn't attract the kind of patients who would want to fix their bodies; or, if it was because the patients I usually took care of had very sick bodies and were ready to move out of them; or, if it was because I did not know how to do that level of healing. I really wanted to know how to do that level of healing. I wanted to be able to cure, to fix, to heal. I wanted to be part of a miracle. I wanted to do miracles.

One patient who asked, "Can we fix it?" was Oscar.

Oscar was a builder. He loved to build things and he understood the process of building things. When I met him in the ICU, his body was very sick and he was unconscious.

When I looked at Oscar in my mind I saw his attention was fully focused on his body. When he heard me say, "Hello", his head jerked around toward my direction; he stared at me and said, "Hey is this real?"

Later, I learned that one of his sisters was psychic, and while he did not totally disbelieve, he had not fully embraced her experiences. *So, when he became aware we could talk to each other he got very excited. He looked back at his body and knew he was separate from it. As he stood there looking at his body, I could see him assessing it. He walked around it and started pointing out problems.*

"See this, it's looking pretty bad, and what about that? I wonder what we can do about all of this."

I could tell he was seeing his body as a kind of remodeling project. He wanted to try to rebuild it and I wanted to help him do it. His daughter, Rose, was into spiritual things and so, I told her about all of this. Through her the rest of the family, with varying degrees of belief, became aware of our efforts.

Oscar and I did everything we could think of, at that time, to help rebuild his body, but, neither of us knew enough of what to do and his disease process outran us.

I had been off work a couple of days and was at home sleeping when he came to me in distress, saying, "I can't do anymore. I can't take it; my body is failing and I have to get out."

I could see he was upset and desperate to leave his body now. He was a practical man. He wasn't afraid to leave his body. He had already explored his beliefs about "the other side" and was happy with it. He had just been curious to see if we could rebuild his body. When he saw that we couldn't he felt like he had to hurry and get out now; kind of like running out of a building that is about to fall on your head.

"Okay, try to relax. I will take care of it in the morning."

When I got to work that morning I looked at his body and saw that he was right. I called his wife and daughter and told them to come to the hospital; it was time for Oscar to go. I called his doctor and told him the same thing. Oscars' whole family came and, of course, they wanted to talk with the doctor about his condition. Fortunately, the doctor concurred it was time. We put Oscar on comfort care and withdrew life support; he died peacefully and quite quickly. He really was ready.

Rose came to see me privately for a while when I was doing Life Coaching and Healing Touch. Among other things, she learned how to listen and to communicate with her dad in a way that brought her peace.

It has been a few years since then and I just recently received this email from Rose:

"Hi Linda,

It's so funny; tonight I drove my daughter Shelly home from the Lake, just the two of us and we talked the entire ride home (90 minutes) about my Dad and what I learned from you. I had never told her before.

One of the stories that really stays with me is when you told me that my Dad told you, in a vision, that he wasn't really sure about "leaving" so he asked you if you would hold one end of a rope while he tied the other end around his waist. You assured him that he could do that. Then he ventured out and came right back filled with happiness and he told you that it was ok, that he didn't need you to hold on to the rope anymore. He knew he would be alright.

The next morning, after our talk, my daughter Shelly woke up and came to me, urgently, to tell me about the dream she'd had that night. In her dream, Grandpa was floating like a balloon and she was holding the end of the string. He lovingly told her that it was ok, that she could let go of the string, he was going to be alright.

That entire time changed my life forever. Losing my Dad and gaining a profound new sense of awareness. I am so grateful you were there to help me listen.

I miss you!

LOVE, Rose"

I am very grateful for my experiences with Oscar and Rose. I am glad to see the ripple effect in motion and that Shelly received some positive effect too. I am glad that I could help a little.

But DANG, I still wanted to cure, to fix, to heal, and do miracles!

****

Another patient was a young woman named Hermonia. She was even sicker than Oscar had been. She would have died weeks earlier; but, her husband's faith in Jesus would not allow him to let her go; and, our technology kept her hanging on.

During her whole ICU stay which was bordering on two months, I took care of her only one day. That day I said, *"Hello"* to her.

"Look, look at me! I am okay, I feel wonderful." She danced around and then looking at her body, she exclaimed, "Oh, look at all those beautiful lights." She could see the energy in her body!

She wanted to try to fix it, so I showed her how to ground her body; how to move the energy in her body along the healthy pathways; and how to clear her chakras, aura, etc. I showed her how to run love through her body and she started doing it. I could see she was such a delightful young woman.

She actually woke up in the next couple of days and was able to nod "yes and no" to her husband and caregivers. We all began to have great hope for her recovery.

I was gone for a week and when I came back her body had declined again. I could see she had done all she could and that she was okay with going now. I knew she was going to leave and told her she had done an awesome job. She stayed long enough for her husband and family to come to terms with it. Then they finally allowed her to have a peaceful passing

Some of the nurses were upset because they'd had real hope she could overcome it all. It was very sad for all of us. I didn't know what to think; I was so frustrated. Could I have made a difference? Here was a patient who could see the energy and was exuberant about wanting to heal her body, but, I didn't have time to work with her. I had other patients to take care of. Did I even know enough to aide in her healing process? Would it have made a difference if I could have worked with her every day? Was there a reason I wasn't her nurse again? I don't know. I don't know if I could have helped at all. I do know that, once again, there was no miracle and, once again, my confidence, and my faith, declined. Maybe I was on the wrong track again, but I couldn't deny the feeling I had that it was possible to cure, to fix, to heal, and to do miracles. I strongly felt this possibility and that I should be able to do it.

But, then again, who am I?

30
Dixie/Homeless Guy/Showing Up

Then Dixie came along.

Wait! Before I tell you about Dixie I have to relate something that happened at the psychic school. Part of our training was to do energy healing. A person would sit down and I would use my hands to find the edge of their aura. I would explore the feel of their energy, smooth it, and encourage it to flow in a healthy pattern. It was possible that I would experience feelings or see images as I did this. As always, I needed to be aware of any of my own matching pictures because this would be an opportunity to release them; or, get stuck in them.

Well, unbeknownst to me, the teachers had a "ringer" that they would invite for healings. This woman sat down and I started to feel for the edge of her aura. She yelled, "OW" and curled her body up into a ball on the chair. What the heck is this?

She said "You're hurting me!"

Really? Yikes, I didn't want to do that. I backed another foot away from her body, and then I backed away more and more until she couldn't feel me touching her aura. I was almost six feet away! At that point, she could allow me to work on her and slowly move closer as her energy relaxed. All of her energy centers were wide open and she was extremely sensitive. I had to be very aware of our matching pictures so that I could clear myself and be able to help her; otherwise, I could end up mood matching and I sure didn't want that!

Afterwards, the teachers told me about her. She had lots of allergies. She shied away from people because she could feel their energy and it hurt her. She was always having odd mishaps and often felt victimized.

It was a good lesson for me to be aware of how the energy I am offering, even though it is with love and good intentions, can be perceived by someone as painful or as an attack as they filter it through their own energy systems, their beliefs, and their perceptions.

I have a friend who recently told me that she has lost several friends by being helpful. She gave more than what they could receive from her. It reminded me of the movie, "The Soloist" with Jamie Foxx and Robert Downey Jr. They depicted very clearly how you cannot give more than a person is *able to receive*. In the end what was most important was to just **show up and care**. Showing up allows a person to take what *they can have* from what you are offering. I think that "showing up and caring" is an important trust building step that helps a person *learn to receive* more.

I have been on both ends of giving and receiving "too much". Have you ever had that experience? I had to learn that it is okay to receive and *not* be obligated to give back. The bottom line was that, in my experience, people often gave to me with the expectation of me returning the favor. There were times I was *afraid* to receive too much because then I would "owe" more than I could, or wanted, to give back. My relationship with Lee and our dog, Sam, had taught me how to give unconditionally, but I also had to learn how to *receive unconditionally*. And you know what? That was a lot harder to learn.

My revelation came one summer when I began to notice an elderly homeless man who lived in my town. He limped around on two crutches from one end of town to the other. I had decided I was going to give him a hundred dollars. Well, after I made that decision, I didn't see him again for weeks. Lee and I were going to move and I still hadn't seen the homeless man. On the day before we were going to move, Lee needed money for something so I gave him the hundred dollars.

The next day, sure enough, I was driving down the street and there was the homeless guy hobbling down the road. I stomped on my brakes and screeched over to the curb. He didn't even notice. I got out of my car, stood in front of him and said, "I have wanted to give you this." I reached into my pocket and pulled out whatever money I had, it was about $30 and I gave it to him.

He said, "Okay." Then he walked around me and took off down the road.

I stood there staring at him. My initial reaction was: Okay?"...That's all?" Then I started laughing, yeah, Linda, what did you want? This is great! He helped *me* out by receiving from me. Giving him the money made me feel good about myself. The truth is I did this for *me*, not him. I'm the one with the big payoff. So, I thank you homeless dude for receiving from me and allowing me to feel good about myself. You have given me a bigger gift than I have given to you.

Freely giving, freely receiving...what a concept.

That was when I truly learned about the joys of giving and receiving unconditionally. I give when it is a joy for me to give; not because the calendar or someone tells me I should. On the other hand, if someone wants to give me something, I receive it joyfully, gratefully, and unconditionally. I do not feel I have to give back. I do not take responsibility for how the giver feels or what they are seeking when they decide to give to me. That is their responsibility. As I became aware of this game and stopped playing it, you wouldn't believe how some people thought I was a selfish bitch. Hey, that is *so* not my problem.

Hmm, I wonder how this will relate to Dixie's story. She does remind me of the sensitive woman. Dixie was also a very sensitive person and crazy mishaps would frequently happen to her too. She also had a big heart and was a friend of mine. It was hard when Dixie became extremely ill and almost died, three times. I was one of her nurses.

It was so apparent to anyone taking care of Dixie that her body often did not respond in the "usual" ways to treatment or to routine care. Also, equipment around her would break, procedures would have complications, experienced people would accidently pull out IV lines, and routine medicines would have side effects. She was sick, dying, and having these weird extraneous problems on top of it.

It was emotionally difficult for the healthcare team to take care of someone they knew. I knew that Dixie and I had some matching energy. I was also very conscious that all of the weird stuff happening was just due to energy, but, I believed I could handle it. I wanted to take care of her and I believed I was a good nurse for her. But, eventually, it got to a point of freaking even me out because I never knew how her body would respond to a routine situation. I couldn't rely on equipment working normally. I became an "equipment control freak", making sure things were handled carefully. It was crazy.

What I want to focus on, though, is the healing she and I tried to do for her. *When I said "Hello" to her, I learned she wasn't sure she wanted to get well.*

I took her over to stand in front of the full length mirror and what she saw was a very nice, cool girl. Someone she liked. Someone worth saving and living for. Okay, good so far. But still, she wasn't sure she wanted to get well.

She went "into the light", came back, and said all of that was cool too; but, still not interested in getting well. Then she flew out into the universe and became a point of light like a star, hanging out with a group of other stars. I started calling her, "Little Star". Still, she wasn't sure what to do.

I finally asked, "What is it that makes you so unsure?"

She said, "It is really hard work." She looked at her husband and daughter and all that was cool; but, her mother...ahhh, that was the really hard work.

I hadn't known how difficult the relationship with her mom was, how it had affected her whole life, and was affecting her decision to get well now.

Dixie was a nurse. She knew that, in addition to the emotional challenge, there was the physical challenge of getting well. She knew how much work and discomfort there would be to recover her very ill body. She wondered whether she wanted to go through all that just to get back to "her crazy life?" That's what was making her so unsure.

I kept having her look at herself in the mirror, seeing the truth of her Self. What she saw there began to give her strength. I asked her if she wanted a friend to be with her and she did. A male figure came to her and would hold her in his lap. I didn't know who it was but he gave her great comfort.

At some point, she finally decided life was worth it and that she could handle the challenges.

The "weirdness" escalated: her body's reactions, relapses, and near deaths; her mother's mental crisis; and the doubts and conflicts among caregivers who loved her. I was part of it; I was the focal point of some of it; and I was being affected by all of it.

The weirdness was getting to me. But, despite all of the drama, I still wanted to take care of Dixie. I wasn't sure how to deal with the mom though; she was breaking me down.

One particularly hard day, my co-worker and friend, Dale, said, "Linda, do you believe the things she is saying about you?

"No."

"Do you believe you are still a good nurse for Dixie?"

"Yes."

"Then don't let her talk to you that way."

OH, DUH! Awareness flared like a light inside of my head. What am I doing? I have totally lost myself. I don't usually let this kind of victim energy engulf me. What kind of game am I involved in here? It came on so insidiously. I'm so sucked into the game, I believe it! Damn, **I am mood matching!** I am **reacting** instead of **acting**.

I had to separate. I took a few days away from the situation to deal with my matching pictures and energy. I had to remember myself and my truth.

After I did that, I could take care of her again and join Dixie's husband, the healthcare team, and the emotional health team who had been trying to support, re-focus, and set limits on the mom's behavior. I set my own limits on how she spoke to me – no more accusations and innuendos. Then I set limits on what kind of energy I would allow her to bring into her daughter's room. This is not how I normally deal with families and it was frakking hard. But Dixie's mom understood exactly what I was talking about. She knew the difference between energy that heals and energy that disrupts. She wasn't allowed to come in to "say goodbye" because she "just knew" I was going to kill Dixie that day. She wasn't allowed to stand in the room and cry the whole day.

One time, after I set a limit with her mom, I could hear Dixie in my head saying, "Oh, that's how to do it."

"WHAT?!" Suddenly, I got clarity of the bigger picture and my part in it. I saw that Dixie was watching all of us as we set limits; and *she was learning!* I began to see that perhaps there was purpose to this whole nightmare. This was probably the lowest point in my career, but, I came back a better and stronger person. I am grateful, now, to Dixie's mom for all that I learned.

Meanwhile, I was trying to have actual physical time to do Healing Touch on Dixie's body, but it was difficult to find time amid all the critical cares she needed. I totally believed that once Dixie had decided to live, she would. It didn't look like it, but I believed it. Like so many of us, Dixie wanted help but she also liked to be in control and do things for herself. I remember, in the beginning, when she was less sick, she had tried to place her own feeding tube into her nose. ☺

As time passed, I could think of no other healing things to do for Dixie except to love her; to tell her she was awesome; to see her as Little Star; and to do my job as a critical care nurse. In other words, all I could do was to show up and care. I realize now how important this is, but at the time, I felt I had failed her.

In my mind I admitted my failure to her, my lack of ability to heal her and she said, "That's okay; I'll take care of it myself." I didn't know what that would mean but I would support it however I could.

So, I was amazed at what happened one day when I was helping another nurse who had been assigned to Dixie that day. I was holding Dixie's hand still while this nurse was doing some procedure to her. All of a sudden I felt a "flash flood" of energy being pulled into me, through me, and into Dixie's body. It was her! She was pulling energy through me to help herself and I let her. I closed my eyes and I almost passed out from the rush, the awesome feeling of it. I had to struggle to stay conscious. The nurse and the tech across from me never noticed a thing. It was incredible.

A couple of weeks later it happened again. This time I was more prepared. I grounded myself and let go. She pulled and pulled. It was wonderful. I'd never had that experience before these two times and I thought, oh, okay, maybe I don't have to know how to fix something, maybe I can just be a conduit for the energy. Maybe it's like showing up and caring and allowing a person to have what they can receive from you. I didn't know. It was a unique experience. Of course it was; it was Dixie.

Dixie is what I call a collaborative miracle. With her strength of will, along with the best that technology had to offer, and the skillful, loving care of her healthcare team, she survived. She was in our ICUs for about 5 months. In just over a year she was able to return to work. She has enthusiasm for life and helps other patients and families facing critical, long term recoveries and she has a new found relationship with her mom. As I said, Little Star is an awesome human being and I am happy to have her back.

31

Stan

Another person I want to tell you about is Stan.

Stan was in his 30's, single, healthy and beautiful. He'd had an accident that cut off the oxygen supply to his brain effectively damaging all of the brain except for the brainstem which kept the vital parts like his heart still working. He was unresponsive and on a ventilator.

After Stan had been in the ICU for a couple of days I was assigned to him because the charge nurse thought I might be able to help the family. His parents had been divorced for a while and the mom was remarried. He had two siblings. Apparently the dad, Joseph, was having a very difficult time with his son's condition and was also in conflict with the rest of the family who wanted to stop life support and let Stan be the organ donor he had wanted to be.

I went into Stan's room and said, *"Hello."* *At first I just saw darkness; then I heard:*

"I fucked up!"

"OK."

"Okay? What does that mean?"

"It means OK, you fucked up."

"But what do I do now?"

"I don't know. Let's go take a look in this mirror over here."

He saw a very young beautiful boy, full of light, love, and joy.

"Oh my God, that's me!" *He began crying and said to the boy,* "I'm sorry, I am so sorry for everything."

The little boy smiled and said "I am still here, you didn't kill me. You covered me up and forgot I was here, but I am still here. I am still you."

He held out his arms to Stan, who reached into the mirror and pulled the boy into his embrace. Stan sat on the floor holding the boy, crying and saying over and over, "I am so sorry."

The boy kept comforting him and said "You did what you had to do to survive and to preserve me. I am still here; I am still you."

Finally, Stan heard this message and pulled the boy into himself where they integrated and became one.

I sent Stan off into the light. He came back glowing with light and said "It's all right. I am more than my body." Then he lay down alongside his body and cradled it in a loving embrace. He had so much gratitude for all of the craziness it had gone through with him.

In my mind, I asked his family to gather around. Stan went directly to his father and told him everything was okay... "I am good and all that matters is our love."

This all happened within a few minutes in my mind.

About half an hour later a man who was Stan's close friend and sponsor came to visit. For some reason, I felt an urge to tell him what I had seen and when I finished he stared at me with his mouth open. He told me Stan had recently found a picture of himself as a young boy and had become enthralled with his "real self"; he wanted to reconnect with him.

When Stan's mom and step dad showed up, the sponsor asked me to tell them the story and I did. O my gosh, they became so happy.

Linda what the heck are you doing? Don't know, not sure, just following my instinct and the urge to say these things.

As more family and friends showed up they wanted to hear the story. I learned that for such a long time they had all been trying to convince Stan of his innate goodness and he just wouldn't buy it. Now, they were so happy that he had finally recognized and embraced himself again.

Okay, cool. So it is relevant.

Then Joseph, with tears streaming down his face, came into the room and draped his body across Stan's chest. He sobbed, told Stan how much he loved him, and that he would never, ever, let him go.

Oy, Linda, how can you help him? I have no idea. Love, please help me now.

Everybody kind of backed off a little, overwhelmed by Joseph's grief and his statement which let them all know he hadn't changed his mind. During a pause in Joseph's remonstration of Stan's condition, the family asked him to hear the story and they left the room. He was willing; and as I told the story he began sobbing again, reaching out and holding me tight. At that point, I think he saw me as an ally, someone who recognized the goodness that was his son. He held my hand and told me he could not live without his son.

"I will die if anything happens to him. I will not stay in this life if he goes. I will go too."

"Are you saying you would make yourself go?"

"Yes,"

"Are you saying you would take your own life if Stan dies?"

"Yes"

"Hmm, let's go sit down and talk."

I asked the secretary to alert the Social Worker and asked someone else to watch Stan for me while I took Joseph into a conference room. We sat down and I encouraged him to tell me about Stan and himself. Apparently, Joseph was a successful man of moderate means who loved his son dearly but had always wanted him to be more than he was.

At an early age and through most of his early adult life, Stan had tried to please his dad with his various activities, but, he never felt his dad was happy with him or what he did. That was because the things he did were not the things Joseph would do. Stan did not follow in his father's footsteps. He was not mainstream, conservative, and goal oriented. Stan was a gregarious, flamboyant, free spirit who loved people and liked to have fun. Yes, he got into drugs and then he got into treatment. He was a good hearted person, kind, generous, and especially attentive to seniors and the disenfranchised. But he never felt he was good enough, in large part, because he had never been able to please his dad. And while Joseph had tremendous love for his son, he never could condone Stan's life or style. Now, of course, he was ripped apart with guilt, grief, and regret; old story, right?

However, during this sad time, Joseph said he had been meeting many people who loved Stan; people of all ages and socio-economic backgrounds who had been affected by Stan's kindness and joyfulness.

I could see this really had an effect on Joseph. I asked him, "What is the possibility that Stan could have done all of these wonderful things for so many people and be so well loved if he had grown up the way you had wanted him to?"

"I don't think he would have. I don't think he would have been so sensitive, aware and compassionate. Yes, yes. I see where you are going with this and it is true. I did not recognize that doing life his own way, his own path, could lead to so much goodness. Yes, yes. I know, I can see it now; but, now he is gone and I cannot tell him."

"But you can tell him, now." Right then, I led Joseph in a brief guided imagery to talk with Stan. They made an easy connection and it went well.

This communication touched Joseph's heart; eased his grieving; and opened his mind to the fact that Stan had a spirit that still existed. He was able to become more engaged with what was happening around him. Over the next few days, he began to actively greet Stan's friends and ask them to share their stories regarding him. He was becoming illuminated by them.

However, he was also still in disagreement with his family about letting Stan go. This family was in conflict. My desire was to unite them in love and peace. Joseph and I had another talk in the conference room.

"I can't let him go. What will I have if he goes?"

I nodded, "I have learned from my patients that we don't always understand why such a tragedy happens but that there can be a higher purpose, a bigger picture, and we must trust, allow it to happen, and let it grace our lives. I am not saying it is easy. I am not saying I could define the purpose of such a tragedy. I am not even saying I could agree with it. What I am saying is that my patients have taught me to trust. Joseph, since this has happened I have watched you come to an appreciation of your son and his life. What is the possibility that Stan's life is an expression of what you could have experienced in your own life if you had allowed it?"

"No, I am not so good as Stan was. We are not the same."

"And yet, Stan came from you, he is a part of your roots. He chose to branch out in a different way, yes, but he is still from you. What is the possibility he has shown you a part of yourself that you could be if you chose to embrace it?"

His head snapped up, his eyes lit up, "YES! He has shown me. He has shown me what is important in life. Yes, it is possible for me to be more like Stan. Yes, it would be an honor to continue my son's legacy of kindness and love. Yes!" I could see he had a new vigor about him, a sense of purpose.

The next day Joseph met with his family then asked for a conference with the doctors. He spoke for the family and asked that we take Stan off of life support and if possible to use his organs to help others.

About a month later Joseph sent me a copy of the words he spoke at Stan's funeral. I will print some excerpts here:

"In the five days that he lay unconscious in the Intensive Critical Unit I met so many friends of Stan's. Each tale that I heard about Stan   coalesces into one story of a beautiful, intelligent, loving, and artistic man who loved people passionately and who in his short-lived life touched the hearts of so many.

Last Thursday, by some miraculous good fortune I found a notebook containing writings from Stan that exemplify the true spirit of his heart and being. During my difficult hours at the Hospital, a beautiful and spiritual nurse who cared for Stan so dearly and passionately took me to a conference room. Linda said, 'Who are we to know why such a tragedy strikes such a beautiful man at the young age of thirty-six. There has to be a higher reason beyond our comprehension.' Well, my dearest family, friends and all, I am totally convinced that Stan's writings will truly save the lives of many tormented drug and alcohol addicts. It is my solemn duty as Stan's father to seek and find a way that his writings end up as a source of healing to drug addicts, and to bring upon them the start of a new day.

I end my tribute to my beloved Stan with the following words he wrote in his notebook:

'We are our greatest challenge.
    Fear is our challenge not our nature.
    Distraction is our challenge.
    Anger is our challenge.
    They block us from the light of the universe

                    from the light of love
                    from the light of God
                    from the light of ourselves
                    which are one and the same.
        One reason why I am so blessed
                    Is that my soul
                    can come so close
                    to the surface
                    and touch people's lives.
        My father and I share more than blood,
                    more than history,
                    more than intelligence,
                    more than creativity.
                    Our souls are of the same branch.'

As of last Thursday, when I found Stan's writings, I know that my soul will connect with Stan's beautiful spirit and be the very same branch."

Did he say branch? Did Stan say branch? Oh my God that was what came out of my mouth. Hmmm, I really *do* think something is happening here.

Still, once again, there was no miraculous healing of Stan's body. I do acknowledge, though, that I am having a helping effect and I am grateful for that.

When my sister, Sue, was reading this for the first time, I asked, "What if I never do more?"

She said, "What do you mean more?"

I said, "What if I can never help more, heal more, do miracles?"

Her mouth kind of dropped open and she looked at me like – are you kidding me? Then she came over, hugged me big time and said, "Just keep doing what you are doing, Linda and keep writing about it."

Thanks, SusaBella, I needed that.

After reading this chapter today, I realize that by writing down my patient's stories I am passing on their legacies to you. I really like that. What an honor it is. Please take what touches you.

32
Don/Mrs. Scott/Mr. Thomas/Mrs. Dooley

Here are more stories, more legacies.

Don was in his 30's. He'd had some kind of an allergic reaction that was destroying his liver and kidneys and was sending him into a severe body failure. He was unconscious, on a ventilator, and also needed dialysis. The doctors and nurses knew that he was suffering; they felt he should be allowed to have a peaceful death. All but one doctor believed he had very little to no chance for recovery; but, his fiancée would not let go. She was having a very difficult time. A recovered alcoholic, she had relapsed, coming to the ICU sometimes with her sponsor and sometimes drunk. I was assigned to Don a couple of weeks into this.

When I said, "Hello" to him in my mind, he showed me a man and a woman dancing together, and, the song playing in my head was, "Can I have this dance for the rest of my life...?" He told me that he was okay with suffering for now if there was any chance he could recover, because he wanted to marry his fiancée."

At that moment, Margie the fiancée, called from the ICU waiting room and asked to come in and visit. As I opened the door to the ICU, I was still in this lovely space in my head seeing the dancing couple and hearing the song. I reached for Margie and gave her a big hug. I blurted out, "Oh my God, Don sure loves you. He showed me this couple dancing and the song, "Can I Have This Dance" was playing and he is willing to suffer if he can just get well and marry you. It is so beautiful."

Yeah, that was my hello to Margie; first contact...very professional, hmmm.

She and her sponsor just stared at me for a minute then Margie got a big smile and hugged me back. She told me how she and Don had bought this figurine of a dancing couple. They always said it was them. My message to her reinforced her decision to give him more time to see if he could recover. The one doctor believed he would if we could keep him alive long enough to overcome his body's allergic reaction and heal.

It took a couple of painful months, but Don did recover to a point that he got out of ICU; out of our hospital; and into an acute rehab hospital. He was able to talk with Margie and they set a date for the wedding. I saw Margie a couple of times. I could see that this experience was somewhat of a healing for her. She had become a stronger person while learning to cope with the ups and downs of a critical illness. She now *knew* she was loved and this allowed her to love unconditionally in return. She was back in her program. She had become the dependable one, the rock that Don could lean on.

Then Don's body gave out and he came back to ICU. When I said, *"Hello"* to him this time, he was tired. He was ready to leave his body and didn't feel guilty or bad about leaving Margie. He knew he'd given his all and had bought time for them to heal, to grow, and to spiritually evolve. I told all of this to Margie. She knew. She was ready too. In that moment, she was strong, her love was strong, and she knew it was the right thing to do this time. She asked the doctors to switch to comfort care and allow Don to have a peaceful death. We did and that is what happened.

****

I have mentioned before, I do not see a victim lying in the hospital bed anymore.

Mrs. Scott had been on the ventilator for about three weeks and had been slowly failing. She had not been conscious or responsive for a week. Her husband, a vibrant man, in his 90's was still driving. He did use a cane for walking and when he would come to visit, I could hear the tap-tap-tap of his cane on the floor. They had a granddaughter they had raised and she called herself, their daughter.

The family had finally decided it was time for Mrs. Scott to be taken off of life support and allowed a peaceful death. I knew this had the potential of being kind of ugly because Mrs. Scott really needed that machine to help her breathe. I knew it was going to take a lot of medicine to keep her body comfortable and I told the family this. They totally understood. Mr. Scott said he did not want to be present when his wife died and was going to the waiting room. Their daughter wanted to be at the bedside.

I have my own method of withdrawing life support and customizing comfort care for a person and it had always been successful. I was attempting to give Mrs. Scott what she and her body needed but it was *not* working. She was lying on her side, facing the door to her room. Her eyes were open for the first time in over a week, but she was still not responding to me or her daughter. Mrs. Scott's breathing was quite labored, noisy, and *sounding* very uncomfortable - just what I was trying to avoid. I told her daughter that I had given her a good amount of medications, but, I thought she might be waiting for something. Her daughter agreed.

Just then I could hear the tap-tap-tap of Mr. Scott's cane and I went out to meet him. I told him what was going on and warned that she sounded and looked uncomfortable. But, now, he didn't care. He was desperate to see her again. As we entered the doorway, I could see Mrs. Scott's eyes were staring right at the doorway. When Mr. Scott entered the doorway, there seemed to be a pause, then, with one more big breath, she closed her eyes and died. The daughter turned and said, "Oh Papa, she just wanted to see you one more time."

****

Mr. Thomas was in the ICU and his family was allowing him to have a peaceful death. His granddaughter had spent the whole night with him in his room. Her dad, Mr. Thomas' son, was at church. When I went into the room to say "Hi" to her I found out she was hungry, hadn't peed all night, and, was afraid to leave her grandfather's bedside.

I told her, "My patients have taught me that when we get out of their way, allow them and God to decide when it is time to go, they will do it in just the way they want to. Some people will want a certain person to be present and will wait until that person comes before they die. Some want to be wearing their favorite hat. Some want to wait for a certain time of day. Some are waiting for the family to resolve issues. And, believe it or not, some folks actually just want to be alone when they pass. I have learned to trust, that if I allow it, the passing will be just the way a person wants. So, don't be afraid to leave or to stay. Don't feel guilty if you're not here when he goes. Do what you need to do and know he will die in the way he wants to because you are allowing him to do it. You have given him this gift of love to have things his way. He and God have got it down."

She looked at me kind of strangely and finally said, "Okay."

She left to go to the bathroom. I walked back to the nurse's station and suddenly the alarms started going off. I looked at the monitor and saw that Mr. Thomas' heart rate, oxygen saturation level, blood pressure and respiratory rate had gone to zero - ALL OF THEM AT THE SAME TIME. I didn't think that was possible but it was there, recorded on paper. I called the aide to go get the granddaughter and I went to Mr. Thomas' bedside. Yep, he had gone as soon as he was alone. I noted the time of death from the clock on the monitor.

We called Mr. Thomas' son to inform him and he came right away. I told him the same thing I had told his daughter. He said, "I was in church and I had the feeling my dad had died. I looked at my watch and saw the time. What do you have as his time of death?"

I checked my forms, but, there was a five minute difference between his watch and the time of death. On impulse I said, "Hey, let's go compare your watch with the clock on the monitor." Yep, there was a five minute difference. He felt his dad had let him know he was going. It made them all feel peaceful; and, they knew they had allowed their loved one to pass peacefully in his own time and in his own way.

****

A lively lady, Mrs. Dooley was in her late 80's and had still been playing in an all-women's jug band before she became sick. I met her the day I was floated out to the med/surg floor. By this time, she was unconscious. The family and doctors had decided to let her pass peacefully instead of going full bore with life support and intensive care. The daughter was a fundamental

Christian lady. She and her mom didn't have exactly the same religious beliefs, but that had never been an issue between them. The daughter and I had to discuss the usual after death plans about which mortuary to call, etc. For some reason, I asked the daughter what they planned to do with regard to a memorial kind of thing.

I said, "Are you going to have a religious service, a party, or what?"

She looked down her nose at me and stiffly replied, "Of course we will be having a religious service."

Hmm. I went about taking care of Mrs. Dooley while her daughter sat there, watchfully.

When I said "Hello" to Mrs. Dooley I could see her playing in her band, then she put down her instrument and started dancing. As she danced she was getting younger and younger. I said, "What the heck are you doing?"

She gave me a little wink and said, "Ooowee honey, I am getting re-borned and I am celebrating!" Awesome.

I started laughing out loud and the daughter frowned at me. Well, I was feeling kind of ballsy so I told her what I saw. She gave me a look like, "Mmmhmm, yeah right, who is this crazy woman?" But then she stared at her mom for a while and I could see she was thinking. Finally, she nodded her head.

Mrs. Dooley passed away peacefully and about a week later her daughter brought fruit baskets, cold cuts and a cake to the ICU where I was working.

On the cake was the number "1".

I cocked my head questioning and she smiled saying, "It's the first year of mom's new life, we had a birthday party for her!" Awesome.

33
Julia

Julia was a beautiful young woman in her early thirties. She was married to the love of her life and she had two beautiful boys below the age of eight. She was a gorgeous girl in every way – physically, mentally, emotionally, and spiritually. I admitted her to the ICU where she was diagnosed with Guillian-Barre. This neuro-muscular disease is usually temporary, but, could take a very long time to get over. The patients I have had took up to a year to recover.

Julia became debilitated quickly and had a hard time adapting to some necessary interventions. She needed an ET tube and ventilator to breathe for her; she needed an NG tube to empty her stomach because it would not drain properly into the intestines; and, she needed another tube into the intestines to feed her. All of these tubes went into either her nose or mouth and down her throat; and, all of these tubes kept gagging Julia and making her vomit. Vomiting is dangerous because it can flow down into the lungs. So, Julia needed a lot of sedating medicine to help her cope with the tubes and to suppress her urge to gag and vomit.

After a week or so, we gave her a tracheostomy, so we could take the breathing tube out of her mouth and put it directly into her trachea. We also took out the other tubes and put them through two small holes in her abdominal wall. One tube went directly to the stomach to keep it empty and one went directly to the intestines for feeding her. She still needed all of these tubes because it was going to be a long recovery. But, YAY, now her nose, mouth and throat were clear of tubes and she could stop gagging! THIS WAS GOOD! This meant she needed less sedation.

It also meant she was now awake and aware of all that was happening to her. Let me tell you, it's much easier to be totally dependent and unconscious in ICU than it is to be conscious and aware that you are totally dependent. It's a big learning curve and it can be an attitudinal/perceptual challenge. Julia could not talk nor move her body and she was entirely dependent upon others for everything. She couldn't move, but she could feel. In addition to the usual pain and discomfort of being in ICU, Julia got incredible hot flashes that were not only very intense physically, they also played havoc with her emotions and she would go into panic mode. She tried her best to cope, but now she needed a lot of attention and, frankly, sometimes we nurses just don't have that much time to give. It was very frustrating for all involved. Thank God for her mom; she helped as much as she could.

It turned out that over the next couple of months, I became a primary nurse for Julia. In addition to the usual critical cares, I spent a lot of time helping her to cope. I taught her visualization and relaxation techniques. I did energy work and massage to calm her and to help her body heal. I massaged her head and combed her hair which she really loved. I talked about perception, reality, spirit, etc. She listened to it all; learned to cope better; and, became more self-aware. We became very fond of each other. Her mom was there much of the time and was such a great support. Julia loved it when her doting husband could bring in the boys. She couldn't communicate or touch them but, they would sit on her bed to touch her and give hugs. It was a very nice, loving family.

Julia slowly got better, but, she still needed to keep all of her tubes. Her stomach just would not empty into her intestines and it needed to be kept empty. She was still a "gagger". It was very easy for her to gag and vomit and the danger of inhaling fluid into her lungs was still an issue.

However, her biggest fear was that she would never be well enough to resume the total involvement she'd had with her boys' lives. She was afraid she wouldn't be able to fully contribute to their well-being and their future. She was used to being "on the go" with them and loved it. She complained of being so weak and tired and didn't feel she was going to recover enough. This really depressed her. She didn't want to be in a wheelchair. I told her she needed time to get strong again and that, if she needed a wheelchair, it would only be temporary; I told her about other patients I'd had with GB who had recovered to their usual self. She heard me, but, I could see she was still afraid. She was so aware of her debilitation and despite the feeding tube, she was pretty thin. She doubted she could be her normal self again.

It was a very happy day when Julia finally got well enough to be out of ICU and transferred to a rehab unit in another hospital. I let a couple of weeks go by for her to get settled and then went to visit. She was off the ventilator! Her trach was capped and she could talk to me! It was so awesome. She was sitting up in bed, had her own cute pajamas on, and seemed to be doing much better. However, she still had the tubes in her abdomen and she was so very thin, worse than before. We talked for a little bit and I could see she still had an underlying fear about not getting well enough to contribute to her sons' well-being and future. I kept encouraging her, but, I felt uncomfortable when I left.

A week later, while I was working, I got a call from a friend who worked in the ICU of the hospital where Julia was getting rehab. They were resuscitating her as we spoke and she was not responding. Apparently, Julia had been fed into her stomach. She had vomited a massive amount into her lungs which started an acute failure of her lungs and heart. They had already been doing CPR for quite a while.

Julia died while I was on the phone.

"I'm sorry, Linda." My friend said,

"Mmm

hmm. Bye." I held the phone and couldn't move for a moment. "Julia just died." I announced to my co-workers. I didn't hear their responses. Time seemed to pause as I stood there, then my feet turned and I headed to the bathroom, not even noticing my tears.

How in the HELL did this happen? How did I not see it coming? I can't believe it. I can't deal with this right now. I have to get back to work. I would not say "Hello" to her in my head. I closed down.

Over the next few days, I could feel her "knocking" at my head, wanting to talk. I refused. I was really upset. Gradually, I had to cop to myself that blocking her was not a good thing for me. I had to face her, so, I finally responded to her, *"Hello."*

"What the hell are YOU so happy about? Do you realize what you did? You fucking died! After all that work to get well, after all

163

that you learned, you gave it all up. What about your husband and boys? Do you realize how destroyed they are right now? And your mom is falling apart. I am so pissed off at you right now, I almost hate you!" She reached out to hold me, but I turned away. She put her hands on my shoulders while I struggled to cope.

Ooo boy, I have lost it!

Somehow, a part of me was still rational and aware of my process. Come on Linda, you have to get it together for your own well-being. I know, but I am so angry. Get over it. I am so sad. Embrace it all and choose Love.

I peeked at Julia; she really was radiant and happy. Happier than I had ever seen her, so, I relented, "Okay, you look good, tell me what happened."

She giggled, "Oh, Linda. You were right. I am more than my body. I am still me. Look at me! I am alive! I feel great. I do see a bigger picture. I knew my body was never going to be normal again or be able to provide for my boys like I wanted to. But, in this form, in my spiritual form, I can help them so much more. I can be with them all of the time as they grow up. I can surround them with my love, and I can support them and, maybe, I can nudge them to make good decisions. I don't know yet what all I can do; I just know I can do so much more in this way." She glowed at me, wanting me to understand and approve.

I resigned, "Okay, I got it. I can see it."

She looked expectantly at me.

"What? What else?"

She held my hand and looked me straight in the eyes. "I want you to tell my husband to sue the hospital."

I snatched back my hand. "What! Are you kidding me? "I can't do that; No way, Jose!"

She took my hand again, "It's a way I can provide for my boys."

"Are you telling me you caused this? What the hell? What are you telling me?"

"Linda, you have to trust. There is a bigger picture here. We are all playing our parts."

"So, what are you telling me? You have to be the victim to the plans of some big Kahuna in the sky? Bullshit! I can't accept it."

"No, you're not getting it. I am not a victim. The more aware I am, the broader my perception is and the more I can be a partner in co-creating my life experience. This is what is best. I want it. It will be so wonderful for my family." Her eyes willed me to understand, *"Please, get this."*

I got to my "overload" point. I couldn't take anymore and maintain my rationality; I surrendered. "Okay, okay, I can't get it right now. I can feel my resistance, but, I do trust and I do think you are awesome; and I will get it together. However, I won't tell someone to start a law suit." She looked so beautiful and radiantly happy.

"Just trust, Linda."

"Ok." I said. As I turned away I thought, *"Can't do it, no way."*

"Trust, Linda!"

Geez, sometimes this mind talk sucks.

I received a request to come to the funeral services. I wanted to go, but, man, what was I going to do? So, I meditated about it and asked for clear guidance to do "whatever was best – the highest good"; blah, blah, blah.

It was crowded, but, Julia's mom saw me right away. She began introducing me to people saying, "Linda was Julia's last best friend." Dang, that kept bringing tears to my eyes. I didn't want to talk to anyone. I didn't see Julia's husband, Dave, except for when he spoke during the service.

At the end of the service I was making a quick getaway when I heard my name being called. It was Dave. Of course it was. He came over and hugged me, thanked me for coming, and asked if we could talk for a moment.

UH OH!

He told me he was thinking of starting a law suit. He said, "You know they should not have been feeding her in the stomach. You know her stomach had trouble emptying. You were always documenting that and telling people to be careful. You know this." He hesitated, rubbing his forehead with his hand, "But, I don't know for sure what to do. I want to do what is right. I need to take care of our boys. I want to do what Julia would want. I want to honor her. I'm not sure, but I keep feeling like I am supposed to do this."

O man. Okay, Love, guide my words, please.

"You know I won't tell you to start a law suit. What I will say is for you to listen to your heart and know that Julia is with you right now. Pay attention!"

He gazed into my eyes for a while. Then he closed his eyes and paid attention; one tear came rolling down his cheek. He sighed, "Okay."

He did sue. They did receive a large settlement which was used to create a trust for the boys. A few years later, I saw Julia's mother. She told me Dave had remarried to a nice woman who had been a friend of Julia's and had kids of her own. It was a happy blended family. She said "We feel like Julia is always with us, watching over us and we are so very grateful."

34
Billy/Little Girl

Yeah...the power of a person's spirit; the power of awareness; the bigger picture; and being One - I am still learning.

The Big Picture can be a difficult thing to appreciate when the character you are playing is always getting the shaft. When we are the victims of tragedies and inhumanities who gives a damn about the big picture? This is where the faith/karma thing is supposed to kick in and tell us there is a higher purpose and that we will be rewarded   sometime, somewhere. Do you believe this? Some do, some don't. Some receive comfort from this perspective, some don't.

I'd had a run in with the "big picture" before Julia. It was with my younger brother, Billy. I won't get into the back story because I don't know it. I really didn't know my siblings when we were young adults because I went my way and they went theirs. Later, when we were a little older, we got back into touch. So, I can only tell you what I do know.

A year before everything came down, I was meditating and I saw Billy die in a fiery explosion. I knew he was driving home from L.A. and I was worried he would be in a car accident, but it didn't happen. He got home and all was well. I decided this vision was just another weird thing in my mind and I forgot about it.

Billy had already been married and divorced, amicably, by the time our paths started crossing again. I knew he had been through trying times but he seemed to be doing fine. He was popular, a college graduate, doing his DJ thing, and planning to go to Hollywood to further his career. The lady he'd been seeing didn't want to go to Hollywood, but, was in total support of him following his dream and they split up, also amicably. This was the plan, but, it didn't happen.

What did happen is that for reasons unknown to any of us, Billy got drunk, bought a shotgun and went to kill his girlfriend. Instead he shot and killed her three year old daughter. Then, while he and the girlfriend were fighting, the police showed up. Billy shot himself in the head, dying instantly in a fiery explosion.

A lot happened after that: reactions of my family, her family, new and old friends, strangers, and newspapers. One thing that was revealing to me is how the girlfriend's parents were trying to comfort my mom. They knew Billy; they had introduced him to their daughter. They knew something crazy must have gone through his mind to have done this.

I had a huge argument with my mother over her grief, pain, guilt and shame. I couldn't give her or the rest of my family the support they needed. I didn't have the solace of grief. I didn't even go to Billy's funeral. I couldn't. Why? Cuz I had a vision of a bigger picture that I didn't know how to deal with and I could not tell anyone about it.

I'd been meditating about Billy and the whole terrible tragedy when the little girl he had killed came into my mind.

She said, "Linda, things are not as they appear to be. There is more happening than you are aware of and everything is all right. I am all right. I am in full agreement with what has happened. I came to this body knowing of this possibility and I agreed to it. I love Bill and everything is okay. That is all you need to know."

"No! No, that's not okay. What do you mean that is all I need to know? What do you mean you came to this body for this and you are in agreement to it? That is NOT all I need to know. I need you to explain this to me."

"Trust, Linda. You have to trust and you have to love no matter what your eyes tell you and what you think you know. Trust, Linda, trust." And she disappeared.

I don't know if I can trust.

I don't know how to feel.

I don't know what to think.

This could break me.

On one hand is this horrible tragedy with a little girl dying; my beautiful brother blowing off his head; and, two mothers left grieving the loss of their children. There is a mother's shame, embarrassment, and guilt, wondering where she had gone wrong in raising her child. There is fear of the unknown - how could someone who seemed so normal and had so much going for him, suddenly go so wrong? There is the impersonality of the newspapers calling someone I love, a killer. There is the feeling of guilt for me, because, I am glad Billy killed himself. Some will think it was the easy way out – and they're right. But...I am still glad.

On the other hand I have the victim, the Little Girl, telling me she isn't a victim. She is telling me to love and to trust no matter what I think I see or what I think I know. I am not sure I can do this and I don't know why I should.

I was so lost.

So, I ended up not feeling the usual stuff that everyone else was feeling. I couldn't. I had a whole different vision of what went down. It estranged me from my family for a while. I knew this was wrong of me, but, I couldn't tell them why. I just stayed away. The best I could do, eventually, was to forgive everyone and everything of my perception and choose to love us all instead. That is how I got by. I tucked this experience away.

Actually, I shoved it into a dark corner.

Years later, someone recommended I read a novel entitled, The Shack, by William P. Young. She thought I would love it because of the spiritual aspect. So, cool, I started reading it, then stopped dead in my tracks after a few pages.

"I can't read this book; NO WAY," my mind screamed. "Why would anyone want to read this book? This is horrific, why would she think I would want to read a book like this?" I tried to remember if I had mentioned Billy to her, but no; I didn't talk about that whole thing.

This book is a bestseller? I don't get it. Why are people reading it? I was going to throw it away; but, instead, I hid it in a corner of a bookshelf. I locked it out of my mind, but, during my meditations it kept coming back to me:

"Linda, read the book."

"NO."
"Linda, read the book."
"NO!"

Over and over it happened, until I surrendered. Oh man, this is gonna hurt. Okay, okay, okay; I'll read the damn book.

I am so glad I did. It lit up the dark corner in my mind, opened the wound in my heart, cleaned them, filled them with love, and healed me. I could never have written about Billy if I hadn't read this book first.

It helped me cope with things I saw but couldn't explain. Stories like Julia's, Billy's, and Mrs. Johns' (the next chapter coming up) challenged me to my soul. Why though? Why am I so challenged? I talk to peoples' spirits. I know we are more than our bodies. I am seeing and hearing that there is a bigger picture. I see there is more happening in our life stories than what we may be conscious of. I have the awareness of wearing the different hats like Clint does when creating a movie. Are we all characters in a movie, an illusion, a virtual reality, a dream? I have heard all of these explanations before. Are we the creators, co-creators, victims of creators? Is it God's mysterious Will, the Law of Attraction, or whatever? Is it conscious Deliberate Creation through Intent, or, creation by default? I guess despite what I have seen and experienced, I still don't know for sure. What do you think?

35
Mrs. Johns/Trial/Big Picture

Okay, one more story along the "Big Picture" line.

In one of my nursing jobs, it was the practice to start the shift by everyone listening to report about all of the patients and then to ask for the patient you wanted to take care of. My usual practice was to ask for patients I had previously taken care of and if told no, then to maybe ask for a patient I felt drawn to. But that was it. I believed that I would be assigned to the patient I was supposed to have, so, I usually didn't push.

This particular day I asked for a patient and was told no because some other nurse was taking him for the second day in a row. I asked for another patient and was told no; another patient - no and no and no. I had asked for five different patients and was told no.

Hey! What's going on here? First, why am I asking for patients and, second, why am I not getting any of them? No se, Jose. (I don't know)

It turned out that I was assigned to a patient who was just waiting to be transferred out of ICU that morning. While I was getting the story on this patient, my charge nurse told me I would be receiving a stable patient from the ER. This woman had been slotted for admission to the telemetry unit but the doctors had decided they wanted her watched a little more closely. Okey dokey.

Well, I never did see my original patient because I took one look at my new patient, Mrs. Johns, and never left her room again. I was even asking my neighboring nurse to run errands for me.

Why? I just didn't feel good about the situation.

Mrs. Johns was conscious, sitting up in bed with one leg crooked and the other straight out. She was writing notes to her husband who was sitting in a chair a couple of feet away from the bed. She looked calm yet had an air of frustration at the same time. It was obvious she wasn't happy about being here.

She was also drooling and would stop writing to dabble at her mouth with tissues. Her swollen tongue was so huge it was protruding out of her very swollen lips. Her neck was swollen too. She was unable to vocalize because of all the swelling. While introducing myself, I set up a suction device for her to use instead of the tissues. I showed her how to use it, but she refused it.

Mrs. Johns was having a reaction to one of her medications and it was causing angioedema. Angioedema is kind of like hives under the skin and commonly causes swelling on the lips and tongue. The danger with angioedema is the possibility for swelling to progress to a point of closing off a person's airway. The minute I saw Mrs. Johns, I decided I couldn't leave her bedside.

I closely monitored her for signs of airway closure. Even though she could not vocalize, she denied having any problem moving air through her throat and nose. She looked comfortable and had no increase work of breathing. Listening audibly and with my stethoscope I could not hear sounds of a narrowing airway passage. I used my hands to get a quick idea of the size of her neck. I watched her behavior. She was neither anxious nor sleepy. When a person cannot breathe out carbon dioxide, they get sleepy; she definitely was not sleepy. I could see she was getting enough oxygen because she wasn't anxious, the color of her skin was normal, the oxygen monitoring device on her finger showed she had plenty of oxygen circulating in her body, and, because she indicated that she was getting enough air. I could feel good pulses in her wrists and feet and the monitor also showed that her heart beat and blood pressure were within normal limits.

Still, I was concerned. During those first few minutes while I was setting up the suction, I spoke with Mrs. Johns about the possibility of needing intubation to protect her airway from potential closure. She vehemently shook her head no; she didn't want it. But, a few minutes later, when the doctor came in to tell her of potential intubation, she didn't refuse. He told her that an anesthesiologist was coming shortly to evaluate the need for intubation.

I stayed in the room watching and evaluating her constantly. I was doing her ICU admission paperwork while keeping my eyes peeled on her. I asked questions about her health history and her husband was trying to answer them the best he could. Truthfully though, Mrs. Johns was making me laugh inside and I was trying to hide my smile. She was so exasperated with her husband's answers; she would roll her eyes, shake her head, and then write down her own answers.

All of a sudden her alarm went off. Her heart rate had slowed way down. I immediately pushed a button to check her blood pressure. At the same time, she clutched her chest and looked very alarmed. I took two steps outside the doorway of her room and told the charge nurse and the secretary that I needed anesthesia stat! I told the group of doctors and nurses doing "rounds", ten feet from the room that this lady was going to code then turned back into the room. Mr. Johns was still in his chair. Mrs. Johns was trying to sit on the side of the bed. I steadied her while she did this. The monitor said her oxygen levels were still normal but she was stressing. I asked the respiratory therapist who had come in to get an oxygen mask on her.

At that moment the anesthesiologist and another doctor entered the room. I left to get some equipment for a difficult intubation. When I got back into the room a few minutes later, she was already intubated and lying unconscious in bed. I didn't know, until later, that the anesthesiologist had easily inserted the tube via the nose while Mrs. Johns had been sitting on the side of the bed.

Her airway was secure, but she had passed out seconds after intubation. The doctors and respiratory therapist were checking that the tube was in proper placement. Other doctors were preparing to put in central IVs.

While the doctors were working on her, I noticed one of the nurses searching for a place to put the oxygen monitoring device that I'd had on Mrs. Johns' finger. I asked her what the problem was and she said she couldn't get a good pulse waveform on the monitor.

That is when I asked, "Does she have a pulse?" I started checking and could not find one. I asked the doctors around me to see if they could find a pulse.   There was none. Mrs. Johns was in PEA. She had an electrical stimulus telling the heart to beat, but, the muscle was not responding so she did not have a pulse or a blood pressure. We began CPR and all the appropriate resuscitation moves. The room was filled with doctors, nurses, respiratory therapists, pharmacist, etc. Her husband was sitting just outside the room. The social worker and the ER nurse who had taken care of Mrs. Johns in the emergency room were there to support him.   We worked very hard on her, but, Mrs. Johns died.

Oh My God. This poor woman walked into the hospital and died. My patient came to me and frakking died in less than one hour! What the HELL had just happened?

The social worker took Mr. Johns to a quiet room to begin help with grieving. I expected that. What I didn't expect was the high intensity of emotions from the caregivers. It was thick and tangible to me. The doctor was crying, the ER nurse was crying, the social worker was crying. The emotions were beating at me. By now you know that I can experience intense emotion and not get lost in it. This was different somehow. I felt almost a little altered, but, that isn't even the right word to describe how I felt. I walked over to our secretary, my friend, Juli, and told her, "The emotion is really running high here. I don't know why, but, I feel like I am supposed to dive right into it. So, I am." And I did.

I went to where Mr. Johns and the social worker were. Holding his hand, I started talking with him and the SW left.

He told me, "I'm afraid I'm going to cry."

I concurred, "Oh yeah, you're gonna cry. You can count on it. You're going to cry when you least expect it; it will just pop out. And every time you have to tell someone that she died you are going to cry. Don't try to stop it, just let it out."

I told him about my husband who had died three months earlier just two rooms away from his wife's room.

He started crying and I held him.

We both cried.

After a while, we talked about the things that had to get done now. I wanted to call a friend or a taxi to come pick him up; but, he wanted to drive himself home. I made him promise to call me when he got home. I told him I was so sorry about his wife dying, that we had done all we could. We held each other and then he left. He did call me when he got home. He had already called a family member to come be with him. He told me he had already had a couple of drinks. I asked him to be sure to stay home and stay safe.

I did firmly believe we had done all we could for Mrs. Johns. I just didn't understand why she had died. We were watching for a potential airway closure. When she went into crisis it was our first reaction to treat an airway problem which we did by intubating and oxygenating. That issue was fixed remarkably easily and fast. It couldn't have been the problem. I couldn't figure it out. Why did she die? No one had an answer for me. Mentally and emotionally I was embroiled.

Spiritually, I was upset because I KNEW I was supposed to be her nurse. Hadn't I asked for five different patients that morning; something I never do? I was led down a path right to her; but what for? I didn't save her. Why was I her nurse! She could have died with any nurse. What the hell? I was drowning in this sea of emotion I had chosen to jump into and I didn't understand anything that had happened!

Days, months went by. Everyone involved had to attend a case review. Then the hospital lawyers began having private interviews with us. I was surprised that I could not speak of this case without sobbing, not just crying mind you, but sobbing. The emotion was volcanic inside of me; it erupted as easily as pushing a button. I didn't understand why it broke me up so totally anytime I tried to talk about her. And, I still couldn't figure out the physiology of why she died.

Time went by and, as usual, life went on. This was the time period I had moved back to San Diego. Another year went by and I was notified there was a law suit pending. No surprise there, I had expected it. I was a key witness and would be subpoenaed to give a deposition. I expected that too. Apparently, I was the last person scheduled to be deposed. The lawyers had been very busy gathering information and building their cases. They sent some of this information to me and this is when I found out that Mrs. Johns had been born with a heart problem. WHAT? I had never finished her History and Physical papers and I hadn't known of all her past medical problems.

This particular heart condition was one that might cause a problem in young adulthood, but if it didn't, then later in life, it could cause right heart failure. The heart has four rooms or chambers; two on the left and two on the right. The left side pumps blood to the body, the right side pumps blood to the lungs which then goes to the left side and out to the body. I also found out she had problems with her liver.

When I read about the heart problem, suddenly my mind could work out a physiological scenario to explain what had happened. It wasn't an airway problem, it was a heart problem! O my gosh, I was so happy to have this information.

I had to fly to Seattle for my deposition. I love Washington and it still feels like a home to me, so I was happy to be there. I was feeling comfortable about the care myself and the doctors had given Mrs. Johns and so I wasn't too worried about the deposition. Still, when I saw my hospital lawyer *prior* to the deposition and she asked me some question, I started sobbing again. *Oh my God, the emotion hadn't lessened one bit!* I still felt the pain. I couldn't explain it; I had no clue! Yeah, yeah, I know, I had told, Juli, the secretary, that I was going to dive in, but geez, it had been two years!

It was a long deposition; we actually ran out of video tape. My lawyers told me I did great. Obviously the lawyers want to win the case; and, one thing I learned is that they will schmooze, baby, support, and do whatever you need so that you can do a good job. Hey you know what? I was really okay with that because it turned out that the prosecutor was trying to blame *me* for Mrs. Johns' death!

I was in shock. I couldn't believe they could even *think* I was responsible. What movie where they watching? How was it possible they could even imagine such a thing? Well, then they told me.

I was accused of leaving the patient's side and not being there when she went critical. The husband said he had to wander the ICU looking for help. And, although I had written a whole paragraph describing Mrs. Johns' respirations, ease of breathing, behavior, color, etc, I hadn't written down the *number* of her respirations per minute, so they accused me of not assessing her properly and that this caused her demise.

Oh my God, I cannot *believe* this is happening! How can my life suddenly turn upside down like this? I try to be a positive influence. I am on my spiritual path. I want to love, to trust, to be conscious, to present a calm, enlightened presence, blah, blah, blah. SO WHAT THE FRAK! I am being accused of negligence and going to court. That is so not me. What is going on here? I am freaking out. On the plane back to San Diego I tried to get a grip.

"I have to trust, I have to trust," I keep repeating to myself. "Pay attention to the energy. Choose Love. Go with the flow. Be my SELF. Hey Big Dude in the sky, a little help here please." By the time I got home, I was calm and trusting again. Still clueless, but trusting.

I was to fly back to Seattle for the trial and be there for only one day. The lawyer prepped me, had recommended the colors of clothes to wear, and, to "Please take the nose stud out of your nose, Linda". Did you know there have been studies to find what things influence jurors? They appear to like the colors, red, white and blue. Go figure...it is America after all. Well, dude, I was wearing navy blue slacks, a navy blue sweater over a white blouse, and I had on red shoes. I did take out the nose stud, but, I was afraid the hole would close. I reassured myself that I would only be gone one day so it should be okay.

After waiting AAALLL day on those hard benches in the hallways of the courthouse and in the cute red shoes that were killing my feet, I finally got called to the stand. My lawyer was up first.

The first question *my own* attorney asked me was, "You spent a lot of time talking with Mr. Johns, what did you talk about?"

WHAM, guess what? Yep, I started sobbing right there on the stand. I don't *think* snot was pouring out of my nose, but it was close. I tried to tell the jury all the things we talked about. My feelings were obviously so totally sincere they could feel it themselves. I heard later that it was impressive to watch. My lawyer, of course, was quite happy with my reaction. Very sneaky.

Then the prosecutor started laying into me trying to create a timeline regarding the doctor's presence at Mrs. John's bedside. I was trying to answer, but, it was like: "What time did you see Mrs. Johns; and, how many minutes until the doctor came and how many minutes til this and what time was that?" On and on, and it wasn't even about the crisis period! I was getting a bit lost in this questioning. Eventually, the judge stopped the proceedings because it was late. I was going to have to return the next day.

I hadn't planned on more than one day. The hospital liaison set me up in a hotel. She and the lawyer asked if I wanted to see my friends and have dinner, but all I wanted was to be alone. I went to my hotel room and cried. I was so emotionally confused. I didn't know how to answer the prosecutor's questions. I didn't want to say something wrong due to my confusion. My lawyer had told me to not let the prosecutor push me around. Also, I was still plagued by why Mrs. Johns had died. Although I could understand all but one aspect of the physiology of how Mrs. Johns had died, spiritually, I still didn't understand why she had died or why I was her nurse. I never had said "Hello" to her. I still didn't. I wasn't even trying to.

I went shopping to buy a different top to wear and I got a red sweater. I ate a good meal. But, none of it was helping me to deal.

I couldn't sleep, instead I meditated all night and my Inner Voice said, *"Linda speak your truth; just open your mouth and the words will come out."*

"Are you sure? What if I say something really dumb?"

"Trust, Linda, just trust."

Dang, sometimes trusting is hard.

I felt like some movie director had come to me two years earlier and said, "Linda, we want you to play this character. You are not going to get a script. The character is a really good ICU nurse; she has had awards for her nursing. She is going to get involved in a case and not know why or what is going on; you will have to allow things to flow and to improvise. Can you do it?

Will you do it?" I must have agreed on some level. And of course, I *did* say "Yes" when I told, Juli, the secretary, "The emotion is really running high here. I don't know why, but, I feel like I am supposed to dive right into it. So, I am."

The next day when I went back to court, I saw two of the nurses who had already been on the stand. They told me that there were two spectators following the case; elderly ladies who came every day. They were psychic investigators. They would go to cases, make predictions of the outcomes, and keep score on how they did. Anyway, the nurses told me that when I had walked to the stand the day before, the psychics said, "Oh, look at her aura, it is so bright and filled with light, she is going to win the case for you."

Yeah, right. I wasn't feeling too bright.

I got on the stand and the prosecutor started in again on her timeline thing. Without thinking, I opened my mouth and out came these words:

"I didn't have a stop watch on the doctor. I was watching my patient. The doctor came whenever he was supposed to. He knew I was there and would call him if he was needed. This is my job; this is what I am trained to do. He didn't need to be there all of the time because I was there." I refused to keep considering her timeline.

Then she began referring to my deposition and statements I had made at that time. I opened my mouth again, "You were very skillful in that deposition, asking me questions, bullying me, misdirecting me, and making assumptions. You were really good and should be proud, but I am not going play that game anymore, so forget the deposition."

Oh MY GOD, WHAT THE FRAK IS COMING OUT OF MY MOUTH!

The prosecutor actually smiled. The judge was smiling, the audience was smiling, and the jurors were all smiling. I wasn't smiling. I felt like I was on trial for my life and I was damned serious.

It went on like that. I listened hard to the questions and I would open my mouth and out would come my answers. I didn't let the prosecutor sway me. I would interrupt when she was making erroneous assumptions. At one point she said, "That is your conjecture."

"No that's a fact." I countered.

When she started in on my incomplete charting, I turned to the jury with firm conviction and said, **"My patient comes first**, then their family, then if I have time, the paperwork. That has always been my practice; it is now and always will be my practice. I won't change it."

Then she brought up my relationship with Mr. Johns. She said, "Obviously, you and Mr. Johns had a relationship, would you say he was an upstanding and honest man?"

"He seemed like a nice man."

"Then why would you say he is lying about the facts?"

"I said he seemed like a nice man. You said he was upstanding and honest." I could hear snickering all around me.

It went on and on. I was on the stand a long time. When all the questions and counter-questions were done everyone seemed to be smiling and feeling good. Not me man; I was drained. I actually stumbled getting down from the stand.

Outside the court, during the break, I saw those psychics and sarcastically asked, "How's my aura looking now, ladies?" They told me it was brilliant.

I'm like, how can that be? I decided to tell them the back-story of how I got assigned to Mrs. Johns; how I had asked for five patients and was told no; how I knew I was supposed to be her nurse. I finished lamely, "I just don't get why I was supposed to be her nurse."

They just smiled at me and said, "Another nurse might have been suspect, Linda. Nobody who knows you would question your integrity, your excellence of care or your devotion to your patient's well-being. You were supposed to be her nurse. It had to be you."

Hmm. I shelved that for the moment. I could see that my reputation was defensible, but, it still didn't tell me WHY Mrs. Johns died. I mean from the spiritual point of view. Plus there was one more physiological piece in this whole scenario that I couldn't figure out.

I flew back to San Diego and I was not happy. I was sooo tired and still with questions pelting my saturated brain. When I got home, I tried to put my nose stud back in and it wouldn't go in. That did it!

I yelled at God, "WHAT IS THIS? I did everything I was supposed to do and now I cannot get this damned stud into my nose. If this is how you reward a person, it's bullshit!"

Hey! I am in my own home, in my own bathroom, if I want to have a meltdown...I can have it! Part of me was thinking oh Linda, shut the fuck up, you are such an asshole, quit whining. But the other part of me wanted a fight; I wanted to explode. I knew it was just an emotional release, but, no way was I gonna give in.

I kept trying to put in the stud and I kept yelling and complaining.

My Inner Voice said, *"Go see Terry and Wael."*

"No, fucking way am I going to see Terry and Wael. I don't want to see anyone. You help me put this damned thing in right now!"

I tried and tried to put it in, but the hole had closed. I tried puncturing it, but couldn't do it. *All the while, the murmuring in my head was "Go see Terry and Wael".* Finally, like a child worn out from her tantrum, I surrendered and agreed to go see them.

Terry and Wael are two critical care nurses I work with who also have their own business where Wael does piercings and Terry does facials. Wael had put my stud in originally. Reluctantly, I went to see them the next day. They knew where I had been. When I saw Terry, she hugged me and nurtured me just like I knew she would; and I started crying. I'm such a baby.

While Wael re-opened my stud hole he asked me to tell him Mrs. Johns' story. Now, Wael is a brilliant nurse and teacher. When I explained the whole scenario to him he asked me the same question that had been bothering me all of this time. Why did her heart rate slow down, initially? I told him that I couldn't figure it out. He then proceeded to explain to me exactly why it had happened.

Just like that! Now I understood the whole physiological process of Mrs. Johns' death. Two years and two states away, I find my answer from a co-worker who pierced my nose. Holy Moly! I called the lawyer's assistant and told her this bit of info. Apparently those suckers had already known it from the expert cardiology witnesses on the case. This was why the prosecution's case had started to fall apart and why they had decided to go after me instead.

Nobody had told me! Yeah, duh, Linda, you were the innocent nurse without the script. If you had known, you wouldn't have been able to play your part so well.

As I was driving home, I was so aware that I really had been a player in a Big Picture; a picture that had spanned over two years. A picture I still don't understand completely and one that I may never understand. I am very sorry Mrs. Johns died. I never have said "Hello" to her and I am not sure why. Maybe I don't believe I could get a clear picture in my head. Maybe I just don't want to know.

I do know my job was to be my Self; to *love* and to *trust* enough to *act* no matter what *appeared* to be happening; to pay attention to Love's guidance and to go with the flow. I did do it despite my insecurities, confusion, and exhaustion. I did it despite the fact I didn't have a script or understand the movie. I did it and in the end I was blown away to finally grasp that there *really was* a big picture, that there was purpose, and that I had played a part in it for two years. From my perspective I am aware of an unseen hand of "direction" guiding me through the whole two years:

1. Me asking for and not receiving five patients then being assigned a patient who did not need me and could easily be given to another nurse.

2. Intuitively knowing I could not leave Mrs. Johns side once I saw her; and, amazingly, having another nurse available who willingly volunteered to run errands for me so I wouldn't have to leave Mrs. Johns.

3. Having had time to write a thorough narrative description of her breathing even though I did not get to the rest of the paperwork. Thank God, although apparently a number is way more important to a lawyer.

4. Having expert multi-disciplinary healthcare givers right outside her door to help when things went into crisis.

5. Being aware of all of that unusual emotion surrounding us; me feeling like I was supposed to embrace it and telling Juli I was going to jump into it.

6. Making the connection with Mr. Johns.

7. Moving to a new state and reconnecting with Terri and Wael.

8. During the trial, falling apart on the stand with ALL of that emotion I had been hanging onto.

9. The next day hearing words coming out of my mouth, as if they were put there, to state my truth with conviction.

10. Having psychic investigators in the court who helped me understand my purpose. (Now *that* was just weird and incredible to me.)

11. Having Terri there to give me the loving hug that I needed but resisted.

12. Having Wael explain the physiology of what had happened.

Wow, now I can read it like a script. Now, I can see a beginning, middle and end.

Even though it was painful and confusing, I never did feel like a victim because I had so much awareness of the energy moving and that I was going with the flow; even consciously choosing to "jump right in". I am conscious that, for at least two years, my life and actions were guided with purpose. It makes me wonder how much guidance and purpose I am unconscious about.

It gave me a big surge in the trust factor. BUT, I wonder if next time I could have the script? Next time could I have more awareness? Next time could I be a conscious partner of the creative process? I am not sure what I am asking. I guess I want to know, do I always have to play the part blindfolded? Cuz, dude, it can be a drag. But, maybe, that's just how I roll.

Oh by the way, the jury voted in favor of us. In addition to the fact it was obviously a heart issue and we had done things appropriately, they apparently appreciated my critical care expertise and my sincerity. They liked that "my patients come first". They liked the comments that "came out of my mouth".

I am so very sorry for Mrs. Johns' passing and the loss her husband felt. I feel great compassion for them.

At the same time, I am happy to say all of that intense emotion is gone.

36
Big Picture/Manuel

Being aware of the Big Picture has been a bit hard for me. I have always wanted to just have a happy life and to love. That seems like a good desire, right? Whenever that wasn't happening, I wanted to fix it. What's wrong with that? To learn that fixing wasn't always the best answer was hard for me to swallow. To become aware that I am being guided down certain pathways is kind of scary and kind of comforting at the same time. Do I want to be more conscious or less conscious? If I know what the Big Picture is about and what is coming down the road toward me, will I play my part, resist, or try to change the picture? Is it better for me to just act on blind faith?

My intent has been to do "the highest good". In my limited consciousness as Linda the "mini me", I don't have a clue as to what is "the highest good", hence, my trying to trust my higher Self. At the same time, I want to be a part of the creative process; so, I keep working on expanding my consciousness and being one with Source.

I am now beginning to wonder if my motivation to have a bigger hand in the creative process has come from wanting to control life so that I won't have to experience so many crappy parts. However, I know that being a control freak does not bring happiness, hence, my repeated choices to trust, to let go and to let LOVE.

Maybe there is a middle ground; a place between controlling and unconsciousness. Maybe, *in this moment*, it is best for me to just to be aware that there is a bigger picture and that I do have a part to play; to be aware that I do have guidance; to be aware of the energy surrounding me; and, to consciously always choose to walk in the flow of Love. Maybe, that is all I can handle right now. Hmm. I need to grow some more.

Meanwhile, life keeps moving and my patients kept teaching me.

I have said that many of my patients would choose to peacefully pass rather than try to fix their bodies. Initially, my intent was to help them become aware that they were more than their bodies and that they would continue on when they left their bodies. Once they got this concept, they could see they had options. They could perceive their bodies as a vehicle like a car. They could choose to try to restore their vehicle or to just let it go and move on. Did they want to go down a "try to fix me" path or a "peaceful passing" path?

My experience had been that when they found their bodies could not be fixed, or, the quality of life would not be acceptable, my patients would decide to have a peaceful death. Many of them were intrigued and happy to explore life beyond their body. They moved on.

Every patient I have been with during their passage journey was a gift of Love. For me, this has been the coolness of the stories I have been writing. Watching and helping my patients as they become aware, explore, choose, and then act, has been informative and inspiring to me. It has helped me to help their families have hope and to bring Love to a time of sorrow. I am honored to be a part of this.

I said this was my experience with "pretty much all" of my patients. Truthfully it *had* been my experience 100% of the time. It happened so much, I was lulled into believing that when people became aware that they were more than their bodies, had options, and had a place to go to, they would choose to move on to their concept of heaven.

WRONG!

In the last four years I have been meeting patients and families with wholly different viewpoints. In a generalized nutshell here are two contrasting examples of what I am talking about:

On one hand is a friend of my Dad's whose body is pretty run down and deteriorating. His doctor told him if he needed to have a major surgery of any kind, he would die on the table. My Dad's friend can see the condition his body is in. He doesn't currently have a quality of life that he enjoys. He knows death is coming and it is just a matter of time. He agreed with the doctor that there will be no more surgeries. He also made himself a No Code and doesn't want the medical system to try to stop him when his body tries to die. He is choosing the "peaceful passing" path rather than the "try to fix me" path.

On the other hand is Manuel.

Manuel was in his 60's. He was obviously sick and from our combined medical/nursing experience we could see he was not going to get better. He had a son and a daughter. The daughter was an RN and *she* knew he was not going to get better. But, Manuel had made his kids promise to never let him go. So, they didn't, even though both kids could see he was slowly and uncomfortably dying.

The one time I was actually Manuel's nurse, I said, "Hello" to him.

He said, "Whoa, how can you be talking to me?"

I showed him all of the usual things and he got the concept that he was more than his body; he got that life would go on for him outside of his body. I could see he got it all. He could see his body was suffering. He could see his kids were suffering, but, he just kept hovering over his body. He wouldn't make a move.

So, I asked him, "When will it be okay for your body to die?

With his hand on his heart, he looked at me solemnly and piously said, "When God calls me, then I will go."

That is what he had always told his kids too. Uh huh, but something didn't feel right to me.

I said, "Okay, cool. I am curious; how loud does God have to call to you? Will you hear it when he whispers, or, does he have to knock you upside the head? Cuz sir, God is yelling at you right now."

He was quite startled and stammered, "Mmm, I don't know, I never thought of it like that."

I left it at that, hoping he and God would have a good conversation. His kids were going through hell. They knew they should let him have a peaceful passing; they *wanted* to, but, they had promised they wouldn't let him go. So, they kept him a Full Code and receiving full critical care.

A few days went by. I heard the nurses saying he was hanging on by a thread. I was curious and so I said *"Hello"* to him again.

He said he couldn't go because God wouldn't want him. He would not elaborate. So we did an imagery exercise in my mind and I asked God if He would want Manuel. What I saw was God lift Manuel up into his arms and hold him on his lap like a child. It looked pretty welcoming to me. Manuel's face was filled with happy awe.

Another few days went by and Manuel still hung on to his body. I had never experienced a patient's spirit doing this before. I was very curious.

I said, "Hello" again. This time, Manuel was hiding. He didn't want me to see him. There was a fog around him. I persevered, saying "Hello" and eventually, he showed himself. What it came down to was Manuel was ashamed of something. It didn't matter that God would want him. **Manuel could not forgive himself**. He was stuck and could not allow himself to receive. He had a secret and did not want to discuss anything with me anymore. He did not want me to contact him anymore. So, I stopped.

I could see he was in fear and crisis and I wanted to help. But, I didn't have the time. I had other patients who needed my attention. I could have probably pushed the issue with Manuel, but I didn't know if that would be the right thing to do. I had never experienced this before. I let it go.

Another few days went by. The son finally let us make Manuel a "No Code" and agreed to not add more interventions above and beyond what we were already doing. We continued the four maxed out IV pressors, Insulin, antibiotics, ventilator, tube feeding, etc. The staff kept saying Manuel could not hang on longer. His vital signs were already below that necessary for the higher brain to live. The nurses were very frustrated having to force his body to stay alive with our critical care interventions. They were upset with the family for making them continue this "torture".

I tried to tell them, "It's not the family; they are doing exactly what Manuel wants. He doesn't want to go. His body will have to whither down to zero vital signs before he will go."

His son was very angry that we kept encouraging him to stop life support and allow his dad to be on Comfort Care. He didn't want to talk with the nurses nor the doctors anymore. I don't think he felt he was doing the best thing for his father, but, he was doing what his dad had asked of him and he didn't want to argue or justify his decision anymore.

On a Wednesday, I happened to see Manuel's pregnant daughter-in-law. She told me she was going to have a caesarian section on Saturday and hoped Manuel did not die on the day her baby was born. She wanted to know what I thought the chances were.

I answered, "I just don't know. His blood pressure has hung out in the 60's, his heart rate is 30. I have no idea how he has managed to stay alive. He could go at any moment. But, he could have gone at any moment these last few weeks."

I was gone from work the rest of the week, but heard that on Friday, the family finally withdrew life support and Manuel died instantly. Apparently the daughter-in-law really didn't want Manuel to die on her baby's birthday.

This was just the first of a lot of frustrating experiences for me. It was the beginning of a bunch of patients with physical conditions that were not going to heal and that I could not help. I could neither help them on a physical nor spiritual frequency.

Many of the patients and families I work with now insist on any and all surgical, medical or technological therapy that can be done, even if they were told it would not make a difference in the end.

In ICU, families watching their loved one, get so excited about the positive steps upward and so disheartened when the steps are downwards. Experienced nurses know we need to keep looking at the whole picture. I tell families, "In ICU there will be steps up and steps down. What you need to watch is the overall trend: are the steps going "up/down, up/down" and trending upward; or, are they going "up/down, up/down" and trending downward?

When the trend is downward what do you do? Do you keep trying to go down the "fix me path" or do you opt for the "peaceful passing path"? I often give this analogy to my patients' families: The tread on your bicycle tire is gone. You get a hole in the tire and we fix it. You get another hole and we fix it. We will try to patch hole after hole; but, you still do not have any tread on the tire. We cannot fix the tread and the tire is giving out. Do you want it to give out with all of the doctors and nurses working on it or do you want it to have a peaceful, loving passing?

What do *you* want? Do you know what your loved ones want for you or for themselves?

37
End Of Life Guidelines

When we believe it is not going to work in the long run, nurses can get very stressed and sometimes pained doing the things we have to do to try and keep bodies alive. Now, I am not saying we are God and know for sure what is going to happen. I am not saying there cannot be a miracle; you know I want that. I am not saying there is zero chance of recovery. I am saying that based on our experiences, sometimes we know the chance for a *meaningful* recovery is as close to zero as it can get. When all we are doing is treading water and we have nothing significant to offer then it will take a miracle for the body to get better. Does God need technology to create a miracle? Is it okay for us to stop our technology of life support and allow God and the patient to decide whether to live or to die *naturally*? Hefty questions. Right now, in the United States, patients and families can still make this choice.

So, nurses and doctors are continuously trying to inform and educate the family about the "reality" of their loved one's situation. Day after day we educate until the family may feel like they are under attack. Then it can become "us against them". Remember Terry's story? Families may feel we don't want to take care of their loved one and that we *want* the patient to die. It is a tenuous tight wire to walk between informing and supporting families through crisis.

My personal intent is to inform and empower people so they can make decisions based upon Love not Fear. I am going to include here three excerpts from my other book, <u>Where do YOU draw the line? – An insider's guide to effective Living Wills, Healing, and Critical Care</u> which addresses end of life issues:

WHY BOTHER?
(why you need this information)

You may be wondering *"why the heck does she want me to think about this scary stuff. It's depressing, who wants to go there?"* Listen, I know that thinking about these things is scary and, believe me, nobody wants to think about it. BUT, it's way scarier to deal with things during a crisis, and then later have to live with results you may not have wanted. It's comfortable to be wrapped in a cocoon of ignorance and denial, thinking, "These things may happen, but not to me." Being in critical care can bring about major life changes, and most changes are hard to deal with--especially if you weren't expecting them.

My mortgage broker is fond of saying "You have to have an exit plan when you buy a home. I think it is empowering to have an "exit plan" for life, but, people are afraid that, *if they think about it,* they will cause it to happen. If you drive a car, do you carry a spare tire and a jack? Getting a flat tire isn't something you dwell upon. No. You just take care of business and then get on with driving. Dying is a part of living. If you're prepared, you can plan for a "good death" the way you might plan for a "good birth", or a "good wedding." You don't dwell upon it. You just take care of business and then get on with the living! We don't always know when we're going to die, we just know we will. Our attitude toward death will determine whether or not we're victims. There's a great line from the book <u>Tuesdays with Morrie</u>. Morrie said, "When you know how to die, you know how to live." I believe that when you face dying you learn what's really important to you and you can change your priorities.

If you knew you had only one hour left to live, what would you regret having not done? What would you regret having not said? **Stop!** Think about this right now.

If you knew you were going to move to another country and would never see your family or your friends again, would you wait till the last minute to say everything you wanted to say? Would you regret not seeing or doing things you wanted to do? Or would you take the time before your move to say and do all that you could? Life is all about choosing. When you choose between two things you want, you pick the thing that is most important to you. In the end, whether or not you got to do everything you thought you wanted to do, you'll still have done all that is most important to you, and there'll be no regrets. It is a win/win situation.

And what of your parents, spouse, or adult children? If you're suddenly faced with the task of making major health care or life and death decisions for them, do you even have a clue as to what they'd want you to do? Would you know how to help them?

In the past, the medical system could only do so much to save your life. There wasn't much to think about because there were few choices, so public education didn't seem to be needed. Today, with transplants, better technology, and better drugs, we can do a whole lot more. And who knows where cloning and stem cell research will lead? You may have more options, but there are still many limitations.

In the old days when a person went on life support we were talking the end of the line. Today the question is *what kind* of life support do I need and *for how long*? In the past we thought only in terms of life and death, but now we must ask, "What will the quality of my life be? Will this treatment bring me back to the way I was, and if not, will it be a kind of life I would want?

In the past, doctors made these decisions. Today YOU and YOUR FAMILY make them.

If you want to have everything done for you or your loved one, we'll be there for you. But you need to understand what that means. You need to understand your options and what you're getting into. To make the best decisions you'll need information. So, where do you begin?

FUNCTION IS THE GUIDE
(How do you know what you want?)

First, let's just ask the big question, if your body is trying to die, do you want us to try to stop it or do you want us to allow you to have a peaceful death? Of course, that answer will change as you live your life. So, if/when you do change your mind, make sure you communicate this. I will give you guidelines regarding communication later in this book.

Now, let's say you want us to try to save your life. Great. Then we need to talk about *what you want to achieve.* Ask yourself what *level of disability* are you willing to live with? What is the *"basic level of functioning"* you need to make life worth living? *Where do you draw the line?* Here is a guideline I use with folks:

1. **Is it okay to be in a coma?** One patient with cancer said that he wanted to keep going unless he was brain dead. Does that mean it was okay with him to live in a coma for the rest of his life? He said, "Yes." He was young with young children and was willing to live in a coma hoping that a cure could eventually be found.

2. **Is it important that you are conscious and can recognize loved ones?** Often when a person is in a "vegetative coma" they appear to be aware of people in the room and appear to respond even though medical wisdom says they are not. This can lead to a lot of conflict in families on what to do. In my experience, if a person has, in the past, stated they would not want to be kept alive if they could not talk, etc. then there is no conflict because a person in this condition will not be doing that.

3. **Is it important that you can talk?** Another patient said that she would need to be able to talk, to share her ideas, and give advice to help other people. It would be okay if she were paralyzed as long as she could talk. What she really wants is not to just talk; she wants to be able to think, to understand what someone is saying to her, and to be able to speak well enough that others would not consider it too great a task to listen to her.

4. **Is it important to you that you can eat food with your mouth?** Believe it or not, eating by mouth is very important to some people. They would rather not live if they cannot do this. For some people the danger in eating by mouth is that swallowing is an issue. They may choke and stop breathing; or, the food/liquid could be slowly going into the lungs which could cause a serious pneumonia and possibly a serious infection called Sepsis and necessitate life support. So, my question is, if you want to eat, do you want us to try to save you if you if something goes wrong and you need life support? Or, do you want to eat and be a No Code?

5. **Is it important that you can move your body in bed?**

6. **Is it important that you can get your body out of bed...with or without help?**

7. **Is it important that you can go to the bathroom by yourself?**

8. **Is it important that you can get around your home by yourself?**

9. **Is it important that you can take care of your home by yourself?**

10. **Is it important that you can get out of your home and take care of business by yourself?** One lady said that if she could not be independent and take care of herself she wouldn't want to live. That allows for a lot of various disabilities including stroke, paraplegia, amputations, some brain damage, etc. Lots of people with disabilities live independent lives.

Another woman said any disability was unacceptable.

You get the picture?

Then, consider this: are you willing to do rehab for a month, a few months, a year, for as long as possible? Do you have an end point? How long are you willing to do rehab to get to that bottom line?

What do *you* need to make your life worthwhile? This may change as your life circumstances change and you get older. Knowing what you're willing to live with will be the guiding light for making health care decisions, including what kind of life support you want and how long you would want it. If you want it all, does that mean you're willing to live with any kind of loss of functioning? Think about it. While we may be able to keep you alive and even get you off of life support, there's no guarantee that you're going to like the life we've saved you for. Maybe you will, maybe you won't. This is why knowing your bottom line can be so helpful.

When you or your loved ones are making these decisions, take time to evaluate *why* you are making the choice you want. Be well informed about your options. That's the purpose of this booklet. If you're choosing to not have life supports for any reason ask yourself, why? If you're choosing this because life seems hopeless or because you feel like a burden to your family, you should talk to your family or seek counseling before making your decision. If you feel your family is pressuring you into making this decision, don't let them, get family counseling. End of life decisions are best made for spiritual and practical reasons.

On the other hand, if you want yourself or your loved one to have full life support for as long as possible, to "go down kicking and scratching", ask yourself why? We will all die someday. How sick does the mind or body have to be before it's okay to let go? One woman with severe Alzheimer's disease came to critical care because she was having irregular heartbeats. She lives at home with a 24-hour caregiver. Her son lives across the state and sees his mom for about an hour once a week. Her mind has deteriorated to the point where she barely responds verbally. She is fed through a tube. She lies in bed in a constant fetal position. It hurts her when we move her. Her hands are tied down because she pulls out her IV's. She's a Full Code. Although they've never discussed her wishes, her son insists everything be done to keep her alive. Do you think she would want us to do that? Would you want it if this were your loved one? Would you want this for yourself? You should know this answer.

STOPPING LIFE SUPPORT

You must stay informed so you can track the progress of yours or your loved one's situation. Always compare the answers you're getting with the "basic level of functioning" you or your loved one desires. Many times you'll come to a fork in the road where you will have a *"window of opportunity"* to choose to continue life support therapy on the "fix me path" or to stop and choose a "peaceful passing path".

One patient, a heart attack victim, upon whom CPR was not started soon enough, arrived at the critical care unit unconscious. There, his blood pressure and heart rhythm were controlled and, over the next week, he stabilized but didn't regain consciousness. Brainwave tests showed that he wasn't brain dead, but his brain functions were seriously impaired. The family was told that, although this man may be able to come off of the ventilator and be able to breathe on his own in a few days, he had extensive brain damage. Right now he was in a coma, but he would probably come out of it and could possibly recover to a point where he would be alive, but he would need total physical care and likely he'd not recognize his family. This was a *"window of opportunity"*. Stop life support now, and he would pass away peacefully. Continue life support and he would be facing extremely limited recovery. There was conflict in the family; the wife and one son did not believe the Dad would want to live with such diminished capacity. The other son said, "We should give him a chance." In further discussions it was revealed that this son and his father had not had a great relationship, and only recently had begun working things out. This son wasn't ready to let go. In helping the son with his personal wishes we kept asking what would his dad want? If we give the dad this chance, would he have the capability and more importantly, the desire to face this challenge? He finally admitted that his Dad would not want to do this. This family chose to stop life support and provide a peaceful passing.

Most of us have heard of heroes who have faced the challenge of disabling injuries or illness. Some are famous, like Christopher Reeves and Stephen Hawking, but most are the people next door. When life gave these people poop, they turned it into fertilizer and grew. You may even know someone who became a happier person within himself and in his life because of the changes the disability made. These people personify the strength of the human spirit. You can never discount the strength of a person's spirit and will to live. Every nurse has seen people recover despite the odds. These recoveries are called miracles because they don't happen every day.

Yet, when you are making decisions for someone else, it's very important that you remember that it is that person who has to experience everything it will take to live, and you need to know whether or not this is a challenge that he or she would want. Too often we save people with life support and then they have to live with results they did not want. They are forced to face challenges they didn't want. Society has adopted the adage, "You don't know your own strength until you are tested", thereby making it right to face every challenge that comes our way. This implies that a person is weak or cowardly if he elects to not accept the challenge. This is simply not true. People should be able to choose those challenges they want to face and those they don't. It's the individual's choice rather than society's. Just because we can keep someone alive, does that mean we should?

Some answers I have heard regarding Technology are:

- God gave us technology to help us live.
- God gave us technology so we can play at being God and learn wisdom.
- God gave us technology so we could have a choice. Then when He calls us home we can go joyfully, or we can whine and say "Aw, do I have to come now? Can't I stay out and play a little longer?"
- God doesn't need technology to make a miracle.

It's always hard to set aside your own feelings and make a decision based on what your loved ones would want, but it's even harder if your loved one never told you what to do. Whatever decision you make, you must live with. You'll always wonder if you did the right thing. When you make a decision based upon Love and what you think your loved one would want, it does help you cope in the future. On the other hand, if your loved one *did* tell you what he wanted, how wonderful is that! This was a final gift of Love he gave to you. So then, know that you aren't making the decision; you're simply honoring the decision he made; you're following his wishes. This is your final gift of Love to him.

38
Culture/Belief/Karin /Dark Days

These past few years, one thing I have really learned is that, often, it is *not* about being informed. Many of our patients and families are quite informed and aware.

For example: one very sick lady had two daughters. One had been a doctor in the Philippines; and one had been an ICU nurse in Los Angeles. I took care of their mom the first few days of her stay in ICU and was one of the first to "inform and support". Her very poor prognosis was not news to them; they were experienced healthcare givers and could see the condition she was in.   But, they insisted she continue to have repeated surgeries and all the technological interventions we could offer even though the doctors felt she would not have a good recovery in the long run. Her daughters kept her a Full Code throughout this time. The mom had a very tough course; I think she was in our ICUs the whole time. She never regained consciousness and two months later when she finally died her daughters were angry about it.

Another example is of a very wonderful family who tried to be as informed as possible. They did not like to see their loved one suffering as he was, but, they believed that for every moment he spent suffering, souls were being released from purgatory. They wanted him to be a witness to the power of Jesus and to be a miracle healing.   In his lucid moments, the patient was in agreement to this. However, it was pretty obvious to his healthcare team that he was not going to make it. We did a lot of work with this family, supporting, informing, and listening to them. They struggled with their decisions. They only wanted to do the "right thing" and they hoped, of course, that the "right thing" meant their loved one would be healed. He hoped so too. Eventually, after several weeks, the patient and the family realized things were not working and requested he go to Hospice where he peacefully died.

Speaking of Hospice, a service I think is so wonderful, there is this story:

An 85 year old man was receiving Hospice service at home and was still a Full Code. So, when he had a problem at home, 911 was called, the EMT's began resuscitation, brought him to the ER, then to ICU, and that is where he lingered while we stabilized him. Once he was stabilized, he was comatose, septic, and in multi-organ failure on top of the *baseline fatal disease* he had been receiving Hospice for. It then took the family several days to decide whether to continue to use all of the life support interventions we were using to keep him alive or to stop, go to comfort care and allow him to have a peaceful passing. Some of them wanted to keep going.

WHAT?? What is wrong with this picture? Hospice **and** a Full Code? In my experience you decide to utilize Hospice when you have a terminal illness and want to be on the "peaceful passing" path. Hospice provides access to wonderful care, services, support, and medicines you may not find elsewhere. In my experience, though, you become a No Code when you enter the Hospice path. The Hospice I know and love provides service and palliative pain relief with the end goal being a "peaceful passing". On the flip side, being a Full Code is on the "fix me path". It means we will try to stop you from dying. We will use CPR, shocking, intubation, ventilation, medicines, and dialysis...every resource we have to stop you from dying. How can a person have both? I don't get it. Is this a lack of communication, education, a political thing, or a financial thing? It makes me wonder if it is a back door way to receive the wonderful services Hospice has to offer while still planning to live as long as technology can make it happen. I have to think there is some kind of rational explanation, but, I just can't see it yet.

There was another patient who had been very sick in our ICU had gotten well enough to go to a rehab hospital while trached and on the ventilator. She did not last long at this hospital, deteriorated, and returned to us, comatose. The healthcare team was encouraging her family to take her off of life support and go to Comfort Care. Her family, however, insisted their mom would want to be kept alive even if she was in a coma. You know what? They were right, that is exactly what she wanted. How do I know? Cause she woke up! I asked her, if this were to happen again, would she want the family to make the same decisions and she said, "Yes." She did make it to rehab again. I don't know what happened after that.

What I began to learn from these and other patients is that these families didn't need to be educated and informed to make a "rational decision in a futile case". They weren't "torturing their loved one." They were doing *exactly what the patient would expect them to do.* The families were choosing what they all, including the patient, believed was the right thing to do.

As one family told me, "God will take us when He is ready to. God gave man science and man is supposed to use that science to save us until there is no more that science can do, then God will take us."

Well alrighty then.

And you know what? In America, we still have that choice and the right to demand all of the technology and resources available to save a person, even when, in our experience, we think it is futile to attempt it. But, here is the dilemma, sometimes a person does get better! So, how do we know when to stop? Do we keep going until there is nothing more that current technology can do? Do we stop after maxing out on three pressors, four, or five? I remember in the early 1980s, I went to a conference on Ethics. I don't remember much from it except that it was presented as having three arms or ideas to be considered. One of the considerations was the financial aspect of healthcare. I totally discounted finances as a consideration. I felt there was no price too high for a person's life. Now, truthfully, I see it isn't a question about how high the price is for a person's life; rather, it is how high a price will we pay to try and stop the unstoppable from happening? I see, now, that we must address these issues. The question is how to make the decisions. I would love to see people in this country have an alternative to calling 911 for emergency care because 911 is on the "fix me path". I would love to see a nationwide number we could call for **emergency comfort care.** What if you could go to the Emergency Room and say, "I am not asking you to save my life, I just need relief from my discomfort while I have a peaceful death."? Wouldn't it be great if they had comfort care rooms right in the ER?

In my own little way, I have written my first book and this book, in part, hoping to broaden people's perspectives about end of life issues, so that they can make these decisions based upon Love while they still can choose. I think, in the near future, finances and government will start making the choices for us. I am sure we are going to make mistakes as the pendulum swings back and forth, but, I am hoping we will find balance and wisdom soon.

In the light of these patient's beliefs, I found myself increasingly frustrated and useless when talking to them or their families on a spiritual or a physical level. More and more, I found that my patients, even on the spiritual level, did not want to make a decision whether to get well or to pass peacefully. They seemed almost content to passively suffer until God or technology would make a decision for them. I finally completely stopped talking to them in my mind. On the physical level, I would take time, only once, to inform and educate the family and then I stopped talking to them about life support or comfort care. I just went along with the flow. The best thing I had been able to offer people wasn't working. The one thing that had kept me from burnout was suddenly ineffective. I felt so unhappy, useless, and ineffective in the ICU.

I began to hate my job. It had already become an escalating challenge physically, emotionally, mentally, and spiritually; and now, the gratification and satisfaction of "doing a good job" had disappeared. Now, my job was increasingly painful to me because the care I had to give my patients was hurting them and I could see no end in sight. Dude, do you *get* how extremely difficult it is for nurses to give care that hurts their patients, all for *futile* reasons? It totally sucks! Most of the nurses I know want to give loving care with every fiber of their being. Just the other day, one of my friends "shamefully confessed" to me how bad she feels because she doesn't care about her patients the way she used to. She said, "I feel so guilty because I feel nothing anymore. Something is wrong with me." She didn't believe me when I told her it's a defense mechanism and that I understood. I hugged her and told her to read this book.

As an example, I will briefly tell just a part of Karin's story.

Karin was in her 30's. She was married and had a ten year old daughter. She had had an inflamed pancreas that led to multiple surgeries and multiple resuscitations. Her stay in the hospital was about 18 months, mostly in the ICUs, before she eventually died. I will be talking more about Karin later in this book, but, I want to tell you this part now.

The first time I took care of her, Karin, was in terrible pain despite being on high doses of continuous IV pain medicine. All you had to do was lay a finger on her and she would moan or yell in pain. She held her whole body and face stiff with pain. Oh man, I did not want to have to touch her and cause more pain, but, that is exactly what my job required me to do.

Before, I went into her room, I said, "Hello", to Karin in my mind. I could see her standing in the middle of a room with her right arm folded over her abdomen and the left one up, hand facing out, as if guarding her body. When I said hi to her, all she would move were her eyes. She wouldn't even move her lips to speak. She wouldn't turn to look at her body which was lying in the bed behind her. I knew it was because she thought it would hurt her. I tried to tell her she wasn't her body. I held a mirror in front of her face so she could see her body behind her. But she did not believe she wouldn't hurt if she moved.

So, I told her a joke and she kind of smiled.

"Does it hurt your face to smile?" I asked. She smiled some more.

Then I started to lightly tickle her. She was horrified and scared to respond, but, pretty soon she was laughing thus making her body move.

"Does that hurt you?"

She gave me a dirty look. She still didn't believe, so I pulled out the big guns. Do you remember the "dancing baby" that was on Ally McBeal and the commercials for a while? Well, I had that baby show up and start dancing for Karin. She laughed even more. Then I took Karin's hands in mine and started making her twist her body side to side. At first only her torso would move; she wouldn't move her feet. So, I suddenly pulled her into a dip making one of her feet fly into the air.

She yelled, "OW".

***"Really?"** I inquired.*

She stopped for a moment to consider then yelled, "It doesn't hurt!" She was ecstatic and began to dance with the baby.

It was great to see her happy. After a while though, I tried to talk to her about her body's condition and her beliefs about dying. She saw the white light off to her right. She went into it and came back saying it was nice, but she did not want to go there and did not want to discuss it further. So, I stopped.

I entered Karin's hospital room then and said, "I know it's going to hurt when I touch you, but, you choose to be alive and I have to touch you to give you the care you need. So here's my offer. You go ahead and moan or yell all you want to. I will not try to shush you or to falsely comfort you. Also, I will not feel guilty and pained about the fact that I am hurting you because the more I beat myself up about it the less I can be of help to you. Agreed?"

She blinked her eyes, "Yes."

And that's how it went. I touched, she moaned. I told her to just let it rip. After a while, I would say, "Karin, I need you to lift this arm, or, Karin, I need you to turn to this side." I knew she wouldn't do it, but I felt that if her brain knew what I wanted it to do, then it would be thinking about doing it and she would have less resistance when I moved her. It turned out to work very well. We did this through the day and by the end of my shift she was moving her own body and not moaning in pain anymore. I knew she still had pain but she was coping differently. I was trying to cope too.

This was the beginning of our relationship for the next 18 or so months. I was only one of her many nurses, and many of us had a very caring relationship with her and her family. But, I had to watch her painfully suffer; I even watched her die right in front of me one day, until we resuscitated her back. It was such a difficult time for all of us nurses. We didn't understand why Karin would want to live in this limbo like state or why her parents let her suffer like this. But Karin did not want to die and her parents supported that decision. I will talk more about her later in this book.

As I have said, Karin was just one of the many patients and families that were willing to go through so much suffering despite the combined expertise and experiences of the healthcare team telling them that nothing we were doing was going to help in the long run. *We could not fix the lack of tread on the tire.*

I felt I had nothing useful left to offer my patients or their families. I never let my patients or families see this and from their comments, I think they still felt my love for them. BUT, for me, the only way I was able to deal with all of these folks painfully, uselessly, wasting away was to see them as job security!

Why do this job? For the money, baby!

O MY GOD, how could I be THAT nurse! So callous; so unfeeling; so not compassionate! I didn't like it. I loathed myself for what I had become. BUT, having to work for the money was a lifeline that *forced* me to keep working. It was a lifeline that *eventually forced* me to be available to opportunities that could enable me to evolve and learn to love my job again.

Yeah, eventually that might work, but, in the here and now, I was dragging my ass to work for the money and to socialize with my friends.

My coworkers and one doctor who knew about me talking to patients on a spiritual level would often ask me, "Linda, have you talked to this patient yet?"

And I would reply, "Nope and I'm not going to either; it's futile for me to talk with him/her."

I had shut it all down.

These were the dark days of "Nurse Linda".

Ironically this was also the time period when I was elected the Nurse of the Year for both of the ICUs and for the whole hospital. Oh yeah, how crazy could things be! Can't they see how undeserving I am? My manager called me at home to give me the good news. I asked him, "How can I possibly be the Nurse of the Year?" He gave me a bunch of reasons. I guess others couldn't tell, but, I knew my attitude sucked. Was this some kind of sick joke the Universe was playing on me? I felt that to be the Nurse of the Year in this environment was a huge honor as we have such amazing nurses in both of our ICUs. I felt guilty and so undeserving.

Just after receiving the award, I went to Washington for Nancy's wedding. While I was at the reception, Sandra, one of my ex coworkers came over to say hi. I had always admired Sandra for her experience and skill as a great ICU nurse. Without any preamble, she told me how much she had loved working with me in the ICU. She said my love and compassion for my patients and families had inspired her to be a better nurse. She hugged me and said goodbye. I just kind of stood there with my mouth open and tears in my eyes. I don't know, maybe God is trying to tell me I am not as bad as I think I am. My patients and families still feel loved by me, but, I know they are not receiving all that I can give. I don't feel like I am a good nurse; *I know* I can be better. I want to, I just don't know how to.

Back in San Diego, after a particularly rough day at work, five of us nurses met for a drink. We got our drinks, sat down and the first things out of our mouths were: "I have nightmares about coming to work"; "I'm afraid to come to work"; "I dread coming to work"; "I cry at work."

Whoa! This wasn't a bitch session. This was a real - "Man this is how I feel and I don't know what to do about it"- session. We acknowledged we have a great management team from our unit manager to the CEO of the hospital and to the CEO of the corporation. We love our hospital, we know the grass is not greener somewhere else.

We are all experienced ICU nurses. We are all dedicated nurses. We *want* to take good care of our patients and we feel it is harder and harder to do it. No longer do we come to work and believe that we are *good enough*; that we can get the job done. We are secretly ashamed that we may not be able to keep up with the work. We are feeling guilty because we have to constantly decide what parts of our job we can get done today. Much of nursing is actual physical labor that is getting harder and harder to do. Our patients are so very sick, many in isolation, and often there is not enough help, *when needed*, to take good care of them. Even worse, sometimes, patient care suffers because the damn documentation has to get done, or, God help us, the government will stop reimbursements or the lawyers may sue us. When you realize we *are struggling to provide the good care that we want to give* and then you add on the spiritual/mental/emotional strain we are under because we are *not sure we are serving our patient's best interests by forcing their bodies to stay alive*, is it any wonder that nurses are not happy? We keep trying, because that's what good nurses do and WE ARE GOOD NURSES! This is a healthcare system wide problem and, frankly, we don't see a light at the end of the tunnel. I know my friends at other hospitals are experiencing the same things. One of my friend's mom asked me why her daughter is not happy being a nurse anymore. I tried to explain it to her. I hope she reads this chapter.

The five of us nurses started problem solving. We know it is a healthcare wide system problem but what can we do for us right now? The first thing was to know that we *are* good enough. Yes, this is something we each have to know inside of ourselves, but it helps to hear we are not alone in our frustration and fear. We are not the only one who feels so guilty about wanting to stop giving care to a patient we believe we are needlessly hurting. We are not the only one who feels ineffective and helpless trying to reason with a family or a doctor when they insist on giving futile care. We are not the only one floundering to get all of our work done. We are not the only one who cannot reposition their patient at this hour because there is no one available to help at this time and we are not strong enough to do it alone. We are not the only one who can't get the patient care and the documentation done before the end of the shift. And, speaking for myself now, I hope I am not the only one who sometimes pees her pants when she laughs or coughs cuz, dang, my bladder is full and there was no time to go to the bathroom. OR, alternately, I am so thirsty because the government says I cannot keep a thermos of water at my work station and I literally have no time to walk to the break room for some water. We need to not be afraid to say to our coworkers, "Hey, I am drowning here" (literally in my case). As coworkers we need to supportively respond to that cry for help without judgment. We need to tell each other, "You are a good nurse; You did a good job." We need to give each other hugs. These were just little things we thought of, but I thought it was a good beginning. At least we all felt better. I am grateful that in most of my career I have worked with such supportive coworkers.

However, when I left the bar, I was still thinking it through. I am 58; I don't know how much longer I can physically do the work of modern day nursing. In addition, my patient's don't really want what I have to offer anymore. How am I going to survive? How am I going to love my job again?

You thought I had an answer, didn't you?

Ha!

39
Renaldo/Angela/Big Death/Gomez

One Monday morning I came to work and, Angela, the night charge nurse, had assigned me to Renaldo because she thought the family needed my "Feng Shui" as she called it. There was to be a family conference with the doctors and she hoped I could "talk some sense into the family so they would let Renaldo go".

When Angela returned to work 12 hours later, she was assigned to be Renaldo's nurse. When she asked me, I told her I did not go to the family conference because it would have been a waste of time. I knew there would be no decisions made and I was right; there weren't.

"Have you talked to Renaldo in your mind?"

"Yes, when I first took care of him about a month ago. He didn't want to make any choices then, either; it was futile and I just stopped talking to him."

"How do you talk to people in your mind?"

"You can do it, we all can." We got into a discussion about this and suddenly I had to stop.

"We have to stop talking about all of this, because I can feel my mind opening up to Renaldo and I don't want to talk to him again." I shut down my mind, finished report and left to go home. Too late; Arggh! By the time I got to my car, Renaldo was talking to me.

"Why am I futile to you?"

"Oh, Dude, I am sorry. I don't mean to offend you. It just means that I don't think we can have a reasonable conversation. It means, that when I show you the condition of your body and that we are not going to be able to save it, you don't acknowledge it and choose to either try to make yourself better or to take your next step and let your body die peacefully. Instead you just lay there; you don't do anything. You don't want to know more, you don't want to explore your options, and you don't want to make decisions. Your family is the same way. You are just wasting away and it is very hard to watch."

"Here is my problem," he said. "How do I know the difference between God calling me and me quitting?"

"Hmm", I mused. "I never thought about it before. Let me think. Well, I guess the first thing you could do, to let God know you are willing to do His will, is to make yourself a No Code. That way when God does call for you, we won't get in the way and try to stop your body from dying. Then, you could ask God to make it very clear that He has called you. Ask Him to make it a Big Death, so it is apparent to everyone that we could not have saved you even if we had tried. No one could ever think of you as a quitter then. How does that sound to you?"

"That sounds like a good idea."

That was Monday evening. It was the first time I had ever used the term "Big Death", I think.

The next evening I was at home. I had to call in to work for something and I heard that Renaldo's body had taken a turn for the worst.

Really?

I called Angela at home. She told me that, Monday night while she was taking care of Renaldo, she had experimented having a conversation with him. Among other things, she had told him, "I don't know if you can hear me or not, I just want you to know that I support you."

On Wednesday, Renaldo's family made him a No Code. I don't know how that came about.

On Friday, as I got out of my car at work, Renaldo was in my mind smiling.

"Guess what I am going to do today?"

"Go away, I don't want to know. I'm too close to your situation. I am not neutral enough to be sure I am seeing and hearing clearly."

He laughed, "Today I am going to die the Big Death."

"Yeah, right. I'll believe it when I see it."

"Linda you are so funny, you just don't trust, you know?"

My patient assignment was across the unit from his room, so I had no awareness when it all came down. But that is exactly what he did. He had the Big Death. No one in his family had doubted that God was calling him.

At the end of the shift, for no good reason, I sat down next to the resident that had been Renaldo's primary doctor. He was typing out a summary about Renaldo. I asked him how he was doing and he said he was trying to figure out if there was something else he could have done. For some unknown reason, I felt an urge to reveal my conversations with Renaldo. The doctor then told me that Renaldo had been sick most of his 40 years and his biggest concern was that his family would think he was a quitter. He really didn't want them to think that way about him. The doctor thought it would help if he could tell the family about the conversations. I said sure.

I don't know what happened for them after that, but for me, I realized I had to start **listening** again. Maybe I was no longer a help to my patients, but, my patients still had things to teach me, even if I didn't like it or agree with them. And so I began again.

Or, so I thought.

Shortly after Renaldo, I briefly had another patient named Gomez. He, too, was slowly circling the drain – not getting better; slowly getting worse and worse. Gomez had previously made his minister his Durable Power of Attorney for Health Care (DPOA), instead of giving the power to one of his adult children. He had given his minister the legal right to make life and death healthcare decisions for him, but, it turned out the minister didn't feel comfortable making these decisions and the kids didn't know what to do either.

The one day I took care of Gomez, I said, *"Hello".*

He was really surprised and interested to become aware he was talking to me while looking at his body lying in the bed. We did all the usual stuff I do with patients in my head. He went and explored his "after death beliefs" and was amazed.

That is where I left him. I wasn't assigned to take care of him again.

Over a month later, one of our doctors asked, "Linda, have you talked with Gomez?"

I retorted, "I did it a month ago and he's still here. I'm not going to do it again. It is futile."

HEY! What did I just hear me say? What happened to my decision to begin listening again? Dang, I think I'm out of practice. After the thing with Renaldo, I knew this was a sign for me to say *"Hello"* again, so I did.

What did I see? Well, there was Gomez lounging, stretched out on a chaise lounge next to the bed his body was lying in. He had on shorts, sunglasses and was reading the newspaper.

What the hell?

I asked, "What the heck are you doing?"

He said, "What do you mean, what the heck am I doing?"

"Dude, you are sitting there enjoying yourself like you're at the beach and your body is over there slowly and painfully dying!"

"So?"

"SO??! Your body is suffering. Your family is suffering. Your minister is not sure what the right thing to do is. Your nurses and doctors are having a hard time forcing your body to stay alive when they can see it isn't going to work and it is suffering. What are you doing?"

"Linda, have you not been paying attention? Have you not learned anything yet? It is my body, it is my life, it is my story, and it is my choice."

"What about your family?"

"It is all part of the big picture, Linda. Part of a story you have no consciousness of. You have to let go and allow. As for you and your nursing, you choose this work and you play your part."

"OUCH!" That pulled me up and brought me to awareness.

I squinted my mind's eye suspiciously, "Hmmm, you've changed haven't you? If you're here as some kind of an angel to help me learn, thanks, I got it and I am grateful. Please don't keep your body going just to teach me anymore; please be in peace."

He smiled at me and went back to reading his paper.

His body died a couple of days later.

Oh my gosh, I cannot let myself forget that I am playing a part in a bigger picture. But, I am not happy with my part and I don't know what to do. One thing I always loved about my job was the "making a difference" part. Whether it was helping someone get well; or, helping families to make the hard decisions and choices based upon Love; or, helping spirits become aware and have peaceful loving transitions; whatever, I felt like I was doing a good job.

Now, after almost two years of decline and wallowing in my ineffectiveness and unhappiness, I became aware that I'd had some kind of an agenda. That was a surprise to me. I had always considered myself to be unconditionally loving, non-judgmental, and supportive of my patients and families in whatever they wanted. **Apparently not!** I think that, on some level, I was trying to get my patients to agree with what I thought was best for them. I think, unconsciously, I *expected* that if I could help them broaden their perspectives and let go of their fears then they would, in love, choose a better quality of life whether that was in their bodies or out of them.

O my gosh, Linda; what makes you think you know what is best for someone else? Who are you to judge their quality of life? What has happened to your perspective; your awareness of the bigger picture? Linda, where the hell are you? I don't recognize myself. Where is my Love, where is my Compassion, where is my Happiness? Damn, I'm down in a hole again, caught up in the game again. I forgot myself... AGAIN!

Okay, okay, okay, think; use your tools for self-awareness. What is bothering you here? I feel like I can't help anyone. It is futile. Not only is it futile trying to make these people physically well, my attempts to work with them spiritually are futile. There is no forward movement. They are just standing still or slowly circling the drain.

Okay, this is what I perceive. Now, where am I matching that energy? What buttons are being pushed inside of me? What beliefs are my patients reflecting back to me; beliefs I don't want to see? Where am I being futile in my life? Where am I circling the drain?"

O MY GOD. WHERE AM I BEING FUTILE IN MY LIFE? WHERE AM I CIRCLING THE DRAIN?

Where indeed?

Once again, my patients have blessed me with a *SMACKDOWN!*

40
Mom/Billy/Little Girl

Futility, circling the drain; the Big Picture being so harsh; there are so many terrible stories in the world. I am reminded of my brother, Billy, again.

When I wrote about Billy, I waited for my family's response and, yes, it was very painful for my mom to read. What if the Little Girl's family reads the book? It would be so painful for them too. I really doubted the wisdom of putting the story into this book. However, despite its intensity and pain, all of my family and test readers said to put it in.

Why? Where do I draw the line? I'm neither into sensationalism nor wanting to do an expose. I want this book to be a *blessing* and to bring hope. What do I do? Just reading the draft of the story knocked my mom out. I know it probably really bothered Sue, too. I need some guidance and I need to help mom.

So, I said, "Hello" to my mother.

I could see her; she was doubled over in pain. Crying, she gasped, "I can't resolve this issue it hurts too much."

I asked, "Mutie, do you want to resolve it?"

She nodded, "Yes."

I said, "Mom look into this mirror and tell me what you see."

She looked into the full length mirror standing in front of her and said, "I see me and I see Billy. He is standing behind and to the right side of me. I see the Little Girl standing in front of me on the left side. She is reaching through my belly trying to get to Billy. Oh, I'm in the way. I'll step back and get out of the way."

Mom steps back until she is not standing between Billy and the Little Girl. I notice she can stand up straight now.

Mom says, "Oh the Little Girl is trying to hold Billy's hand but he's not responding. Now she jumps up and is hanging onto his neck. She is demanding, 'Bill look at me, look at me.' But, his eyes are closed, he won't look at her. Instead, he turns his head toward me."

I ask, "Is there anything you want to do, mom?"

"Yes." She turns toward my brother and demands, "Billy look at her."

"What does he do, Mom?"

"He turns his head towards her and opens his eyes. They are sightless, in shock. He finally sees her and tears start rolling down his cheeks. His arms come up, reflexively, to hold her. She puts her hands on his cheeks and kisses away the tears. She says, 'I am still here, Bill. You didn't kill me. You didn't kill yourself. We are still here. It's all okay.'

Now he is sobbing and crushing her to him. She keeps holding him and soothing him. I want to hug them. Is that okay?"

"Absolutely."

Mom puts her arms around Billy and the little girl. Mom is crying too, kind of cuddling them, rocking herself and them, murmuring, "it's okay, it's okay."

I say, "Mom turn away from the mirror now and look behind you."

She turns; she sees Billy and the Little Girl who is standing at his side, holding his hand. They are smiling at mom. Then Billy lifts the Little Girl up into his arms and they start walking toward the light.

Just before they disappear, the Little Girl looks back at me, Linda.

She blows me a kiss. "This is my blessing, Linda; now send it out into the world."

Then they are gone.

A blessing!

Now I'm crying.

My mother is elated. She is jumping up and down yelling "I did that, I did that. I helped them heal. It really is all okay!" She is so happy and I am hoping she can bring this into her consciousness somehow. I ask her to try to do it and then tell me about it.

Still in my mind, I ask my sister, Sue, if she saw all of that? I see she is sitting down on the path through the wetlands where she usually walks. She did see it and I hope that somehow it helps her and that she can help mom too.

I really wanted them to have some awareness. Eventually, I told them I had done this thing and asked if they wanted to hear what had happened. I wasn't sure if they would want to go there anymore. But, they did want to hear.

A couple of days later Mom and I got this email from Sue:

"Mom - at some point this week, I don't remember the exact day, I WAS out walking in the wetlands and became part of something that included loving YOU...I felt the need to talk to you in my head and hug you and forgive you...NOT BECAUSE THERE IS ANYTHING I NEEDED TO FORGIVE, but I felt you needed this from me. I nearly cried when I suddenly saw you, big as life, as you were in your 20's...so young and alive and beautiful and I hugged you and was very happy and hoped that something good had happened. I hope you felt this...it must have been what I call, a shared enlightenment. Since I don't usually have these types of moments, it must have been the 3 of us together."

Thank you, Sue.

So, my mom finds some healing and the Little Girl gives me her blessing and tells me to send it to the world. Part of me wants to find out what her name is. I want to show her my respect. *I asked her how she felt about it. She appreciated my desire but she wanted to be anonymous; she wanted to "bring hope and peace to others who have experienced tragedies."*

Once again, the Little Girl is trying to tell me that there is more to life than what I think I am seeing. Sometimes a role that appears to be so terrible, perhaps, isn't.

41
Big and Little Pictures

Big Picture, Big Picture! I admire the people who can take on the large issues of the world. Part of me feels like I would want to do this or maybe I should do this; but, right now, it's too much, I feel overwhelmed. I am frakking tired of thinking about the Big Picture. What about the Little Picture, *my picture*, my story? I can barely deal with it right now.

Obviously, I am being futile and circling the drain in my profession. Being ineffective in my job makes me unhappy and being unhappy affects the quality of my life in so many ways. But, I wonder, was I already being futile and circling the drain in my life? Where else have I been unhappy and feeling ineffective? The questions are getting bigger and scarier; pushing my buttons even more.

Are the problems in my job just a reflection of problems in my life? Is my Little Picture a microcosmic reflection of the macrocosmic Big Picture? Do I take the Big Picture global and ask where is humanity being futile and circling the drain? What about man's inhumanity to *everything*? What about the destruction of the environment? What about the destruction and abuse of life forms throughout the planet? What about all of the suffering, hopelessness and ineffectiveness in the world? How do you get life's foot off your neck, your mouth out of the mud, that dick out of your ass, the gun out of your face? Do I go universal with the Big Picture and ask is it all about Good versus Evil, God versus Devil; Fate versus Self Determination; Love versus Fear? How big of a picture am I talking about? It's starting to look mighty damn BIG and I am starting to feel very small.

Shit, I am losing it; I am futilely, circling the drain in a whirlpool of helplessness and hopelessness. I am just a broken cog in a broken wheel. I can't fix it. Quick! Where is a sandbox I can stick my head into?

Yeah it's all cool having a lofty awareness of the Big Picture and agreements to act out a particular role in a life story unless it is your character that's getting the shaft. I have been in a victim role before and what victim wants to say, "Wow, maybe I *did* agree to play this part in a Big Picture. Maybe my choices have been unconscious. Maybe I have been *living by default*, allowing others to make my choices, directly or indirectly. Maybe, I *have* actually been making the bad choices that lead me to this pit of shit. Maybe I *did* create this situation for myself. SO THE FUCK WHAT! I am still hurting. I am still afraid, I still feel hopeless. I still don't know what to do. SCREW THE BIG PICTURE!"

What can I do? Do I cop out and say well, dude, it's the **Big Picture**; it's too big!. I can't even deal with my own Little Picture. Do I hop on a surfboard, read a book, or take a walk while the atrocities, defilement, pain, and fear keep happening? Is my head already stuck in the sand? Do I really have to pull it out? Don't know if I want to. Am I futilely circling the drain in my evolving Beingness as a Human? This picture is getting bigger and bigger!

Where does all this leave me? What the hell am I supposed to do? I have pretty much just freaked myself out and feel like a loser. This concept of the Big Picture has been shoved into my face over and over and what the frak am I supposed to do about it? My *Little Picture* is getting harder. The job of nursing is becoming harder. I am getting older...now what?

Whine, whine, whine...sounds like a burnout flaring, doesn't it?

Naw, I can't live like that.

I can't keep my head in a sandbox - been there, done that, didn't work. Why? Because I *do* believe that the well-beingness of the smallest cog in a wheel is essential to well-beingness of the whole wheel. I do perceive my Little Picture being just a small reflection of the Big Picture; I wonder if it is even possible to separate the two. If I don't think in terms of Big versus Little will I see there is no difference? Do I face the problems of the world, the universe, every day in my own life but on a smaller scale? If I cut away the varied manifestations of the problems, do I see they are all the same problem? If they are all the same problem, do they have the same core issues? Can I get to the core issues that created the problem? Can I get to the beliefs that created the core issues? Are they the same beliefs in both the Big and Little pictures? Can I distill the beliefs down to one or two manageable core beliefs? Do I distill all the manifestations of "goodness" in the world down to a "positive energy flow" that appears to move Life forward? Do I distill all the manifestations of "evil" in the world down to a "negative energy" that appears to stop the forward movement of Life? If so, then I have to ask are those statements even true? To move the blood forward in our bodies we need the pulse provided by the squeeze and relaxation of the heartbeat. Is it possible that the flow of positive energy and the supposedly no-flow of negative energy are the manifestations of the heartbeat of Life? Is it more like a Sine Wave where energy moves up and down in a dualistic pattern creating an oscillation, a pulse, of forward movement so that energy always flows whether it is perceived to be positive or negative? Is the energy of Life like the people movers at airports? They keep moving whether we want them to or not. We don't even have to do anything. Whether we stand still, take baby steps or giant leaps; whether it appears to be positive or not, life keeps moving forward and we keep moving with it. Evolving; consciously or not; willingly or not.

Intense, man; hefty thoughts and questions. What are the answers? Well, you know you can find different answers in every part of the world.

I don't have YOUR answer. Your answer is INSIDE of you.

MY first answer is to quit trying to "get rid of it" and, instead, to EMBRACE all of it in LOVE and to say to myself, "I am sorry. I am sorry for my pain, my fear and my loss. I am sorry for all of the big, the little, the everything. I am sorry for my expectations, my self-righteousness, and my judgments. I am sorry for sometimes wanting something so much that I forget to ask what Love thinks is best. I am sorry for the quality of energy I have been bringing to life."

Then to say, "I forgive me. I forgive me for my pain, my fear and my loss. I forgive me for my own contributions to the big, the little, the everything. I forgive me for my expectations, my self-righteousness and my judgments. I forgive me for sometimes wanting something so much that I forget to ask what Love thinks is best. I forgive me for the quality of energy I have been bringing to life."

Then to ask, "Is there a better way to perceive it all? Is there a better way to be?"

Once again, I had to be open to the possibility that there could be a better way to perceive not only myself, but, everything. I knew that whenever I asked for it, a new way of perceiving would always come. I wouldn't have to look for it; it would come to me, from a song, a book, a stranger, or from the voice in my head.

I had to allow myself to have a new perception because with a new perspective I could make new choices.

I had to ask what my core belief was. I imagined the best, the most pure, the highest frequency of energy in the world that I could think of. I realized some would call it God/Source/Spirit. I called it Love. I perceived that the fundamental energy, the core energy, that all of life was built upon, was this foundation of Love energy and that everything else was a belief, a perspective, and an agreement. I saw it kind of like Love being the operating system of life and everything else was a program someone had created on top of it, for good or bad.

I decided to put my trust in this Love energy. So when I wanted a better way to perceive I would ask what Love's perception was. I would choose Love's way. I soon realized that this worked for not just my Little Picture, but also, it worked for the Big Picture. Oh my God, could it be that easy?

Actually...YES!

However, I often still found the ALLOWING part to be a bit of a challenge. Just as in the past, when I found there were things I wanted that didn't match Love's way, I would have to choose what I wanted most. I would still often choose the "what I want" instead of Love, hence, the *backward steps*. It always turned out to be a dead end because I discovered Love is Life and Life moves forward while anything else will end sooner or later.

Dang, doesn't all of this sound familiar? Haven't I expressed this problem before? You'd think I would have learned this lesson by now. I need to remember to always choose Love because I know that when I let self-righteousness, judgment, expectation, and wanting go, I can move into the groove of Love and go with the flow. It is cliché, but it works for me.

Thank God my patients have brought me back around. They have helped me to see where I have been stuck, futilely, circling the drain. I am so grateful to them

42
Moving Through Burnout - Reframe

I acknowledged to myself that maybe I can't be the nurse I was 10- 20 years ago. The work is harder; I'm older; there is so much paperwork; and my patients don't want what I have to offer.

My expectation of what I could achieve at work had to change. I had to remember my Self; reframe; and create a new intention. I could perceive my patients as not needing me anymore or I could perceive my patients as challenging me to look deeper into myself so that I could clear myself more. I could perceive them as encouraging me to *show up more*; not just for them, but, for myself and for life.

Shortly after my patients' smackdown gift, I was at work when someone asked me how I was doing. I responded, "Partly cloudy with a chance of sunshine."

Wow! That was a cool metaphor. Yeah, I liked it. Hey, you know what? The sun is still there even when I can't see it. A light house is a light in all kinds of weather and it is particularly needed when the weather is bad. Yeah, that's what I want to be. I like being Love and shining its light. I like being Happy. I know that feeling happy is an emotional manifestation of Love. What do the wise folk say? Something like: "Be the change you want to see."

Voila! I decided that my primary intention would be that I am an expression and communication of Love, shining its light and being HAPPY! Being happy would be my *emotional compass* of whether or not I was in *alignment with Love* and on the right path for me. From this place of being happy I would be the best nurse and person I could be. And you know what...it's working!

I have met some people who seem to be naturally happy. Consciously or not, they live so close to the truth of their Selves it seems like they just can't help but bring sunshine into a room. Others live so far from their Selves they live in a perpetual dark cloud. I find myself somewhere in between. The bottom line is I choose to be happy within myself. Someone asked me, "Linda, how do you do that though? I want to be happy, but how?"

I told her, "This is my answer. Sometimes, I need to remember what happiness feels like, so, I think of a situation where I feel happy. I pay attention to how happiness feels. I dive into it; really get into it and wear it, until that is all I can feel. Then, every morning, and as often as I can remember throughout the day, I choose to *practice feeling* that way. I don't look for something to make me happy; rather, I choose to feel it no matter what I perceive happening around me. A light house doesn't look around to see what can light it up – it's just lit! The Sun doesn't ask "What can make me bright today?" It just is...no matter what the weather is. The wonderful thing is, the more I practice it, the easier and more natural it is becoming. It is bringing me closer to my Self.

Someone told me that happiness is a by-product. For me happiness is a source. It is the internal beingness of Love. I learned that it is not the job of my Little Picture nor the Big Picture to make me happy. My happiness is not born from my reality or my actions. Rather, my *reality and actions are born* from my happiness. My life is happy because my choices are being made from a foundation of choosing Love and Happiness. It is a choice for me. And, yes, I have to REMEMBER to make the choice!

Re-living all of these stories, I can see that along with my conscious desire to help and to love, there was an underlying, unconscious, motivation of self-protection. In trying to help, to fix, and to heal, part of me was also trying to control myself, the people around me, my environment and my world, so that I could *feel safe, worthwhile, effective, validated, and happy.*

If I have learned anything from my patients it is that THAT does not work. Trying to control the story doesn't work. Trying to control someone else's story is even worse. I cannot control Life. Instead, I can live life by letting Love be my guide. In this way my choices are better and I feel *safer*. I perceive expressing and communicating Love to be a *worthwhile* and *effective* venture and so I *validate* myself. And, duh, I am *happy* living a life of Love.

How does that help the part of me that wants to help the Big Picture? I love the words from the song, "The Man in the Mirror":

"If you want to make the world a better place take a look at yourself and make the change."

I love the words in this Chinese proverb:

"If there is light in the soul, there will be beauty in the person
If there is beauty in the person, there will be harmony in the house
If there is harmony in the house, there will be order in the nation
If there is order in the nation, there will be peace in the world."

I love these words from Mother Teresa:

"We cannot do great things; we can only do little things with great love."

Maybe I can or cannot do great things, but for sure I can do little things with great love.

I recognize that loving myself and being happy is the important first step. I have to remember "Love's Light" shining inside of my Self. Even when there are storms around me and I can't see this light, I have to remember it's there. I have to take a "Quiet Meditation" as my friend, Dale, recommends and remember my happiness. I have to acknowledge that *being Happy is a service, too.*

From this place and perspective I can flow with Life. I can stop trying to control my story and other people's stories; I can allow us to live our lives. I can let go of my expectations, my self-righteousness and my judgments; I can choose what Love thinks is best; I can love unconditionally; I can act with compassion. I can be like a light house...not trying to change the weather around me, instead, just be Love's Light and... shine.

Will this change the Big Picture? I don't know for sure. I *do know* that the combination of Love and Happiness is a good fertilizer. If I let my Little Picture be nurtured and grown upon this fertilizer and allow my actions to be born from this fertilizer, then I think I can create a pretty damn good story. I suspect that living a Little Picture created and maintained by the energy vibration of Love and Happiness will have a positive effect on the world around me. I suspect that by choosing Love and letting Life flow instead of trying to control it, I will have a positive effect.

I could be wrong, but it sure can't hurt and it is a lot more fun than the alternatives.

What do you think? What inspiring words help guide your life?

43
Moving Through Burnout – Rediscover

Now that my attitude was in better shape, I still had to figure out how I was going to find meaning, joy, and effectiveness in my job again.

Break it down, Linda. What do you do in your job? Break it down into its various aspects:

1. Talking to my patients' spirits
2. Healing energy work
3. Therapeutic Psycho-Social interventions with the patient and/or family
4. Increased knowledge /education
5. Critical Thinking
6. Technology
7. Teaching student nurses at the bedside
8. Basic care of the physical body

Okay, well we have already established that talking to my patients' spirit hasn't been too effective lately. I rarely have time to do energy work in the ICU. Therapeutic interactions have been okay, but I have not been having the deep conversations that gratify me. I am not into getting my Bachelors or Master's Degree in nursing. I still like critical thinking, but there isn't always a lot required. The technology is okay, but truthfully, I quickly forget how to use it if I don't use it very frequently. I actually like teaching basic critical care to student nurses, while we work at the bedside. Basic physical care... whoa! To be honest, the basic physical care like baths, washing hair, turning, etc. has never been my turn-on in nursing.

Hmmm, I'm losing my aspects.

The only ever-present aspect is the one thing that I have never been that interested in: basic physical care of the body. But, Linda, it's Nursing 101! I know, I know, but, dude, I'm sorry, it's never been my thing. Are you listening to yourself, Linda? Physical care is nursing; everything else is built upon it. DUH! I know you're right. Okay, okay, I hear you; but, if that's all there is left for me, how can I reframe it, make the most of it and enjoy it?

Got it!

HA!

Love must have been waiting for me to ask that question.

I love to love and to touch in Love! I love to give hugs. I love to feel Love in my hands and to touch people, animals, plants, wood; whatever, with love. Sooo, I will start taking care of my patients' bodies with Love in my hands. Whether I am turning them, lifting them or wiping their butts, I will do it with Love in my hands.

This will work!

The basic aspect of my job has been reframed and aligned with my intention to be Love and to be happy. It will be very satisfying for me and I know my patients will definitely receive a benefit from it. Yay, I feel great! I am grateful for the inspiration.

The very next day I went to work with anticipation. I was assigned an elderly, homeless man, who was stuporous. I put my hand on his arm and he reacted with a kind of whining moan, pulling his whole body into a fetal position, trying to get away from me. HE DID NOT WANT TO BE TOUCHED!

I grinned and shook my head... yeah, it figures. Out loud, I said, "Mr. Wells, I can see that you don't want to be touched, but you are here in the hospital and I have to touch you. Neither of us has a choice about this. So, you are going to feel my hands on you and I am going to be as gentle and loving as I can be. If there are things I have to do to you that will hurt you, I will warn you first. Otherwise, you can trust that I won't be hurting you.

After about 15 minutes, he stopped trying to get away from me. In another 10 minutes, he just laid there, breathing easily, and looking very comfortable. By the end of the day he would move his body toward my hands so I could easily touch him. Meanwhile, I focused on feeling happy and being the Love I was sending him in my hands. All in all, I'd say we both had a great day and I found a new way to love my job. In its most basic aspect, where I had never before felt satisfaction, I was now immersed in the joy of taking care of the physical body of my patient.

It was as if I had unlocked something deep inside of me; suddenly I had a new lease on the joy of living. Within a very short time period, several things happened to help propel me on my new pathway. One was while I was listening to a book on CD. It was <u>The Power of Intention</u> by Dr. Wayne Dyer. I had first read this book back in 2004, I think. It had been very inspiring to me at that time. But, this time, there was one little thing in the book that slew me. I will have to paraphrase it: Wayne's daughter, Sommer had received an "act of kindness" when the driver ahead of her at a toll booth paid for her toll. She wanted to extend the act of kindness. One day at the supermarket, behind her in the checkout line, there was a woman with a lot of groceries and an antsy toddler. Sommer invited the woman to move in front of her in line. It turned out that the woman and her family were new to the area. She said she hadn't met many thoughtful people and wondered if this was going to be a good place to raise her children. She was ready to give up and move back to her old state despite the huge financial burden it would be. She had promised herself that if she didn't see a sign by the end of this day she was moving back. She told Sommer, "You are my sign, thank you so very much." The checkout clerk told Sommer, "You just made my day." Sommer was so surprised that such a small gesture had had such a large impact.

I found myself literally sobbing as I listened to this story. It touched my heart and seemed to heal a big hole inside of me. I had wanted to do miracles with my healing work; I had wanted to do big things; and have a big impact. Here I was being reminded what a miracle a simple act of kindness could be. I suddenly realized, I have been doing miracles all along. They are easy for me to do. Being kind is easy and being kind is its own reward. Oh my God, being happy is just getting easier and easier.

During this time period, I also got back into Healing Touch (HT). It was very synchronistic with my decision to do my patient's physical care with loving hands. Suddenly, I was volunteering to help with a Level 1 class and then deciding to go for my certification again. My inner voice warned me not to get too stuck on this idea. It told me that this involvement with HT was a healing activity for me to do while I was taking my next steps on my path; but, that Healing Touch in and of itself was not going to be my path. I said okay, but kept going gung-ho anyway. I was making my way out of the dark days and didn't want to look back.

It was sunny in Linda-Land again. And in the light of this new sunshine, I realized there was *no more futility*! At the end of every day, I ask myself: "What did I learn today as a professional? And, more importantly: *"What did I learn today about myself as a human being?"* In this way, no matter what happened in the day, whether I was nursing or not, **I LEARNED AND EVOLVED!** I do not experience futility at work nor in life anymore. Everything is a blessing!

Burnout can happen in any job or in just living life. I hope sharing mine with you and the steps I took to get out of it can help you or someone you know.

While all of this was happening, I met my new patient, Bella.

44
Bella

Bella was in her 70's. She'd been treated for cancer with good success for a while. Now, she was in my ICU having difficulty with her breathing. When I walked into the room, I introduced myself to Bella and a couple of her good friends.   For some reason, it was love at first sight.

She could barely breathe, but, Bella was keeping up a continuous stream of conversation.   She appeared to be just a short, sick, little, old lady, but oh my gosh, I could feel the energy radiating from her. I could tell she was a powerhouse of a woman. She was funny, bossy, and highly intelligent; but, also earthy - my kind of an earthy woman. At one point, when I was demanding that she stop talking and just breathe, she rolled her eyes, quit talking, and gave me the finger. I burst out laughing. We had met our match in each other and there was an immediate mutual fondness and respect.

I loved her friends too. They were Bella's second family. They could see how much Bella and I liked each other and they embraced me as a new member. Bobbie, who was also Bella's Durable Power of Attorney for Healthcare, said, "You're one of us now." I think she meant that, like them, I had fallen into the web of awesomeness that was Bella. Another friend told me that if Bella had been a nurse she would be just like me. I took that as a compliment.

Bella was very ill. I was trying hard to keep her from being intubated and put onto the ventilator. I suspected she would not be able to come off of it, once she was on. So, I teased, loved and bullied her to "shut the fuck up" and breathe. She loved this. It elicited all kinds of responses from her: sometimes, she just ignored me; sometimes, she rolled her eyes at me; sometimes, that finger would show up again; and sometimes, she would actually stop talking for a brief minute. I told her friends that this was their opportunity of a lifetime - to do all of the talking while Bella was quiet. They laughed because they knew it was the truth. They loved Bella so much and were trying to help me keep her quiet and breathing. It was like trying to stop a moving train with your hand.

That night, at home, I said my first "Hello" to Bella.

We were looking at her body and discussing what we could do to help. Neither of us was sure what to do or even if we should do anything, but, she sighed, "I don't have a chance if we don't try."

In all of my healing experiences, I have never worked with anyone who had the awareness, experience, and strength of spirit that Bella had. Usually, I have to begin at the beginning: first making a spirit aware that they are a spirit, separate from their bodies; and then, progress to whatever level of information they can assimilate and experience. I didn't have to teach Bella a thing. She already knew. I could see that the light in her spiritual body was brilliant.

She stood on one side of her body and I stood on the other side. We both held our hands out over her body. I saw Bella become a powerful white light which she sent down into her body. I was doing something similar. I told her I called this light my "Love Light".

She said, "I call it my, "Light within."

I questioned, "Did you say your Light within?"

"Yes."

I showed her my process of healing and she wanted to do it too; so we did that as we continued to send light into her body.

The next day at work, Bella was still her conscious, sassy, self. I shared that I had talked to her in my mind the night before. She nodded, waiting for more. It didn't even faze her that I had said such a crazy thing. I asked her if she uses the phrase, "the Light within"?

She nodded yes and got all excited trying to tell me something. I was having a hard time understanding her through the oxygen mask. Bobbie came close to the bed and was able to interpret. Bella was telling me to read the book, Out On A Limb, by Shirley MacLaine.

I told her about the spiritual work we had done the night before. She was as excited and happy as I was. I asked her to, now, bring the light of her spirit into her body and to fill her cells. She closed her eyes, got peacefully centered and did it. Thereafter, I did not need to cajole her into being quiet and breathe. I had only to encouragingly whisper into her ear to be in touch with her Light within. She would calm down, become peaceful, and breathe.

Despite all of this, Bella was at the end of her ability to breathe on her own and we had to intubate her. One of the doctors asked me if I thought she would make it.

I told him, "Based upon my nursing experience, no, she will not make it. But, I have never worked with such a knowledgeable, powerful, and willful spirit before. Based upon that, I don't know what will happen."

This was the last day I was Bella's nurse, taking care of her physical body. But, every day and/or night we continued to work with each other on the spiritual level.

That night, as Bella and I worked on her lungs, I saw the most beautiful color in them. I didn't recall ever seeing such a color before. It took me a moment to realize it was the color of her wellness. We were giving our love to each cell and space in between. We were thanking them for aligning with Bella's wellness. We were tickling them and bringing them to happiness. I had never gone this far with a patient before. Bella's energy was supporting and catalyzing me to be more.

We worked on her lungs for quite some time it seemed. I eventually needed to sleep. In the morning, I checked upon Bella in my mind.

She told me, "We've done all we can. Now we need to maintain an attitude of wellness and allow whatever is best, to be."

The night before, I had watched the healthy spiritual energy entering her ill cells and transform them back into healthy cells. I could see the cells change into her color of wellness. I had never seen that kind of transformation before. I'd had the concept in my mind that I should be able to go to a cellular level and help them return to their natural wellness. I had been trying to do this for several years; however, I never could quite get there. I had given up. BUT I AM THERE NOW! Bella's energy combining with my own energy has been like a step- up transformer, amplifying my energy and awareness, empowering me, and enabling me to evolve to my next level.

I do not know how this will manifest in the course of Bella's physical experience. Will it make her body well? I don't know. I have to remember that "whatever is best" for Bella, is what's important. I have to remember the Big Picture. But, now I know I can communicate with a cell and promote its wellness. I have seen it. And, I know that this is just the beginning! Like peeling back the layers of an onion, my mind is already seeing deeper information. I am aware that, this time, I am not afraid of knowing. I know that Love will guide me to utilize the knowledge appropriately. I feel blessed, excited, and revitalized by this work with Bella. I am so grateful.

This morning, as I meditated at home, I said, "Hello" to Bella. I found her considering her options of "what is best" now.

She said, "I know I said I wanted two to three more years to live and to finish my book. But, my book could get done without me now. My writing partner has enough information to get it done. I have lived a FULL life and maybe this is the right time to exit."

We both looked over at the very inviting white light that had been hanging around in the periphery.

"You could go check it out and come back."

*"But what if I like it too much and don't come back? I **want** to come back, Linda"*

"You could tie yourself to me and be anchored here."

She didn't look too sure about this.

I admonished, "Bella, do you want to base your decisions upon Love or upon Fear?"

She squinted her eyes at me and snapped, "You don't fucking hold back do you?" Suddenly, there was a light golden chain around my waist. Bella demanded, "If I am not back in five minutes, you pull me out!" Then she stomped off into the light.

I walked over to her body, held it, and reassured, "Don't worry, your spirit is going to figure out what is best for you both and she will be right back." Then I held her body in Love and waited.

Soon, Bella came back, glowing in Spirit – a BRIGHT body of light. She laid down into her body while telling me, "However much my body can align and hold this energy of my spirit will determine how much it lives." After a minute, she got back out of her body.

I could see that her body was lighter. It sat up, and then laid back down again. I raised my eyebrows at Bella.

She explained, "Spirit will determine what happens next."

Sooo, I guess we wait and see.

I asked, "Bella, is there anything else I can do for you right now?"

She got a big, mischievous, smile and said, "Contact Shirley; tell her I love her and that I am grateful for all of the insights, gifts of growth, and opportunities to love. Tell her she provided me with a platform I would never have had without her."

"You know I am not comfortable delivering messages. I am never sure I get them right."

Her smile turned into a wicked little grin, "I know."

"Biaatch! Okay, I'll do it."

I sent the message, but I have no idea if it was relevant or not.

The next day, I saw the nurse taking care of Bella and asked how things were going. She said Bella's body had made some incremental progress, but it might not be enough. The doctors were feeling less hopeful. The nurse hesitated, "I don't know, she seems better today. We'll see, you never know."

The next day, I found Bella sitting beside her body in deep thought.

"What do you think, Bella?"

"Not looking too good. Now my kidneys aren't working.

"Do you want to do some healing work on them?"

"I don't know. I don't know what to do."

"You were going to let Spirit decide."

"Yes." But she didn't look too sure right now.

"Bella, how will you know what Spirit has decided?"

"Well, if my body dies, I would know."

"Yes, but you look like you want guidance; guidance about whether or not you should take any action now; action, as in trying to heal your body. So, how would you know what Spirit would want you to do?"

"Shit, you always ask the hard questions." She looked at her body.

I can feel the love in me.

She says, "I could do what we did before and if it feels right, then continue; if not, then stop.

"Let's do it then."

We got on either side of her body and once again we forgave and released her body of our perceptions and beliefs, and chose Love's truth instead. We brought our energy up to full light and held our hands out over her body. But, after a few seconds, Bella stopped being lit up and sat down.

She told me, "Keep going, Linda."

So I grounded her body, ran her energy, cleaned and spun her chakras then, in my mind, changed the picture of her body being ill into a picture of her body being well to its full potential and highest good.

I heard her whisper encouragingly, "Keep going, Linda."

I felt the energy in me ramp up and I poured it into her body.

After a bit, I felt her hands upon mine and she said, "That's enough."

I looked at her and she elaborated, "See how you've amplified the energy in my cells, now we will see how well they can hold the charge."

So, once again, we waited.

"Bella, how will you know whether Spirit is telling you to stay or to go?"

"Again, with the hard questions!" She thought about it. "I am not sure; I think I will just feel it."

"What do you feel right now?"

"You are fucking relentless!" She thought about it some more and her face softened, "Okay, yeah, it's not time to go." She looked at me and smiled, "Cool, that settles that question for now."

"What do you want to do now?"

"I'm good. Take a break. You know you need to believe in yourself more."

"Yeah, I know. It's my old conflict of trust versus proof. I still have the belief that "seeing is believing" and I want to see it. I want to take a healing, transformative action and see it manifested in the body now. I want to see the physical body change solely due to my intentional use of energy. I am not talking

just about human bodies, either. I would love to be able to heal/transform any physical form, including the environment. I have done it once or twice, but inconsistently and it took too much effort. I was beginning to think it was too big for me, but, working with you, I have taken a step in seeing the energy transform. I can see the picture change energetically. Now I want to see the transformation manifest in the physical realm.

Bella, I would love to see your physical body heal due to all of this healing work we are doing. Gosh, wouldn't that be awesome! At the same time, I want whatever is best for you. I am aware that what might be best for you is to take your next step out of this body. I cannot, in good conscience, insist that your body heal just so I can watch it happen. I wouldn't intend or pray or wish for that, no matter how much I would love to see it. So, I will do what we did before – take action then trust Love to determine the best outcome."

"Listen, it's always a give and take."

"What does that mean in relation to what we are talking about?"

"You gotta give of yourself and take what the Universe gives you. You gotta trust that that is what is best in this moment."

"Is that what you did when you were being such a big activist for women's rights and all?"

"I didn't have the awareness then that I developed after. At that time, we had to fight and I thought that fighting would make the difference. It did make a difference, but, now I think there might have been a better way."

"Better than activism?"

"More of an activism through the soul. You already know this, Linda."

"Well, what I think is that you change within and then reality changes around you – the dream shifts."

"Exactly."

"But, then how do you know when, or if, to take an action?"

"Set your intention to the highest good for all; allow Spirit to guide you to whatever action is best; and then do it to your full potential. Next, allow the Universe to manifest whatever is best."

"Okay." I responded "I am feeling like I need to make a decision, to take a stand now; so, how about this: my intention, for our mutual benefit and highest good, is that you and your body be well now. Then, if you decide to leave your body, you will do it later, in a way that is of your highest good. How does that sound?"

Bella took my hand and said, "THAT'S how activism is done. Someone has to take a stand, set the energy, initiate an action, hold the energy, and allow the Universe to manifest. Then take responsibility for the outcome, learn from it and move forward. It will serve you best if you set the energy with the intention for the 'highest good' and/or, 'whatever is best'; then, allow Spirit to guide you to the best action to be initiated; and then, be open to ongoing guidance from Spirit."

My suspicious spiritual eyes narrowed and stared at her. "Hmm, Bella, I don't know if you really think this way or if I am making this entire conversation up. But, I feel like Love is using our relationship to break through my blocks and to communicate with me. So, I am going to quit resisting, doubting, and questioning whether or not these words are something you would actually say to me. Instead, I am going to accept this gift of communication and clarity. I am grateful to allow Love to utilize our relationship in this way. If I am supposed to share all of our interactions and communications with someone, I am asking Love to guide me and to help me know with clarity and certainty when, where and with whom to share it. Whatever the truth is, I am grateful for you, Bella."

The next evening, when I say, "Hello" to Bella, I see that she is pacing the floor.

"God, what is taking so long? No wonder people decide to leave their bodies. It takes too long for the body to change."

"Yeah, well that's what they say, right? Time flows differently on different planes. I don't know. I don't have an answer. But, maybe we can accelerate it."

"How?"

"Don't know for sure." I thought about it for a bit then suggested, "Probably, I would start with letting go of any beliefs that cause resistance to healing. I would visualize creating a rose balloon and put into it all of my thoughts, emotions, behavior –

any energy, on any frequency, that would hinder healing. Then I would say to all of that collected energy, 'I forgive you all of my perceptions, you are just my beliefs, not the truth. It is possible there is a better way and I choose that possibility. I choose Love's way'. Then I'd put the energy of that "statement of intention" into the balloon. Next I would send the balloon out into the Light, release it, and allow Love to return the truth to me. Yeah, that sounds good. Okay, that's how I would start, how about you?"

Bella deadpanned, "How about –'Spirit show me how to accelerate my body's healing'?"

"Hmmm", I mused seriously as I carefully considered her suggestion for about a nanosecond. I grinned, "Nice, easy and to the point!"

Yeah, I think I may be way too intense!

We both held our hands out over Bella's body. I saw Bella doing her thing of becoming light and sending it into her body. I did the same thing but, this time I sent my consciousness down into her body to the cellular level and I started talking to the cells.

"Hey there little loves. What can you do about shifting the excess fluid out of the tissues and back into the blood? The kidneys need fluid and the whole body could use better circulation. And what can you do to let go of all of the junk in the lung tissues and bring them back to wellness?"

I see the cells kick into action, they look kind of like doorways opening and closing along the walls of long hallways; leaks were stopping. Suddenly, inside the hallways, which I now recognize as blood vessels, big balls of something like sponges appear and they are pulling fluid from the tissues back into the blood vessels. The blood vessels are filling like flooded riverbeds and circulating fluid to the kidneys. Next, I look at the lungs and the congestion in the lung tissue. "What do you want to do about this?" Different images skip through my mind as if sifting through ideas. Finally, the best one was to just "change the picture" and simply see the image of congested lungs fade and the image of healthy lungs become clear.

I am aware that part of me is wondering if this could actually work and I realize that that doubt is part of my problem. Maybe, it is my **entire** problem! Hmm. I refocused on what I was doing.

As I was working in the lungs, I kept having to move around a very forceful column of white light coming out of the heart and up into Bella's hands. I started pulling the light back into the heart.

Bella protested, "Hey what are you doing?"

"I am bringing all of that energy back into the heart so it can spread Love out to your body. You need to love yourself."

We stopped the healing work.

"Don't know if I can. I mean, I understand the need to center myself and to be in touch with my spirit, but, I always do it to help others. I pour the energy out, not so much in.

"O, Dude, I understand that." I replied. "It took me a while to reconcile the, need to "give all" of myself, with the supposedly, "selfish" need to give **to** myself. I would bounce back and forth between periods of giving, with periods of, 'hey, what about me?' I finally realized that I **had** to give to myself and to keep myself full or, not only would I have **nothing** to give others, I would also be **needing** from them. So I try to be like a water fountain that keeps itself so full its pool is overflowing with water and others can use the run-off. Also, one day, I heard a talk by Abraham, an entity channeled by Esther Hicks. In just a simple passing phrase, he said the words, "mutual benefit". Wham! That phrase hit me and I knew that instead of trying to balance between my two intentions, I could **merge** them. I could just say, 'for our mutual benefit, or, the highest good for all of us'. It has worked great since. Soooo, how about when you are using all of that heart centered energy to help others, you create the intention that it is for all of our highest good and let your love be for you too?"

Bella glowed at me and patted my cheek, "Little girl you're a wiz."

"Are you mocking me?"

"No, I am loving you."

"Love you too. Now, what else should we do? Do you want to go explore the light again?"

"No, no, no, no. This time I wouldn't come back. I'll hang out and watch what happens with my body. Go back to bed now."

The next day, Bobbie told me a couple of the doctors were thinking that we were prolonging Bella's suffering. They wanted her to consider allowing them to stop Bella's life support and to put her on comfort care, in the next day or two.

I did a quick check in with Bella. "So, what do you think?"

"What the fuck do they know? You and I know. We'll know when to stop and you will tell them. Promise?"

"I can do that, Bella; I don't have a problem with that as long as you are very clear with me."

"Listen honey, what could go wrong? So, they take me off and I go commando - buck naked, without the life support. Spirit will either help my body to live or I go. Either way it's a win/win situation for me."

"Okay."

"Don't forget what you promised."

"I won't."

That night when I said, *"Hello"* to Bella, I could see her slumped down next to her body, looking sooo bored.

I asked, "Bella, would you like a friend to keep you company?"

"Yeah, I would."

A man appeared. He was an older, black man with short, beginning to be white, hair. He was tallish and very attractive. Bella, being the huge flirt that she is, was happy to see him. I don't know if she knew him. It obviously didn't matter.

I went to bed.

The next morning, Bella woke me up. I could see she was very happy. She and the man were laughing and talk, talk, talking. Bella was herself again. I thought I would ask the man what his name was, but I don't have a lot of confidence in myself to get that kind of information correct.

"His name is Damon," Bella said spontaneously.

Hey, was she reading my mind?

"Damien? As in, The Omen? Ooooo that's scary." I teased.

"Linda, get your head out of your fear and see with Truth. His name is Damon."

"Okay, lo siento, sorry, mi amiga; just joking... uh, sort of." I laughed. "Still joking! So, what's up?"

Damon looked over at the Light. Bella smiled and informed me, "I am going with Damon."

"You said you liked it over there too much and if you went there again you wouldn't be coming back."

"That's right I did."

"So, you are leaving?"

"Yes."

I shook my head, "Well, Bella, I have heard that before from a patient, but, after several days, she came back."

"Ahh, did she do this?" Bella reached over and pulled the cord out of her third chakra.

This is the line that is supposed to connect the spiritual body to the physical body.

"Nope. She sure didn't do that."

Bella smirked, "Now **THAT'S** pulling the plug on life support!"

"HAH, it's just like you to beat them to the punch! Okay, Bella, if this is truly you taking your next step, then I am freeing you, in love and gratitude, and I say, Bon Voyage. I won't try to contact you. However, I will be available to you if you need to talk to me. I will let Bobbie know about this, so that if the doctors ask again about taking you off of life support, she will know it's okay. Have fun, love."

I watched as she put her arm around Damon and they walked together towards the Light. Damon hesitated as Bella lead the way into the Light. He turned toward me and said, "Good job, Linda." Then he followed Bella into the Light.

I am crying.

Bella was taken off of life support and her body died in just a few hours.

I hadn't really known Bella except for the interactions I have told here. She was a catalyst for my evolution. She pushed me to do more, be more. All during this process, I had been sharing our communications with Bobbie. Part of me wasn't sure how much was real and how much was just me. When I went to her memorial service, I found out just how real it was. Bella had many friends. She had been an activist, a mentor, a stimulus for so many people, pushing them to be their full potential. She had catalyzed social evolution. She was spunky and irreverent in her ways. She described herself as a loud mouth, pushy, little broad. I saw her as a thundering train, a dynamic power house; a compassionate, conscious, earthy, pushy, controlling, flirtatious, get things done kind of a woman. I feel like I was her last save; her last project. And, boy, am I grateful.

45
Karin, again

Remember Karin? After all of this time, she was still hanging on. I had not been her nurse for several months, but, I had been continuing to, intermittently, check in with her on a spiritual level. Nothing had changed; she still did not want to make any changes or choices. Her nurses continued to be stressed by the situation; one nurse was even found crying in the hall way.

I didn't know how to tell them that I believed Karin had a purpose for being in this condition. I knew they would think it bizarre and just too crazy that anyone would want to be experiencing the terrible condition she was in. I didn't believe Karin consciously wanted to be this way; but, I had begun to believe that somehow there was a purpose to it.

Finally, it occurred to me to ask, *"Karin, how does it serve you to be in this condition?"*

She smiled wistfully, "Really, Linda, the best situation would be if I could be in a coma for the next 8 years then wake up and start my life again."

What?? I don't think I was really expecting an answer; certainly not this answer!

Karin proceeded to tell me about a huge life change she had wanted to make. She had started taking steps toward the change, but couldn't go through with it because she realized it would cause too much chaos and pain in her family. She really just wanted life to pass her by until a better time came for making the change.

Oh my God. I can hardly believe what I have just heard. I don't know. Could she really have this agenda? I know I thought there was a purpose, but, holy moly, this is waaay more than I could have imagined.

I saw her parents in the hallway a couple of days later. They knew I often talked with Karin in my head. I wasn't sure what they thought about it, but, I felt a huge urge to tell them about this last conversation.

Cautiously, I started, "I know that you aren't really into these things, but I had another talk with Karin."

Her mom took my hand and said, "Linda we believe the Holy Spirit communicates to us through you, so go ahead and tell us." The Dad nodded his head.

Wow! I had no idea, but dang, I am grateful.

I proceeded to tell them this latest news. As I finished, the mom got tearful and the dad's head drooped a little. Mom said, "It's true, Linda. Just before she got sick, she had taken a few steps to make the change, but, she told me she just couldn't go through with it. She didn't want to cause so much pain."

I felt an overwhelming need to say some things.

I told the Dad, "You are Karin's champion. She trusts you above all others to support her choices. If the time comes when you perceive there is nothing more we can do to help her body stay alive, can you tell her it is time to let go?"

"No."

I took his hands and stared right in his eyes with all of the love I could communicate. Gently, I repeated, "**You** are the only one she will believe. You are her father, you are her champion. I am not saying the time is now. I am asking you, if, the time comes will you do it?"

He looked deeply into my eyes and said, "Yes."

This was HUGE!

Later that day, I had a talk with Karin, physically, in our bodies. I held her hand.

"I know you have a change you want to make in your life. I know you believe it will cause too much pain in your family and that you are afraid to do it. I know you are hoping life will pass you by until a better time comes to make that decision."

She nodded, "Yes."

"Karin, I know you know that I love you."

She nodded, "Yes."

"I perceive you as a strong, beautiful spirit; and I believe you can create whatever you want. I am concerned because you keep your body skating so close to the edge. Be careful that it doesn't spin out of your control."

She nodded yes and gave me a little smile.

Oh my God, she knew exactly what I was talking about. This was blowing me away! What if I had known about this issue a year ago? Could I have helped her create a better way to deal with it spiritually, mentally, emotionally, and physically? If I had, would her body have been allowed to heal? I don't know; I think it is possible; but, I don't know for sure.

A few days later, while I was meditating at home, Karin came into my mind.

She said, "I am afraid to go alone; will you come with me?" She held out her hand to me and I took it. She turned to look at the luminous white light that was there. We started walking into it. I saw a beautiful path in front of us with lovely vegetation on either side; Karin saw ugliness, burnt out bushes, and bugs crawling on the path.

I said, "Karin, you are seeing your Fear, choose to see your Love instead."

Instantly, the path cleared up and was beautiful again.

We kept walking and, ahead of us I saw a brilliant light and in it was a male figure sitting upon a gorgeous throne.

Karin saw a grey color and a man with a scary, disapproving face, watching and judging her.

Gently, I whispered, "Karin, choose Love, let go of your Fear."

Instantly, she saw the light and a male figure who shone only Love out at her. He opened his arms wide, welcoming her.

I asked her, "Who is that?"

"It's God."

"What do you want to do?"

"I am so tired." Her shoulders slumped. She looked exhausted. "I want to rest."

She hugged me then turned and walked toward God. She climbed onto His lap, put her arms around his waist and lay her head upon his chest. He wrapped His arms around her. She sighed, smiled, and closed her eyes.

I am crying.

It was Saturday morning; I called the hospital to see what was going on. I was told, that the day before, Friday, the doctors had finally told Karin's parents there was nothing else we could do for her. The parents had made her a No Code and put her onto comfort care. Karin was awake and aware of what was happening. Word got out around the hospital about what was coming down. A steady stream of hospital employees began showing up to share their love and to say goodbye to her: Nurses, Technical Partners (aides), respiratory therapists, Physical and Occupational therapists, X-ray techs, housekeepers, etc; all came. Karin had been with us for almost two years. She had been taken care of and loved by so many people. She was surrounded by family and friends as hymns were sung and prayers were done. Then she had closed her eyes and drifted off in peace.

46
Endgame/Entertainment/Indaba

Right after Karin died, the next patient I took care of was a man named, Roger. I am not going into his story except for the fact that when I said, *"Hello" to him, he said, "Don't mess with my end game."*

END GAME? What the frak?

Remember the fetus who didn't want me to mess with her *pre-game*? Karin didn't want me to mess with her *mid-game* and Roger says no messing with his *end-game*!

Okay, okay, okay; I got it dudes; NO MESSING WITH THE GAMES!

After my initial surprise, I was reminded of my experience as a young woman trying to move back home after having left when I was 18. I needed a place to live temporarily so that I could go to a Nurse's Aide training course. My mom was okay with me coming back, but my siblings were adamant, "No you can't come back". They had just spent a year being free of our step dad Joe's tyranny and did not want to deal with my bossiness.

They were free, independent teenagers who didn't want me messing with their games. Initially it hurt me that they didn't want me back, but, then I had an incredible feeling of liberation. I was free from having to feel any responsibility for their well-being. I could relinquish control. They could live their lives their own way; come what may. And, more importantly to me, I was free to live my life. Of course, my mom told them to cool it and to let me come back home. They were happy to find out that I was chill and not interested in controlling their lives anymore.

For almost two years, my patients had been telling me to not mess with their games. Initially, I was upset and confused about what I was supposed to do. I am a critical care nurse, for God's sake. I am also a human being who cares. But, with Roger's blatant message, I GET IT. I am not responsible for my patients or for their stories. I am here to take care of them, to inform, to educate, to support, to respect, and to love them. I am here to flow with them while they play out their lives and their deaths.

I thought I had already learned that lesson!

Once again, my patients have reminded me that I am not responsible for other people's lives. It is not necessary for me to fix, to heal, to change, or to make them and their lives be what I think is best. Once again, they have reminded me that I am free to love unconditionally and without expectation. What a wonderful gift!

I am here to love and to be happy. Someone said, "But, Linda, you cannot be happy in an unhappy situation!" Well, here is the funny thing. I know that the happier I am, the closer I am living to my Self. The closer I live to my Self, the more comfortable and secure I am that I will not lose my Self-awareness again. This allows me to enjoy experiencing other emotions and to not get lost in them. It's like a happy actress who loves to play really deep characters. She gets to experience all the fear, sadness, anger, jealousy, pain, illness etc. but never forgets who she really is. She can sink her teeth into an experience; can embrace whatever is happening; and then bounce back to being the truth of her Self, enriched by having had the experience.

When I was much younger, I used to take LSD. I would use a tape recorder and a notebook while I asked questions and explored myself. One time I was particularly depressed and really getting into the boo-hooing. It occurred to me how much fun I was having and started laughing. Eventually, I started crying again, and once more, realized how much fun this was. I started laughing at myself and the ridiculousness of the whole situation. It was a good lesson in appreciating how satisfying a good cry, a good scare, or a good anger could be. I learned to embrace my emotions in Love and to be enriched by them instead of being afraid or controlled by them.

What kind of books and movies do you use to entertain yourself? Do you watch them *knowing* you are going to cry, to laugh, to tease your brain with problem solving, be scared, be outraged, be inspired, or whatever? Dude, are you getting into the emotion and *enjoying* it?

What kind of movie do you live in? What kind of character are you *being*? Are you *embracing* it all; learning, evolving, putting on your director's hat, *shifting* your point of view and writing new chapters to experience?

After all I have learned from my patients, I have begun to see our world as a kind of an amusement park, with all of the thrills and chills I might want to experience. In fact, it's got a lot more than what I personally want to experience; but, what I don't want, someone else may love, or at least, find useful! So guess what? *I don't need to control, to fix or to heal an amusement park.* **It's not broken!** Frankly, if I find myself on a ride that is too frakking scary or sad, dude, I am taking myself off of it and going over to "It's A Small World" in Disneyland. I am gonna use my tools of: forgiveness, reframing my perceptions, my beliefs, and choosing Love, to get myself on a better ride. If I cannot find a way to get off the ride, you can bet I am gonna surrender and holler, "UNCLE! I GIVE!" and ask Love to help me. I have learned to trust that, somehow, Love will get my butt out of the frying pan, if I let it, if I listen, and let Love guide me to better and better rides!

Above all, I know that no matter what thrill or chill I am experiencing, I am STILL ME inside; I am still Love, still Light. I can still choose Love and Happiness and return to my Self again. If worse comes to even worse and I die, I know that my physical body is not me; it is only a wonderful tool for me to play in; to communicate with; to express and experience my Self in; to learn, to grow, to evolve; and to use for enjoying the experience of Life on the physical frequency. After all I have seen, I don't believe in death anymore. Knowing this has made life a hell of a lot more fun.

I love the words in the song "Indaba" from the CD, <u>Into The Heart Of The Sangoma</u>, by Ann Mortifee:

"If you cannot hold the dark
Then you dare not touch the light
For they belong to one another
As day is wed to night."

I am not afraid of my emotions. I believe *Love can hold all emotions*. In the end, after all my playing around in emotion, I will always choose Love and Happiness because I found that living close to my Self and being happy is way more fun for me.

My friend, Lisa, says, "It feels good to float in the ocean but there is nothing to hold onto."

I say, "Yeah, let go, merge with the ocean and let it hold you."

Viva la pura vida!"

47
Robbie/Grandmother/Submit to the Lord

I am getting to the end of the stories I will be sharing in this book, but, here are some vignettes I want to mention:

One is about Robby, a teen age boy who was in a fatal car accident. Initially he appeared to be alright but then had a seizure that left him severely brain injured. I'd heard the doctors had told his parents he would be in a vegetative coma for the rest of his life.

I was never Robby's nurse and met him only one time when I helped his nurse turn him in bed. The minute I touched Robby, I found myself saying, *"Hello."*

It was all dark and there was no answer. I said, "Hello" again.

I heard him say, "I'm here."

"Why are you in the dark?"

"Am I not supposed to be?"

"Not unless you want to be."

"My brother died. Am I not supposed to stay here in the dark now?"

"Not unless you want to."

"I don't want to."

Then turn on a light, Robby."

Suddenly, there was light and there he stood. And, just as suddenly, a little boy and a woman appeared. It was Robby's mother and brother. The little boy walked over with his arms stretched out, reaching for his older brother. Crying uncontrollably, Robby knelt down and held his little brother. The little boy returned the hug and tried to soothe his big brother. The mother watched sadly. Eventually, the little boy told Robby he was fine and to not worry about him, then, abruptly disappeared. The mother was gone too.

Knowing I had to get back to work, I apologized, "Robby. I don't know what else to do to help you right now, I'm sorry."

He smiled at me, "Linda, you brought me out of the dark. That's a lot right there. Thank you."

I felt then that this kid was going to be alright.

A year later I was walking by the rehab waiting room and there was Robby sitting in a full support wheelchair with his head and limbs safely secured. I went to him and was so surprised. "I remember you! You were in an accident and in our ICU for a while. O my God, look at you!"

He beamed and I *knew he understood* me. HE WAS AWAKE! I learned later, that with the help of his family and his community, Robby had been receiving a special treatment to his brain called Hyperbaric Oxygen Therapy. He could now count with his fingers and he had said his first word, "Mama".

Of course, Robby is a fictional name; however, with his mother's permission, I am giving you the web site with this young man's story, in case you would like to read more: http://wakeupraguel.webs.com/.

****

A co-worker, who is reading this book, told me her Grandmother was deathly ill. For some reason, I felt drawn to say, *"Hello"* to the Grandmother.

She said, "I don't want to talk with you. You are the bringer of death."

Yikes! "I am sorry..."

"No, no, not like that," She interrupted. "You bring the light of truth that causes the death of illusions and lies. I am not ready for my lies to die."

"Oh, okay," I lamely replied. "Well, let's just visit then."

Afterwards, I wondered what lies and illusions I was afraid to let die. Suddenly, a big one blared into my mind:

"The price of being one with Source is giving up the illusion that I am not already Source."

That was followed by:

"Don't fix. Instead, BE; CREATE! Fixing requires that I hold onto what I don't want while trying to reconstruct it. Instead, let go. See the picture of Love's truth and allow it to BE. From that, CREATE what I want to express and experience."

Ai, yi, yi, yi, yi! The illusions are falling by the wayside. Take a deep breath, Linda.

****

I met a very religious family whose loved one had incurred a stroke so large that half his brain had died and swelling was compressing the rest of it. To me they were a unique religious family. Yes, they had tremendous faith that the Lord could do anything, but they expressed it in a way I had never heard before. The Mom told me, "We have *submitted our request* to the Lord and now we will step back and *watch His will manifest.* Also, we will respect the wishes of my husband and make him a No Code/Full Care. We will keep the feeding tube in him. We know the Lord can work a miracle if it is His will. If my husband gets worse, we will *acknowledge* it as God's will; remove the feeding tube and go to comfort care." All of the adult children were in total agreement with these sentiments.

Oh my God! I thought that was the most wonderful statement I had ever heard a family of faith make. It was so right on.

This man did get worse, quickly. The family did acknowledge it as God's will. They put their loved one onto comfort care and allowed him to die peacefully. The family, too, was at peace in full certainty that God's will had been done.

I was amazed at the family's perception and the way they expressed it. It was so different from the other times I have heard families of faith say, "We want God's will to be done." Yet, when the patients continued to get worse and worse, the families would not acknowledge it as God's will. Instead they would insist we keep forcing the patient to live, until we could not anymore.

After all I have learned from my patients I have realized that these situations were a challenge to my faith; my faith in knowing that Love is working here; and that, by my own choice, I am a tool for Love. Now, I remember there is a Bigger Picture. No more do I war between medical wisdom and people's beliefs. My job is to inform, to care, to do my nursing, and to flow with Love, using the opportunities to learn and evolve.

48
Agnes

Mrs. Agnes Meriwether was a 66 year old woman with cancer. She'd been treated for several months; already had a tracheostomy and was on the ventilator; but, had recently decompensated. She had a PEG feeding tube going through her abdominal wall directly into her stomach. When a person is "trached and pegged" it tells me a story right there.

Agnes was somnolent, very sleepy but not comatose. She was receiving continuous intravenous pain and anti-anxiety medicine. This told me more of the story. Along with other details of her condition, I could see that Agnes was dying in the ICU, but, she was still a Full Code. This told me more of the story. Neither she nor her family had acknowledged or accepted that fact of her impending death.

Agnes liked to have her "stuff" just so; the call bell here, the oral suction there, the tissues there, the washcloth on her forehead, etc. Her kids knew what she liked and they were continuing to do it all despite the fact that she was barely conscious. They were very attentive and at her slightest frown or movement they would be at her side asking what she needed, at which time, she would struggle to bring herself out of the depths of near unconsciousness to make sure her mouth was cleaned just the way she liked it, the call bell was here, the wash cloth was on her head, and so on. This told me more of a story.

I watched this go on for a couple of hours then, at one point, I sat at Agnes' bedside and said to her somnolent self: "Agnes, I am giving you medicine to help you with anxiety, and medicine to help you with pain, but, you are unable to embrace the comfort these medicines can provide because you keep trying to control what is happening around you. You can do that if you want to, but you will not be as comfortable as you could be. It's your choice.

She chose control. In that moment, I knew she would never yield control.

The next day, while I was instilling some meds into her PEG, I suddenly found myself saying, *"Hello."*

She was distraught, *"I never got to talk to them. I never got to tell them all of the things I wanted to say. I didn't get to say goodbye,"* She lamented, *"Now it's too late."*

"You're right! It is too late to communicate the way you wanted to."

Oh my gosh, what was coming out of my mouth? That was no sugarcoated response, I'm not sure it was even a therapeutic response. I wasn't cutting her any slack. Hey, dude, just keeping it real. Okay, but why? Don't know.

I know we said other things to each other, but, I don't remember them. I do remember asking her, *"What do you think you're gonna control in Heaven, Agnes?"*

She just rolled her eyes and reproved, *"Shut up, Linda."* I started laughing.

Two of her adult kids, Jim and Mary, were in the room unaware that I was talking with their mom in my mind until I started laughing and blabbing to them about it. Their mouths dropped open then verified that this sounded just like their mom. Jim said that she would never talk about her failing health even when they asked her about it. She would always change the subject. They laughed when I said she told me to shut up. I don't remember what else I said to them, but I promised Mary, I would make sure her mom was at peace. Then I left the room.

I had about fifteen minutes to take care of my other patient before I was sent to lunch. During my lunch break, a large part of my mind was still with Agnes. I was spaced out and I ate while staring at a wall, My co-worker, Dottie, was sitting across from me. I could hear her talking but I was focusing on Agnes.

At one point Dottie asked, "Linda, are you okay?"

I blankly looked at her then said, "I'm talking with my patient."

Her face went, HUH?

"Oh, did you know I talk to patients' spirits? No? Well, I do and I have to get back to it now." I didn't even wait for her response, I spaced out again.

Yeah, another well done spiritual coming out.

Things were zooming so fast in my mind. It seemed like a life review on crank. I could grasp only snippets of sentences, fragments of pictures. I couldn't make any sense of it. Truthfully, I could only watch. When there was something to say, it just spilled out of my mouth. I felt pushed and, in turn, I pushed her. Sometimes I felt I was harsh with her. I didn't let her waste time on recrimination, whining, or, guilt. It was like there was no time for pussyfooting around. I said things like, "You're right, it is too late, now what will you do?" If she got angry I didn't feel regret, instead, I admonished, "There's no time for being angry."

What the HELL is going on here? No clue.

Agnes called her kids in to talk with them. I saw Jim and Mary come to her side, but, I couldn't make out anything being said. The movie was still in fast forward. Then, suddenly, it all slowed down to normal speed. I could see that Agnes' second daughter, Judy, had arrived. Jim and Mary disappeared; now, only Agnes and Judy were there.

Judy lived with her parents. I knew that she and Agnes were very close. However, what I was seeing was strangely in opposition to all of that. I expected them to be hanging onto each other in grief, but instead, there was a breach between them that was so charged with emotion, it appeared impenetrable. There were angry bolts of energy flashing from Agnes and a fog of confusion coming from Judy. I could hear Agnes screaming, "We were too close. We could not be free."

The sounds and images in my head began to speed up again as my mind was grabbed by Tornado Agnes. There were disjointed, fragmented scenarios of Judy and Agnes together. I didn't understand what was going on, but for some reason, it didn't feel right. The pictures kept changing, moving from one bullshit scenario to another as Agnes and Judy interacted.

Energy erupted out of me as I watched. "What the FRAK are you two doing?" I reprimanded. "None of this makes sense; you two don't make sense. I'm not buying it. What kind of games are you playing with each other? Nothing either of you are saying is the truth." I didn't let them explain; I kept pushing. I kept demanding, "I don't believe this bullshit, what is the truth?" The scenes sped up!

What the HELL am I doing? I don't know, I've never done this before, but, it feels right to push and to push hard. I'm going for it.

SCREECH! Finally the fast forward braked down to normal speed again. Agnes was collapsed on the floor, sobbing. She moaned, "I stole her life from her, I stole her life."

Somehow, I knew she meant that she and Judy were so close neither of them knew how to create a life without the other; she felt guilty because she believed she had stolen Judy's life.

But, Judy kept reassuring, "Mom, I wanted to be with you."

Agnes kept crying, Judy kept reassuring, and I kept pushing them to get past the melodramatic bullshit, until finally they were laughing at the ridiculous drama of it all.

Out of all the people in the family, Judy was having the hardest time with the thought of Agnes dying. They had been like Siamese twins the last ten years of their lives. Judy had been refusing to come to grip with her mom's pending death and was creating a lot of discord in the family.

I wasn't sure whether or not to tell Judy about any of my conversations with Agnes. I asked Jim and Mary to not mention them; that I would follow my intuition about it. Soon after, we were all standing at Agnes' bedside and I felt the urge to tell Judy about my earlier conversations. She took it all in stride and felt they were valid. I decided to tell her about the conversation specific to her. We stepped outside of the room.

I told her, "Your mom feels she stole your life from you."

She started crying. "My mom regrets spending that time with me?"

"No, that's not it at all. Your life together was limited by her body's restrictions. Neither of you could really live the way you wanted to."

She interrupted, "But, I don't regret it. I love my mom; we had a good life together."

"There is no doubt you two loved being with each other. Now, though, she wants you to be free. She doesn't want you to hang on to her. I perceive your mom as coolness and you have that same coolness inside of you. She wants you to go create a cool life for yourself.   Now that she is free of her body's restrictions, she is free to love you without limitation. She will always be with you in love. So, go and be your awesome self."

Hmm, do I have any clue where these words are coming from? Nope, but they appeared to mean something to Judy. She started smiling, and then gave me a big hug. She was finally able to accept her mom's pending demise and agreed to change the code status.

But, apparently, Agnes and I were not yet done as, once again, my mind was seized by Tornado Agnes.

I took her to the mirror. Her reflection was that of a young woman and there was a young man standing behind her. She screamed, "I don't trust you," and pushed him away; he disappeared. She collapsed onto the floor, hugging, rocking herself, and sobbing, "I don't trust anyone!"

I softly asked, "Is there anything you do trust; any higher power?"

She vehemently shook her head no, "I don't trust God. That's why I have to be in control. I have to make sure things are done right."

I suggestively asked, "Can you imagine any energy that you could trust?"

Suddenly in the mirror, there was a radiant golden white light and Agnes' eyes widened in awe. She stood up in front of the mirror and reached toward the light.

I could feel the enormous, awesome, energy coming from the light. I asked, "What is that Agnes?"

She whispered, "It's me!" Unhesitant, she strode directly into her light, fully embracing it; and, allowed herself to be fully embraced in return.

*It was incredible! I could feel what she was feeling. It was immense peace and love. None of the issues in her life mattered anymore; her slate was wiped clean; she had let it all go. She was beyond peace. She had taken a **leap of transformation**. All was okay.*

As her Light, she began reaching out to her family, friends and coworkers, enveloping them with her love and radiance; sending peace to them all. She wanted them to know that the love she'd had for them while in her body was restricted by the issues she had

in her body. But now she was free from her body and so was her
love. She was with them now and would always be with them in
love. She began to call them to her.

They started showing up! Over the next two days, people just began arriving. It was eerily awesome.

Meanwhile, Mary had asked me to talk to her Dad. Apparently, although they had been married for over 30 years and still lived together, Agnes and her husband had not been close for the last ten years. I don't know what the issues were. I do know this was the time period when Agnes and Judy had become so very close.

When I met the Dad, I told him about the mirror and the man standing behind Agnes. He confirmed that Agnes had had a bad relationship before he had met her. He had questions and I began to answer them, but instead, what was coming out of my mouth was totally bypassing all of his questions. Once again, I felt pushed. Once again, there was no time for all that questioning and answering process. Once again, no time for bullshit!

I stopped him mid-question, looked him straight in the eyes and said, "Agnes wants you to know that any issues between the two of you don't mean anything anymore. She forgives everything that ever happened and she loves you. Agnes has transformed, she is beyond peace."

Again, do I have any clue what the hell I am talking about? Again, NOPE! But, it meant something to the dad. He hugged me tightly to his chest and cried until he could smile again.

What a crazy, frakking day it had been!

I know there is no time and space in my mind's eye and things can happen quickly, but I have *never* experienced anything like what had been happening this day. The images came so fast, I only saw fragments. I felt a compelling push to speed through them and to push Agnes like there was no time to waste. There was no time to understand; there was no time to process. I had to let go of control; witness what was happening; and then speak whatever came to my mind.

I didn't understand why I was doing this. I had no time to think about it. I was at work in the ICU. I had a second patient I was trying to take care of. I also had personal business I had to attend to. My mind was multi-tasking in a huge way. But, the dominant focus was the fast running movie of Agnes that I was witnessing.

At one point, I had walked back to Agnes's room and was standing outside of her doorway. Her son called out, "Linda does my mom have anything to say to her sisters?"

Does not compute; I was confused. I blankly stared at him and Agnes' sisters then asked, "Who's your mom?" They roared with laughter. It took me a heartbeat to realize what I had said then I started laughing too. O my gosh, I need to ground myself and get my head back into the game.

I still cannot recall everything nor understand all that was happening in my mind with Agnes. I was not able to screen what came out of my mouth when I spoke. It just spilled out; I had to trust and hope that it meant something to whomever I was speaking.

Holy Moly.

I finally knew though, that the family would make decisions based upon Love and not Fear. Over the next two days, even though she was unconscious, Agnes looked like a queen holding court as her family, friends, and co-workers came to say goodbye. She was still in control and taking care of all of her loved ones.

This experience left me wondering if processing my own experiences, thoughts, and feelings is necessary. Then as I meditated about it, I realized Agnes *had been* processing, but it was at such a fast pace, my mere mortal mind couldn't follow it. I wondered, whether my own spiritual higher Self was continuously processing my life experiences at a speed I could not register. If so, then maybe I didn't have to spend so much time diligently processing; maybe I could just follow my internal guidance. With that thought, I became aware of how *my mistrust would slow down communication* between my higher Self and my consciousness. It would hinder my Self's ability to create within and through me. My mistrust would block the smooth flow of energy from spirit to thought to feeling to physical manifestation. I know my fears cause me to be cautious so that I won't make a mistake that will hurt me, or, even worse, hurt someone/thing else. I know my child-like demands to have whatever I want when I want it, slowed down or obstructed the creative flow that provides me with what I need to happily, successfully, be my full potential. I am aware how this constant, distrustful, resistance would definitely filter and dim the flow of Love, Light and Life within and through me.

TRUST...that's the biggie. I asked myself, "Do I trust Love or don't I?" Suddenly I became aware that, hey, I actually do! What a revelation! I could feel a gap filling inside of me. Now, knowing that I do trust, and, having awareness about all of the processing that gets done on a spiritual level, I realized I really could let go of trying to control my life, and just enjoy flowing in the river of Life created by Love.

Dang, this brings me right back to my original conversation with God thirty years ago, doesn't it? Yeah, but I know me. I know that I will still state my intentions; probably argue and give feedback (read as whine and complain); but, it will be different now because I really do trust. Wow, how awesome is this?!

49
Pulling It Together/Mamie

Hmmm, as I review the stories I have written recently, some things are coming together in my mind.

See through the mask to the truth. I remember Lee was very good at seeing the person behind the public face we all have. He said that behind the public face is our home face, the one we wear with our families and friends. This face could be cool or it could start to become ugly. Behind the home face is our private face; perhaps, even our secret face. Lee always perceived *this face* to be the "real person". He was very good at seeing the "real person".

I understand these concepts, and I agree with them in part; but, I perceive it differently. I perceive all of these faces as being the faces of our beliefs rather than the truth of our Selves. I perceive them as the precepts, concepts, parameters, limitations, boxes, desires, and fears that we have created, by intention or by default, in which to experience ourselves.

I perceive another face deeper within; the face of Love. I perceive this to be the *true face*. What would happen if I *saw only the true face and communicated with only the truth of a person?* What would our interactions be like? What would our relationship be like? What gets in the way of me doing that? I think it is my desire to **not let my lies die** and to hang on to my beliefs.

What if I want to change all of that? Do I spend years, maybe a lifetime, trying to fix, to heal, and to process my illusions, lies, and judgments in search of truth? Wouldn't it be more effective to just take a **leap of transformation** and let go of them, by **trusting that Love has already processed** them and has freed me to **Be**, to **Create** a new me, a new life that is in **alignment** with **what Love thinks is best**? I am thinking this is so.

Without the burden of continuous processing, I could just **make a choice, a decision, an intention** to align myself with Love. I could simply let my intention be and know that, like a lighthouse, Love's Light will draw me to it. Or, I could be more proactive and take an **action** that will align me with Love; and then, as I act, **pay attention to Love's guidance, and flow with it**.

What would I, Linda, be like then? I have no idea. I don't know what Linda, created by Love, would look like, be like, do.

In order to be the Linda, Love would create, I would have to let go of every belief, limitation, expectation, fear - EVERYTHING. I would have to wipe my slate clean and take that leap of transformation. I would have to pay attention to my inner guidance at all times and be completely in the NOW. Man, then I would really be on a Love guided "walk-about".

I LIKE IT!!! I AM EXCITED ABOUT IT!

What would I be like if I could just BE my true Self, living Love's Life, communicating with only the truth of Love in the world? What if I communicated to only your true Self? What would we be like if I did that?

Does any of this make sense to you or is it just Linda out in la-la land again?

****

Mamie had been ill for a year and had been back and forth between the ICU and the rehab hospital. She was like a bald bike tire that we kept trying to patch but could never fix. This time was the worse she had ever been.

I had taken care of her a couple of times and remembered some of her family. Some of them remembered me too. She was still a Full Code, but, there was to be a family conference with the doctors that afternoon. The doctors were hoping the family would let Mamie go to comfort care and have a peaceful death because we could not help her this time.

I was in the room, doing something with Mamie. Her husband and some of the family were there. Suddenly, I was with her in my mind. (Of course, I was!)

I said, "Hello, Mamie." I couldn't see her, she was in the dark. I asked, "Why are you in the dark?"

She said, "I don't want to hear anything you have to say."

I reassured her, "No problem. I am just going to stand over here and love you."

The moment those words came out of my mouth, I felt and saw that my body had become such a bright white light I could barely see its outline. I felt full, radiant, loving, peaceful, and patient as I stood there, loving Mamie.

I could see a spark of Love's Light in Mamie's body so I said, "Hello" to it. A little Light ray of communication went from my light to her light. Her spark of Love was amplified and began to grow. Pretty soon, I saw Mamie's worried look go away and her facial expression began to soften.

I didn't move.

As her Light grew, her body began leaning toward me then she raised her hand toward me. I realized that Mamie was feeling the Love and she liked it! Soon, she began walking toward me.

I didn't move.

She placed her hands on mine and then moved her arms to encircle my waist. She sighed.

I did too.

At that moment, the white light appeared across from us and we could see a bunch of people all giggling and waving at Mamie. I asked her who they were. She got very excited. She said some were family, some were friends and others she didn't know, but they looked happy and welcoming.

Mamie walked over to that light and wanted to go into it. She explained, "I was afraid before, Linda. I didn't want to leave my family and go to a place I didn't know. I didn't want to be alone. But, look, there they are. They look happy, they are waiving at me, and they want me to come. It looks like fun. I am a happy person. I am so tired of being sick and unhappy. I want to go, Linda." She was getting giggly as she waved toward people she recognized.

"What about your family, Mamie?"

"I will miss them, but, my body is dying. I have just been hanging on to it, being afraid." In that moment, she called her family to her and showed them the crowd of people waiting for her in the Light. "See? You see, it is okay. I won't be alone, it is happy there. I know you will miss me, but, you see? When it is your turn, I will be waiting for you too." She hugged them all and they left.

Mamie walked into the Light, laughing and giggling.

I told her family this story. They loved it and were brought to peace. They made Mamie a No Code and allowed her to go to her new home and friends, knowing she would be there for them, someday, too.

Wow, I was literally being the Light of Love! I guess I don't have to do anything except BE MY SELF. It really is plenty!

Is that the Linda, Love would create?

SIGN ME UP!

50
Harriett/James/Me

This last story is an experience I shared with my co-worker Harriet. We'll relate the story in the sequence in which it occurred.

Harriett:

It always makes me anxious whenever I'm assigned to care for a dying patient. I usually feel like a tremendous task is placed upon me and I often feel inadequate or unworthy, somehow. That is, up until recently, when a patient care situation helped me realize how empowering compassion and a true spiritual connection can be.

When I walked into the unit, I was very much aware of the musical alarms emanating from the room I had been assigned to. I had not yet spoken with the off-going nurse, but, somehow, I already knew I was in for a busy night. Looking into the room was an eyeful. I saw several staff members, all of them with grim expressions on their faces, busily adjusting equipment, adding medications, silencing alarms, and speaking with physicians. Amidst all of this chaos, I saw a grieving family standing next to the patient, holding his hand, and crying.

I felt my insides tighten.

Listening to report only confirmed my feelings of a dire situation. I quickly made mental notes to approach the family to clarify their wishes. As I re-entered the room, I introduced myself and expressed how I was going to do the best job I could in caring for their loved one. Noting the patient's dangerously low pressure, I also started to prepare for a code blue. As I began connecting the defibrillator to the patient, the family wanted to know why I was doing that. I explained to them that based upon the patient's vital signs I could see he would need CPR and shocking very soon. After a short conference with the family, they decided to change the patient's status to "No Code". In this particular situation, it meant we would not add CPR, shock, or use some "code" medicines on him. However, we would not stop the life support he was currently on, i.e. the ventilator, pressors, and the intra-aortic balloon pump (IABP).

All night was a constant struggle to find the right balance of medications and other treatments. It was a true miracle to see how he hung on. The family kept a close watch--- never leaving him alone even for a few minutes.

When it was time to relinquish my care to the day shift nurse, I was relieved to see who was going to care for him next. Linda is the best nurse for situations such as this. I knew the family was emotionally in a better place --- most likely relieved that the patient had survived the night. I also knew that Linda was the best person to continue the emotional and spiritual support that I had worked tirelessly to provide overnight. I went home that morning truly believing the patient and the family were in good hands.

Linda:

James was only in his 60's and was deathly ill. Harriett told me his wife, Kathleen, had made him a No Code with no acceleration in care. This meant we were to continue with the level of life support he was on, but, to not add on more life support. James was already on a couple of pressors, the ventilator and a balloon pump machine to support his heart. When I walked into the room, I could see that this level of support was not going to keep his life going much longer. I was surprised it had lasted this long.

Kathleen and her sister, Madge were sitting at the bedside. I introduced myself, then went to James. Surreptitiously, while doing my assessment, I said, *"Hello"*.

James was very calm. He said, "My body's dying."

"Yes, it is. How are you feeling about that?"

He sighed, "I am okay, but Kathleen is not ready. She needs more time."

"Okay, we will do what we can, you do what you can."

After my assessment, I squatted in front of Kathleen and Madge. "How are you doing?" I asked Kathleen.

"He made it through the night, so that's good. It seems like he is getting better."

Uh oh.

"Why don't you tell me what you understand is going on."

She explained her understanding to me and it was pretty good. Harriett had done a great job of keeping her informed. But, despite appearances, James was not really improving. His latest morning labs were worse.

"It is pretty awesome that James has made it through the night, unfortunately his labs results are getting worse. The level of technology we are giving him cannot correct his body's condition. I understand you made him a No Code and that we are not to add more interventions. Is that correct?"

She nodded.

"Okay. We need more information about what James would want. If we see that what we are currently doing is not helping, how long do you think he would want us to continue doing it? What would James want? Would he want to keep fighting or to have a peaceful death?"

Waaaah!

I could hear the scream in my mind. I could see the retreat in her eyes. She definitely was not ready for this! I acknowledge it by holding her hand and saying, "I can see you are not ready for this kind of talk."

She interrupted and stammered, "No, no, I'm not. He seems better to me. I think we should give him a chance. He is a strong man."

"No problem." Then I started to explain the different paths that we could follow and I saw her eyes glaze over. I actually chuckled, gave her a hug, and said, "In all of my experiences, I have met only a few people who do worse when given information. I think you may be one of them."

She smiled wanly and nodded yes. Madge burst out laughing and agreed.

"Okay, here is what I propose. We won't talk about possibilities. I will just keep you informed as we take each step along the way. How does that sound?"

"That sounds good, just tell me what is happening as it happens. I can handle that." She smiled, feeling safe again.

"Okay great. Now will you guys help me stand up? I'm too old to be squatting like this." They started laughing and helped me up.

In that moment, the doctors came in and told her about James' failing lab results. They said it was all looking very grim and that he had absolutely no chance to survive if he did not get dialysis, so, Kathleen agreed to dialysis. Since she agreed to that acceleration of life support, I asked for more pressors and fluid because, not only did he need them now, I also felt there was no way his blood pressure would handle dialysis without them. So, we accelerated James' care and our trek down the "fix me path".

I checked in with James. He showed me a funny image of himself being in a racer's "ready, set, go" position. He was still ready to leave his body; but, then he shrugged, "She has to feel she has given me a good chance, that we have done everything we can do."

And so we went on through the day. I started the pressors, the dialysis catheter was placed and we attempted to filter his blood. But, it wasn't working. His body could not handle even the gentlest of dialysis and the toxins were building faster than we could remove them. His blood pressure had been extremely low all day despite our interventions. I kept Kathleen informed every hour about what we were doing. I didn't realize until near the end of my shift that she was judging his progress by watching the blood pressure on the bedside monitor. Unfortunately, I had to show her that the true blood pressure was on the balloon pump monitor and that it was reading a blood pressure in the 60's. I think that was the turning point for her. As my shift was coming to an end, we had to turn off the dialysis machine because it was not helping and his labs were worse.

I wanted so much to tell Kathleen about my conversation with James, but the words would not come out. It was the complete opposite of my experience with Agnes. It wasn't so much that the words were blocked as it was that I never felt the *urge* to say them. It never felt like the right time.

I saw that Harriett was back for the night shift and I was glad. Saying goodbye, I stood in James' room, with my arms around Kathleen and Madge's waist. We were looking at the whole scene.

"I am sorry our technology hasn't been able to help James." I paused, hesitating, listening to my Inner Self.

Nothing.

"I really want him to be comfortable now." I hesitated and listened again.

Nothing.

I wanted to prep her for the inevitable, but, all I could do was to make her conscious of the fact that everything had been done. "Do you feel that we have done everything we can do for him?"

"Yes, I do."

"Do you feel like he has done all he can do to get better?"

"Oh yes, he has fought hard."

"Okay, good." Oh man, I really wanted to tell her, but now I could feel the blocking; I didn't know *why*, but, I *knew I was not supposed to tell her*. I sighed in resignation.

Kathleen heard my sigh and squeezed my waist. "You worked hard to help him, I know that and don't think I haven't notice your tender loving way with him, Linda. I see how you hold his hand, or, place your hands on his stomach or his head to comfort him. Thank you for that. The nurses in this hospital are so very caring."

"Yes, they are." I agreed. "It's why I work here. This hospital was founded upon Love and Service by the nuns. It draws certain kinds of people to work here. Your Harriett will be back tonight to take good care of you." Then I hugged them and left to give report to Harriett.

Harriett:

I came back that night prepared to see an empty room. Instead, I saw a distraught spouse urging the patient to "keep fighting" and to "be strong". Then I saw Linda talking with the family. A few minutes later, she came out to tell me what was going on.

While receiving report, I asked Linda, did you "talk to him"? I was referring to the non-verbal/mental communication style she is gifted with. She said she did. She said he was hanging on because he felt his wife wasn't ready to let him go yet and that she needed to know everything had been done. Linda told me she had just asked the wife if she knew that everything had been done and the wife had said she did. I made a mental note of how useful all this valuable information was and felt oddly empowered being equipped with this knowledge. I put the thought away hoping I might be able to use it later somehow.

Looking into the room I saw even more life-saving equipment. Somehow, in the back of my mind I felt the need to attempt a more direct approach with the family. I greeted the wife and family like old friends. They looked hopeful; yet, I saw in their eyes the deep sense of sadness, somehow knowing that all of our efforts were futile. I knew then that I had to muster up more courage to be truly honest with them. I prayed that I might have the eloquence to delicately explain how none of our actions would change the outcome.

I began by telling them that in my experience with similar situations, I've noticed that people "hang on" for various reasons. They told me they were waiting for his daughter to come from out of town. I encouraged them to call in other friends and family for further support. It then became a waiting game. During this time, the patient was surrounded by people who obviously loved him and they kept encouraging him to "hang on"; that his daughter would be arriving soon.

I felt a mixture of both relief and cautious excitement when I overheard the family say their much awaited family member's flight had just arrived and that she was en route to the hospital. A second later, my adrenaline kicked in because, to my horror, the patient's blood pressure suddenly took a nose dive at the same time the family had mentioned their relative's arrival. Luckily I still had some ammunition to use, and I cranked everything up, as I anxiously willed the daughter to hurry.

Almost like an epiphany, I knew it was the right time to tell the wife about Linda. There was something about the look in her eyes and the way she spoke. She would look at me, asking for vital signs and medication updates, yet, her expressions seemed more like she was asking just for the sake of asking. It didn't seem like she was really paying attention to the details. Our interaction felt almost as if she wanted me to reassure her that it was okay to "let him go". It was at that moment that I felt a *strong urge* to be completely honest and upfront with her. I felt that if she knew about the spiritual connection Linda had made with the patient, she would be more accepting of the dire situation, and have time to make peace with her decisions.

I began by saying to her, "I don't know if you are aware of the day nurse, Linda's, special gift." She looked at me with a puzzled expression. I continued by saying, "She can talk to patients even in their comatose state." She continued to look very curious YET receptive, so I went on to explain that Linda had a "talk" with the patient and he had said he was still hanging on because Kathleen wasn't ready to let him go and that she needed to know everything had been done. Upon telling her this, I could feel and see all of her emotions. She broke down in tears and began to sob. Her expressions looked like a mixed bag of emotions == sadness, guilt, horror, relief, comfort, and maybe a hint of determination and resolve. She had the look of someone who knew what she needed to do. I tried to comfort her while at the same time commending her for her strength and the courage she showed during this most difficult time in her life. I also reassured her that, if she chose to go the comfort care route, I would do everything I could to keep him comfortable; and, to allow him a peaceful passing, if and when, she decided it was the right time. I think that she took solace when I reassured her of my dedication to ensuring his comfort. Her face changed and the vibe around her lightened. Upon hearing my story, as related by Linda, she went over to the patient and spoke to him. I didn't hear what she said, but she seemed calmer and at peace.

Finally, the much awaited daughter arrived. The patient was surrounded by all of his family and friends while they said prayers and their goodbyes. I heard the wife saying to the patient, "It's okay, we're going to be okay." Then, just as the she came to tell me to turn off the medications, I looked at the monitor and saw that the patient had peacefully passed. I didn't even have time to start or stop anything. It was as if he knew the whole family was together and that they were okay.

I truly felt that I connected on a spiritual level with the family, and that they were at peace with the decision they made. I know end-of-life discussions and decisions are never easy, but somehow, by the grace of God, I felt like I was instrumental in helping both the patient AND the family. This was the very first time I experienced feeling like I had done things right.

Linda's "gift" inspired me to do my part by relaying a message. I don't know how I knew that it was the right time or that this was the right family to share the information with. I guess I just listened to my gut. I truly believe I fulfilled my purpose that night and it sure felt great to know that I played a big part in helping a family go through the denial, bargaining and acceptance stages of grief. They did so with grace and appeared to be at peace with their decision.

Thinking about what happened has helped me become more introspective and intuitive. I don't think I've really ever taken the time to truly think about family actions, facial expressions, or my own reactions. I feel like this whole experience has added another dimension to my care. I've always believed I was a compassionate person, but it was enlightening to see the responses to my interventions and to receive feedback about my efforts. I felt validated and appreciated.

Since having that experience, I feel more confident in handling end-of-life situations. I think I know what to look for in terms of family's responses, and have a more solid grasp on how I should communicate and advocate for the patient.

There really is no specific formula. I'm just glad that things fell into place--- just like they were meant to be.

Would I do the same things again? It's hard to say. I would have to see what I'm given. But it sure doesn't hurt to have Linda on my side!

Linda:

When I returned to work the next day, I noted that James' room was empty. I saw Harriett waiting to talk to me. I could see the anticipation in her smile; she wanted to tell me what had happened.

She began to relate the events and I found myself stunned. I could hear her voice, but, I was overwhelmed with what I was experiencing. My mind was racing. She had *believed* the story I had told her, and, she had *used it in a therapeutic intervention!* She felt *empowered*, had *listened* to her gut and let it inform her when the time was right. She had felt the *URGE* to speak! She described Kathleen's reaction to the message and how she had then given James permission to go. Then James died before any changes could be made in his therapy. I was very happy for James and his family, yet, I knew there was more going on here.

My mind was thinking how awesome is this, how validating, it really works!! What do I mean, it really works? Didn't I know that already? What is going on? Shussh, Linda, Shussh.

I stopped trying to analyze and just allowed myself the experience. I felt satisfied, accomplished, completed. I felt full, kind of floaty and altered as if I had just finished a very long race, a long struggle, to reach a pinnacle, a peak; no, **a fork in the road**! For thirty years, I have struggled between what I want and what Love thinks is best. Suddenly, I saw the two forks of the road merge into one and everything inside of me went still as I filled with a quiet sense of...Grace. Tears spilled from my eyes and streamed down my cheeks. In this moment, I gratefully realized it isn't about me, Linda; the picture is so much BIGGER than me. I am just a link in Love's chain.

Now...I believe!

Afterword

It has been two years since I finished writing this book. There have been so many changes. I did reach a point in my practice where I had to evaluate whether or not I still had the ability to be a good ICU nurse or was I just not competent anymore. That is when I realized there was nothing wrong with me except for my resistance to the path that the future of nursing was on. I had to choose to quit or to get out.

I chose to quit resisting and rediscovered that I am still the good critical care nurse I always loved being.

Also, I was really going strong on my spiritual path, going so far as to secluding myself in my condo and calling it "Little Tibet". I was meditating a lot. Finally, one day, I said, "Okay, I surrender! I give up everything. What do you want to do with me Love? How can I best serve the Highest Good for all of us?

I told my bosses, family, and friends that I was leaving...I did not know when, where I was going, or what I was going to do...It might not even be nursing.

Then I did not initiate any other action, and just allowed Love to let me know what to do. There were long periods of inaction except for work and meditating. Then I would get a strong urge to take an action which I would do even if it didn't make sense to me. Step by step, over several months, a new reality was shaping up until, now, here I am!

I live in Sedona, AZ. This place encourages my "crazy" and I am going with it! In fact, I am getting even MORE crazy! Ha ha! I have retired from bedside nursing. I am creating my own consulting, teaching, and healing practice. I am revising both of my books and may create MP3s. I am even thinking about doing a BlogTalk radio show. And, yet, I know that all of these plans just might be what my logical mind needs to think because it needs a direction so it will not be afraid. I will take the initial steps and, as always, let Love guide my feet. I know that wherever I am will be what is best.

I am very happy. My spiritual path is bright and I am happily following Love.

I am loving all of me and all of me is loving you.

Xo,

Linda

Feel free to contact me if you want to talk with me.
imlindai@gmail41.com
www.lindaingalls.com

About The Author

Linda Ingalls RN CCRN has been a nurse since 1975 and in 1981 began her ICU career. She has a background in Psychiatric Nursing, Life Coaching, Healing Touch, and is a graduate of The Berkeley Psychic Institute. Linda has received several nursing awards. She likes movies, books, travel and wishes she was a real surfer!

She is currently living, happily, in Sedona, AZ creating her own healing/teaching practice and continuing on her bright spiritual evolution!

Made in the USA
Las Vegas, NV
31 January 2024

85014172R00154